Charles Lambrou
The Alchemist's Way

Health, Happiness and Wellbeing

ACKNOWLEDGEMENTS

People often ask me how long it took me to write The Alchemist's Way. My answer is: my whole life. I have had to travel through all my experiences from conception till now to sit and write this book.

Along my journey I have met some wonderful people and some who were not so wonderful. I take this opportunity to thank the not so wonderful people, for they have provided the challenges and wake-up calls which have assisted me in my journey and transformation. Some people have been both wonderful and not so wonderful at the same time; I honor you and thank you all for having been part of my life. Thank you to all my friends for just being my friends.

I am grateful to Arnavah for helping me to write this book. He has done much more than just edit and has helped me share The Three Steps in a clear and concise manner. Thank you, Arnavah. Your input is invaluable and highly appreciated. A huge thank you to Prashant Hirlekar for the superb paintings, they have been an amazing gift to receive. Prashant is a popular artist in Mumbai and he graciously took time from his busy schedule to create in his own unique style, all the paintings for this book. A picture can really say a thousand words, and these paintings are great resources for us to remember some of the concepts especially in a time of need. I am fortunate to have many of these paintings, hanging on the walls in my home.

There are too many people for me to thank here individually, so I shall keep the list short. I honour and thank Siddhartha Gautama, the Buddha, for setting the light aflame 2500 years ago and sharing Vipassana meditation with the world. I thank S.N. Goenka for amazingly availing Vipassana meditation worldwide free of charge. His teaching eliminates barriers to learning and practicing Vipassana, and I personally have benefitted greatly from it.

Thank you, Peter Levine, for your pioneering work in the field of trauma and for making this knowledge accessible through your faculty of trainers. Thank you, Diane and Raja, for your invaluable wisdom and sharing. I have gained so much from the Somatic Experiencing trainings.

Life has brought so many people to help me on this journey: in my former businesses, in all the therapies and sessions in which I have learned. Thank you to you all.

Thank you to my mom and dad for bringing me into this world. My relationship with my mother has gone through many shades. I am proud to share that she too has been a guiding light for me. And I take this time to bow in honoring you, Mom; thank you for everything. Yvette, my elder sister has been of great support throughout much of my life and we have navigated some difficult times together and Chantall, my younger sister, has taught me many lessons. Thank you to both of you.

My greatest lessons have been learnt through my relationships, especially with those I love. Zia, thank you for joining me in this life and on my journey in opening my heart. You are an amazing woman and I am happy that you are the mother of our little girl. You are a great mother. To my daughter, Sufia, my little princess, I love you and thank you for being you. I love being your father. You too have taught me so many things; most importantly, how to love and how to have fun.

And to you, the reader, for reading and letting me share: Thank you.

For Reasons of Legality

The author of this book, Charles Lambrou, does not advocate the use of any particular form of healthcare but believes that the facts, figures, and knowledge presented herein should be available to every person concerned with improving his or her state of health and wellbeing. Although the author has attempted to give a profound understanding of the topics discussed and to ensure accuracy and completeness of any information that originates from any other source than his own, he and the publisher assume no responsibility for errors, inaccuracies, omissions, or any inconsistency herein. Any slights of people or organizations are unintentional. This book is not intended to replace the advice and treatment of a physician who specializes in the treatment of diseases. Any use of the information set forth herein is entirely at the reader's discretion. The author and publisher are not responsible for any adverse effects or consequences resulting from the use of any of the preparations or procedures described in this book. The statements made herein are for educational and theoretical purposes only and are mainly based upon Charles Lambrou's own opinion and theories. The reader should always consult with a healthcare practitioner before taking any dietary, nutritional, herbal or homeopathic supplement, or beginning or stopping any therapy. The author is not intending to provide any medical advice, nor offer a substitute thereof, and makes no warranty, expressed or implied, with respect to any product, device or therapy, whatsoever. Except as otherwise noted, no statement in this book has been reviewed or approved by the United States Food & Drug Administration or the Federal Trade Commission. Readers should use their own judgment or consult a holistic medical expert or their personal physicians for specific applications to their individual problems.

Copyright © 2011 by Charles Lambrou

All rights reserved. No part of this publication may be reproduced, stored in a retrieval system, or transmitted in any form or by any means, electronic, mechanical, photocopying, recording or otherwise, without the prior written permission of the copyright owner.

ISBN: 9780985687564

Published by

Cover Artwork by Prashant Hirlekar

Cover Design by Amanda David

Edited by
Arnavah

Contents

Introduction ... 12

SECTION 1 – Lambrou's story

CHAPTER ONE: My story ... 18

SECTION 2 – The body and its sensations

CHAPTER TWO: The importance of the body ... 32
   Survival and wellbeing
   Elements of experience
   States of being
   The body as a biological musical instrument
   The heart, our sun
   The Gut
   The autonomic nervous system

CHAPTER THREE: Losing and Regaining the Body ... 51
   Fight, flight and freeze
   Dissociation
   Symptoms

CHAPTER FOUR: Re-membering Ourselves ... 61
   Memory
   Implicit memory
   Engrams
   Priming

CHAPTER FIVE: Patterns ... 72
   Habit Patterns
   Neural constellations

Operant conditioning
Re-enactment

CHAPTER SIX: The Source of our Patterns　　　　　　　　　　83
   The womb: our initial, formative environment
   The miracle of birth
   Early interactions with our parents

CHAPTER SEVEN: Mirror Mirror　　　　　　　　　　　　　　92
   Projections
   Relationships as mirrors

CHAPTER EIGHT: Sensations and Awareness　　　　　　　　98
   The sensory system
   Awareness: The secret key to freedom
   Beginning the process of awareness
   Awareness of sensations
   How to observe sensations
   Awareness: the key to transformation

CHAPTER NINE: The Three-Part Brain　　　　　　　　　　113
   Intuition

SECTION 3 – An Alchemical Process: The Three Steps

CHAPTER TEN: Preparing to Practice the Three Steps　　　123
   Exercise 1
   The language of sensation
   Exercise 2
   Exercise 3

CHAPTER ELEVEN: Practicing the Three Steps　　　　　　132
   Discharging

What if discharge is not occurring?

CHAPTER TWELVE: How to Start with the Three Steps — 145
- Small steps at a time
- Observing the 'lost' body
- Curiosity
- Patience and tolerance
- Equanimity
- Pendulation and cycles
- Inclusion
- Resilience
- Resources
- A new way
- Slowing down is speeding up
- When to process
- The spiral effect
- Catching the wave
- Integrating the Three Steps into daily life
- The paradoxical theory of change
- Intention

SECTION 4 - Working with emotions and states of being (emotional Alchemy)

CHAPTER THIRTEEN: The Alchemy of Emotions — 165
- Working with emotions through the body
- Emotional alchemy via the Three Steps

CHAPTER FOURTEEN: Working with fear — 171
- Thwarted flight responses
- Befriending fear
- Examples of working with fear
- Starting on the small waves

CHAPTER FIFTEEN: Working with anger 183
    The importance of feeling empowered
    Empowerment exercises
    Becoming aware of anger
    Restoring Fight Responses
    My personal journey with anger
    Working with anger: a recap

CHAPTER SIXTEEN: Working with states of freeze and dissociation 193
    What does freeze feel like?
    Brace, collapse, rebound
    Working with dissociation

CHAPTER SEVENTEEN: Working with Guilt, Shame and Sadness 201
    Shame
    Working with sadness
    Some tips for working with sadness

CHAPTER EIGHTEEN: Working with Habit Patterns 208
    Working with habit patterns of illness
    Working with our social engagement system

CHAPTER NINETEEN: Opening to the Heart 215
    Making space for love
    Making space for gratitude

CHAPTER TWENTY: Catching the Moment 220

EPILOGUE 222
    The singing bowl
    The writing of the Three Steps
    The inner revolution
    Using the Three Steps

INTRODUCTION

I believe that the answer to health, happiness and wellbeing is in having an open, loving heart. I know the answer to all our misery and suffering is within us. I have seen how the body holds the secrets to our health and wellbeing and I believe the road to riches resides within our unique constellation of mind and body patterns. I believe that an inner revolution has to take place for us to achieve harmony, abundance and wellbeing in the world. For this inner revolution to occur there needs to be an integration of our instincts, emotions and intellect. When this occurs a new way of being unfolds. I have written The Alchemist's Way to share some of the alchemical secrets that have helped me to transform my life.

The legend of the Alchemist is about turning lead (base metal) into gold. The Alchemist's Way shows you how to do that at the human level, the base metal being a metaphor for our difficult emotions like anger, jealousy, hatred and grief and the gold being a metaphor for the opening of the heart and experiencing, love, joy and gratitude. The Alchemist's Way introduces an alchemical process called the Three Steps which shows you how to go inwards and turn lead into gold.

There is a kind of glue holding our unwanted thoughts, emotions and behaviours in place. The Three Steps not only dissolves the 'glue that binds' us to a seemingly endless cycle of re-enacting stories in which we no longer want to participate, but it also re-configures the whole body-mind nexus and

INTRODUCTION

leads us towards physical, mental, emotional and spiritual liberation.

Everyone I have met who has integrated the Three Steps into their lives has benefited. I have taught people from all walks of life: mothers, fathers, businesspeople, professionals and schoolchildren. Because the Three Steps is a natural approach to supporting the body-mind towards health and wellbeing, it has deepened the practices of yoga teachers, tai chi masters, psychologists, massage therapists, and Feldenkrais and Alexander Technique practitioners, as well as physicians, dentists, psychiatrists and counsellors. If all doctors could share the Three Steps with their patients, many ills, which medication only manages, would be cured.

By prioritizing awareness of bodily sensations—and because the body is consciousness, always in the present—the Three Steps helps people become more conscious. Meditators of all disciplines will benefit from the knowledge within these pages. In particular, Vipassana meditators will profit tremendously because they already have some sensitivity and tolerance towards sensations and know of their importance. The Three Steps will give them a new understanding about the relationship between sensations and our various states of being.

Parents can give no better gift to their children than to master their own emotions. Children learn much more from what parents do than what they say, so through the Thee Steps you will give them a strong foundation upon which to build their lives.

Familiarity with bodily sensations will add a new dimension to the practice of tai chi and yoga, and will give that extra 'edge' to sportspeople, dancers and performers of all kinds. Martial artists, boxers, and all ilks of fighters will benefit hugely from increasing their inner knowledge of their bodies and minds. They will be able to transform bodily patterns that hinder them in that crucial moment during the heat of a fight.

With the Three Steps, businesspeople can master their negotiation skills, transform their strategies and manage their stress and health. If you are a businessperson, do you aggressively 'go for the kill' and lose out on great possibilities because the other party walks away from the deal? Or do you cave in when pressure mounts, always getting the short end of the stick? How much conflict and discord are you constantly handling? If you were to examine your life, how many patterns could you identify that waste your time and energy?

ot just walking heads. All of our patterns and strategies, includ-
conduct our business, are based in our bodies; and the Three
key to transforming the body and, with it, the mind.

Walking Heads

The Alchemist's Way also takes us on a journey to open our hearts. We all protect our hearts and shy away from feeling sadness and hurt. We do anything so as not to feel the pain and anguish of the heart, and instead resort to strategies of fighting and fleeing. In order to open the heart, however, we must also master the emotions of fear, anger, shame and sadness, and learn how to be in love, joy and gratitude. The heart will only feel safe to open to its infinite nature once we have done this processing work.

How to open our hearts and work with various difficult emotions and states of being is explained in the book's last section: Section Four: Emotional Alchemy. The key to this work is the Three Steps, which is fully explained in Section Three—Alchemy in action. In fact, you may want to begin with Section Three in order to familiarize yourself with the Three Steps before proceeding either to Section Four or the previous sections.

Section Two—The Importance of the Body—explains the theory behind the Three Steps and why it is so successful in transforming our thoughts, emotions and behavioural patterns. It explains that the root of all our patterns is our bodies' physiological, biological and chemical processes, and that the healing journey involves restoring our bodies' regulatory mechanisms to support the release of trapped energy in a safe way. In this manner, many common symptoms—including migraines, digestive disorders, heart palpitations, hypertension, chronic fatigue syndrome, chronic pain, attention deficit disorder, as well as emotional imbalances such as rage, anxiety, shyness—can be resolved.

Section Two not only gives us an understanding of how difficult physical, mental, emotional and behavioural patterns develop and maintain themselves, but also gives us a newfound appreciation of them. We understand that these patterns are our bodies' means of pointing the way towards attaining wholeness and wellbeing.

Although the insights of Section Two are very important, the real gift of the Three Steps is its practice. Although the intellect can contain a vast amount of knowledge, it cannot, in and of itself, lead us to knowing. Through the intellect we can read in a book that an orange is round, orange in colour, and that it has a sweet citrus taste. But until you experience the texture of an orange skin through your hand's touch receptors, until you smell an orange through your nostril's olfactory receptors, and until you taste an orange via your mouth's taste buds, you cannot really know what an orange is. Similarly, we can sit down with our friends and discuss swimming all day long: how to swim, which strokes are best, and what fun swimming is. But we would merely be theorizing if we never jumped into the water.

Jump into the water! This is the main message of The Alchemist's Way. This book is an invitation for you to delve into the wonders of your being and investigate with a sense of curiosity whatever you may find. I offer the Three Steps as a guide, a set of propositions for you to enquire and explore for yourself. Don't take my word for it; see for yourself that The Three Steps is a tool that will take you to the root of any issue, behavioural pattern and belief system, and effectively transform it.

By changing our body-mind patterns, we reshape our futures. We transmute our self-images, how we respond to life events and how people see us; and we begin to attract people, circumstances and situations that enhance our wellbeing.

As you proceed through the book, you will notice that I share many of my personal experiences on how I have coped with challenges, which led me to explore my body-mind and formulate The Three Steps.

Many spiritual and self-help books place the authors on a holier-than-thou pedestal, leaving the reader feeling unworthy and relegated to the ranks of sinners without hope. With this book I want to emphasize that I am a regular person who has experienced a great deal of discomfort, pain and difficulty. I have persevered and taken many small steps over a long period and have evolved the hard way. I have investigated my interiority and continue to do so. Using my body-mind as a laboratory, I have made my greatest setbacks catalysts to evolve and heal. It is precisely because I have explored and experimented, I am now able to offer you a natural method of transformation which is subtle, gentle and very powerful.

The Three Steps cultivates and hones our awareness. It is the answer to the perennial questions: How can I become more present? How can I stop this habit? How can I manifest what I want in my life? How can I feel more love? How can I be happy?

Just like deep roots sustain a tall tree, the foundation for our personal and spiritual growth is our body's capacity to self-regulate. The Alchemist's Way explains this and shows us how. As we become more established in awareness of our bodies, they become portals to the beyond, to the now (present), to knowing God. This is why Jesus said, "the Kingdom of Heaven is within all of us." Heaven is not something to believe in; it is an actuality, an experience. It is always here. We merely need to work with our body-minds so that they become receptive to it.

Gaining mastery of the body-mind is part of the spiritual quest, and it makes it possible to find heaven on earth—right here, right now. The Three Steps is therefore the key to riches beyond money. It is a simple technique, but it takes time, effort, persistence, perseverance and courage to master. The simplest things are often the most difficult. Having said this, fortune is on our side. Our body-minds contain a blueprint to return us to a state of health and wellbeing; all we have to do is honour the body and it will lead us to wholeness.

SECTION ONE

LAMBROU'S STORY

"Knowing others is intelligence; knowing yourself is true wisdom. Mastering others is strength, mastering yourself is true power."

- Lao Tzu

CHAPTER ONE

MY STORY

I owned a big house, drove a Porsche and an SUV, ran a successful clothing distribution business and had lots of money—all this by the time I was in my mid-twenties. At the same time, I was constantly under high stress and fearful of not meeting my huge business expenses. To make it through the day, I would smoke a cigarette, and then another one—in all, between thirty to forty Camel Filters a day. Smoking a cigarette was the last thing I did before going to sleep, and I often woke up with one in my mouth.

I had a short fuse. To compensate for my underlying fears—fear of conflict, fear of abandonment, fear of failure—I walked around with my fists clenched, transmitting a message of "don't mess with me". I was friendly with my fifty employees, but they were also scared of me, knowing that if something was not done to my liking, I would likely call one of them into my office and start shouting. Never far from the surface of my genial face was an underlying state of grumpy annoyance. There was likewise lots of aggression in my relationship with my girlfriend, who then became my fiancé.

Physically, I was falling apart. In my teens I had been super-fit, practicing martial arts, playing squash and regularly going to the gym. All the discipline I had previously devoted to physical exercise I now threw into my work. I realized how out of shape I was when, one day, I was walking my beautiful Rottweiler in the street and had trouble breathing and became dizzy. Although the event shook me, I continued working too hard and smoking too much.

I was clearly unhappy, but, possessing no awareness of my emotions, if you had asked me how I was feeling I would have said 'okay'. Born under the sign of Scorpio, I am good at masking how I am feeling. Most friends, and even my sister, perceived me as being carefree. Later, I came to realise that to a large extent I was dissociated, but this word meant nothing to me at the time.

I became engaged to my girlfriend because she wanted to get married;

but I had no intention of marrying her. My first girlfriend, when I was sixteen, cheated on me. Since then I have had a deep-seated fear of girlfriends cheating on me. So, of course, according to the Law of Attraction—which we shall explore further in this book—I attracted girlfriend after girlfriend who was likely to cheat on me. My fiancé had a promiscuous past and lied a lot. When our relationship deteriorated we went to a couples' counsellor. I quickly realised that I wanted to end the relationship, but my fear of abandonment was too strong. So I worked with the counsellor individually. This was my first experience of introspection, but I was still so detached from my emotions that I could barely explore them, even at an intellectual level.

Finally, after catching my fiancé in a lie, I broke off our engagement and ended our relationship. I felt sad and depressed. Throughout the turmoil of ending our relationship I had not been keeping a good eye on my business, and some months later I realised that my business partner was stealing from me. He was funnelling our merchandise into stores he had opened with his brothers, where he would sell it.

I was physically strong, having built up my physique as a teenager to compensate for my fear of conflict. I could bench-press a hundred kilograms. Nevertheless, when I went to confront my business partner in one of his stores, I had ten bouncers, or bodyguards, with me. As we stood there waiting for my partner to arrive, inside I was trembling with fear. The bouncer-in-charge pulled me aside and offered to kill my business partner for a sum that would have been easily affordable to me. I declined his proposal, and went ahead and dissolved my business partnership. However, my desire for vengeance was so great that I fantasised about my business partner's death, and for a few days I had nightmares.

I perceived a change happening in the clothing industry, and with the South African rand depreciating heavily, all signs pointed towards selling the business, but out of fear of change I clung onto it a while longer. Around this time I started to meditate with the Theosophical Society. I had become interested in meditation several years before, but had consciously decided to put it aside and devote myself to making money. Now, I was able to establish a daily meditation practice, but because my nervous system was hyper-aroused, sitting in silence was hugely uncomfortable for me. In silence, there was simply no way to avoid the big constant buzzing inside of me. It was only many years later that I would begin to understand the natural regulating mechanisms of the body and how to support them. I was also to learn how to allow my body to release the huge energy stuck inside of me and the big buzz eventually quietened down.

One day, as part of ridding myself of my fear of heights, I went to the highest diving board at the Ellis Park swimming pool. I stood at the edge of the board looking down and froze, unable to move my legs. After twenty minutes of standing on the board I managed to jump. It was exhilarating. That jump—a step into the abyss—opened the door for me. Within three months I sold my house, cars and business, practically everything I owned, and left South Africa. I was twenty-nine.

I travelled and started to regain my health. In Israel I worked on a kibbutz and cleaned floors, windows and toilets. In one month I cleaned enough to make up for all the years other people had cleaned for me. Having cleaned enough, and unused to working for someone else, I only stayed on the kibbutz a month. I went to Egypt, where I ate well, got fit and lost weight. I meditated on the beach in Dahab every day and began to read spiritual and personal development books, which provided motivation and offered techniques for changing behavioural patterns.

In Southeast Asia I devised a plan for giving up smoking—slowly but surely. I started to only smoke in isolation, never socially. Also, I knew that after eating I wanted to smoke, so I would wait for at least half an hour before having a cigarette. After a cigarette, I always wanted something to drink; so I wouldn't allow myself to drink for another fifteen minutes, which soon became half an hour. In this way I created increasingly longer gaps between cigarettes. Of equal importance, I began to smoke more consciously. When I had a cigarette, that's all I did. I sat and watched myself inhale and exhale smoke. It was my 'smoking meditation', and I quickly realised what a horrible habit it is: the taste of the burned tobacco, the burned throat and dirty, stained fingers and the chronic cough.

My stop-smoking plan went on for a month and then, in Bali, I climbed up a cliff where, below, waves were smashing into the rock face. In a personal, sacred ritual, I asked the ocean to forgive me for polluting it and then threw my pack of Camel Filters into the water and never again took another puff. It was a huge turning point and one of the most beautiful things I've ever done for myself. Smoking had not only been destroying me physically, but it had also been a crutch which I had used to mask my fears and anxieties. As my commitment to my emotional growth and spiritual journey deepened, there was no chance I would ever return to smoking. I wanted to develop self-mastery by exploring my body, mind and emotions; not to conceal them.

I returned to South Africa. I still had considerable savings from selling my clothing business, but my fear of not having enough, my desire to be safe later on, drove me to make more money. So I launched a new business.

At the same time, I launched myself into self-growth through therapy, books and groups. Part of this exploration—and the intensity with which I pursued it—was driven by my back pain. The pain had started as a niggling sensation between my shoulder blades, one that never went away but rather progressively worsened. I tried practicing yoga, but that only made it worse. The back pain eventually became debilitating. I would get up and need to lie down again within a couple of hours. With a sense of irony, I remembered how, years before, when my ex-fiancé had told me that she had a sore back, I hadn't been able to understand; I had wondered what it might feel like.

In the search to cure my back pain I went for sessions in chiropractics, osteopathy, Hololographic Breathwork, kinesiology, Rolfing and Postural Integration. I approached this work—as well as the other spiritual and emotional work I was doing—with a tremendous focus and commitment to heal, transform, attain self-mastery and even enlightenment. I was determined to achieve a state of relief from all suffering. I changed my diet and, for a few years, became vegan. Every weekend I was in a group or workshop. Each day I did something, in addition to my regular meditation practice, to further my wellbeing, be it a session or reading. Looking back, however, I realise that my intensity and discipline was driven by fear. Change had to be now. Only later did I learn patience and an understanding that it takes time and trust for our journeys to unfold. Eventually, I was to learn to be more relaxed and enjoy the process.

Throughout the time of my second business venture, much of my energy went into my personal and spiritual growth. Existence reflected my energetic focus and kicked me into my next stage of life by shoving me out of the business world. My new business partner defrauded me—along with several other investors—and fled the country. I was left in debt, with huge overheads and no income stream. Every door I tried to open to generate cash slammed shut, and I was technically bankrupt, losing practically everything that I owned.

After striving so hard and then losing my business, I was at wit's end. I surrendered and said to existence, 'Okay, now you take care of me.' By letting go, it was a huge turning point in my life, and the beginning of my transition from the business world to that of being a therapist.

When I quit my business and moved on with my life and left my sister in charge. It was then that the business finally started to generate money. In hindsight, it was obvious that I was meant to move on. Now that I had taken the dreaded steps, existence began to support me financially.

By selling an old Mercedes Benz and, for a year, receiving a regular salary from my former business, I temporarily had enough money while I explored my spiritual path. I went to a spiritual commune in India, one of the largest centres in the world for meditation and transformation. There, I continued my intensive psycho-emotional work and meditation.

I went on a fourteen-day meditation retreat in Chennai, and afterwards took a pilgrimage around Mount Aranachula in Tiruvanumalai, where Ramana Maharishi had become enlightened. Three days later, I met and had lunch with Zia, the woman who—a month later—would become my wife. Little did I know that I was about to enter a seven-year 'marriage workshop', one of the most important workshops in my life.

Zia and I were at a friend's house. A marriage procession was making its cacophonous way down the street outside.

She turned to me and said, 'Look at those people destroying their lives.'

The next morning I woke up beside her.

'Do you want to destroy your life and marry me?' I asked her.

I was in love. She was a beautiful, talented woman. We were both on conscious, spiritual paths. I saw us as soul mates, and that ours was a true love which would last forever. I cried, a poignant moment in which I deeply felt the immense beauty of being so in love, and simultaneously a tremendous fear of loss. I was also aware of the practical difficulties of our sustaining a long-term relationship, she being Indian and I South African. I was determined to cement our relationship and I wanted to do it now.

A few weeks later we had a beautiful marriage ceremony in a healing sanctuary in South Africa. The first few months of our marriage were also the blissful honeymoon period of our relationship. We were deeply, romantically entwined and, having both recently experienced intensive heart-opening processes in India, were in expansive, loving states. However, anything that expands, naturally also contracts, and as our individual habit patterns came to the fore, our difficulties began.

Life, in its uncanny way, picked precisely the right match for me out of the billions of people on the planet—just like two pieces needed to complete a puzzle. Even though we were from two different cultures and lived on different continents, Zia and I had so much to share and teach each other. Admittedly, many of these lessons have been painful and difficult for me.

I was to later learn that one definition of trauma is 'too much, too soon, too fast'; it can overwhelm the nervous system. In my marriage to Zia, a lot happened in a short space of time. Immediately after the wedding ceremony in South Africa, we returned to India for another ceremony. We planned to move to Europe within a couple of months. It was then April, the month in Mumbai when the monsoon starts to build up and it becomes oppressively hot and humid. I felt drained and lethargic. It would have made sense for me to go for a few weeks to Pune, which is at a higher altitude and cooler than Mumbai. But my fear of abandonment crept in and my co-dependent behaviour towards my wife began.

We discovered that Zia was pregnant. Overnight, I went from a relatively carefree space—one in which I was looking forward to being playful for a while—to the pressure of providing for a child. Being an expectant father brought up a lot of fear in me, especially because I had recently lost all my financial wealth and was in a career transition.

My daughter Sufia has been an amazing gift and an incredible catalyst to open my heart. I will not dwell here on all the happiness and sadness I experienced in my marriage. In short, my nervous system was overwhelmed. I couldn't think straight. My mind started to freeze, and so did my body.

Chronic fatigue set in. If I exercised a moderate amount every day I was fine, but if I did just a little too much my body would shut down.

My short fuse came to the fore. I would sit in blissful meditation and afterwards, as I was walking out of the room, my wife would make a remark and I would freak out. Uncontrollable anger would arise and I would feel this overwhelming pressure throughout my body. The next day I would be exhausted, feeling as if I'd been hit by a truck. With a sense of irony, I remembered all the groups in which I had worked on my anger; all the catharsis and pillow-hitting. And here I was, in my marriage, together with the person I loved the most, and I didn't seem to be able to prevent myself from directing my anger at her. My emotions were hijacking me.

As I said earlier, in terms of my personal growth, my marriage to Zia was one of my most important learning experiences. This is because it acted as an inescapable glaring reflection, or mirror, of my outstanding issues, the ones that were preventing me from achieving a sense of wellbeing. My marriage served as a huge motivator, a conjugal kick in the pants, to go more deeply towards working with and coming to terms with these issues.

Always at the core of my issues was my fear of abandonment. Zia and I would argue, she would threaten to leave, and as she turned to walk out, great fear would well up inside me and I would cling to her. I literally would physically take hold of her in an attempt to keep her with me. Over time I learned to be with my fears, and to let her walk out without holding her back. Then I would go inside of myself and explore how I could shift my behavioural patterns. I learned this through the work I formulated and describe in this book: the Three Steps.

There are two techniques which underlie the Three Steps. One is a trauma healing therapy called Somatic Experiencing, and the other is Vipassana meditation.

Between 2003 and 2006 I travelled to Italy twice a year to pursue and complete a course in Somatic Experiencing, a naturalistic approach to resolving trauma. I am lucky I had not altogether avoided trauma therapy after my initial negative exposure to it. Back in Pune, India I had seen an ad for trauma-release sessions. I spoke to the therapist and said to her, 'I'm sure that I've been through trauma…'

'Well,' came her careless response, 'if you had been traumatized you would know about it.'

Her remark was not only flippant but, I later realised, also inane. I am now aware that I have gone through every category of trauma—including abandonment, loss, physical and emotional abuse, sexual trauma, high impact accidents and surgery—except natural disaster. Contrary to what the Pune therapist told me, trauma survivors often do not realise that they have been traumatised.

Trauma is more of a physiological problem than a psychological one. The reason why Somatic Experiencing works so well is because it prioritises the body and works with bodily sensations. As a person recounts a traumatic event, his or her body activates itself in preparation for a fight-flight response. The trauma therapist notices when the body is activated and helps it to deactivate, often by completing the fight, flight responses or through resourcing—having the client recall a person or place to which he or she has positive associations, and this creates a soothing mechanism. Going back and forth in this way—exploring trauma and soothing the body—allows discharge to happen and the nervous system to become more resilient. Blocked or pent-up energy causing the client difficulties—rage, for example—releases, and the body naturally returns to health, to a place where the person can be more present, feel more relaxed and comfortable, and achieve a greater sense of well-being.

I gradually came to see how trauma was the source of my highly charged, intense personality, my inner directive of "it has to happen now". Trauma work gave me an understanding of how traumatic events—even just a single event—can have a profound effect on the rest of our lives. It gave me hope that there was a way of resolving these deep seated issues. Somatic Experiencing is based in the science and observed experience of how the body, particularly the nervous system, works—how it goes from a relaxed state to a charged one, and vice versa. This is observable in others and experienced in oneself as a felt sense.

I also began to see why all the therapy I had done before—especially the workshops and meditative therapies based in catharsis—had never solved my huge anger and insecurity issues. Many gurus and therapists pay lip service to the concept of the integrated body-mind nexus. But until I explored

Somatic Experiencing, none of the more than one hundred workshops I had attended had delved into the inner workings of the body. Even many highly regarded bodyworkers and massage therapists, who seemed to have a keen intuition and understanding about people's anatomy and were able to perceive holding patterns and blocked energy in others, did not seem to have much sensitivity towards the inner workings of their own bodies, or much capacity to be with whatever sensations arose in them. These therapists encouraged catharsis, a process that never worked for me. By overcharging my system, it exacerbated the damage already done. Regular catharting kept me in a constant state of overwhelm, so I never had adequate time and space to really discharge; I now know that this is a sure-fire way to strengthen and more deeply ingrain traumatic symptoms.

Somatic Experiencing works slowly—a little bit at a time—and respectfully, creating support for the body's own wisdom and mechanisms to return us to balance. Somatic Experiencing recognises that we all carry a blueprint for returning to a state of wellbeing; and, as many of my behavioural patterns started to shift, this was my experience. Because I was living in India, I had no Somatic Experiencing therapist to work with, so I worked by myself, visiting and working with each of my main traumas, making use of the techniques I learned in Italy.

I worked a lot with my anger, fear and insecurity, developing my body's capacity to be with these feelings and the uncomfortable sensations they evoked. Previously, I had always wanted to control my environment, but now I was able to be more at ease with unknown possibilities. I had been extremely possessive of my wife, always wanting to know where she was going and what she did; of her too I was able to let go more and more. In the beginning of our relationship, Zia and I had fought all the time and hurled much verbal and emotional abuse at each other. After a fight I used to obsess over all the past similar incidents in which she had done the same thing that was now making me angry; this obsessing would keep my anger fuelled for hours, even days. Now, I naturally did not dwell on past instances and stayed with the current ones. This helped me to be more present. The frequency and intensity of our fighting decreased and I stopped calling her names. Eventually, when Zia and I separated, I faced the hurt and pain of loneliness and abandonment, emotional and physical states against which I had formerly and instinctively protected my heart.

I still felt insecurity and fear, but I was able to acknowledge and be with these feelings, without always reacting to them. Before, a small incident had sparked a big fire. Now, it would spark a small flame. Whereas I used to binge-eat, my diet and eating habits normalized. No longer being in constant pressure-cooker mode, I felt physically more comfortable and at home in my body.

The very fact that Somatic Experiencing prioritises the physiology is one reason it works so well with clients in India, where psychology is still taboo. Most Indians view someone who consults a psychologist in the same way they would look at a person with an I am crazy sign glued to his forehead. Not just Indians, though; with people from every cultural background, it is generally far easier to teach them how to explore their bodily patterns as opposed to their mental processes. I quickly found that, after teaching my clients how to go inside their bodies, what to look for and how to support their body-minds, they could help themselves and were not necessarily dependent on me or another therapist.

In 2008, a cyclone hit Myanmar (formerly Burma), killing 140,000 people. The Catholic Church invited me to run a trauma healing program in Yangon. An archbishop, two bishops and sixty priests attended my first training. In the beginning, the training was very difficult because none of the priests wanted to be there; the archbishop had ordered them to participate. The first day was like pulling teeth. All the clergymen were stressed from working with cyclone victims, and many also displayed traumatic symptoms themselves.

I persevered in teaching the clergymen the Three Steps I detail in this book, and worked to help them heal both their own symptoms and those of others. Afterwards, the archbishop told me that it was the first time so many priests had been in a workshop in which no conflict had arisen among them. He was so impressed with the results of the four-day training that he supported a yearlong program in which I trained two hundred and fifty participants, all of whom had been affected by the devastation.

The outcome of the workshops were spectacular. I was awestruck by how dramatically the participants' wellbeing increased in such a short time. These simple people from the villages picked the technique up so fast because they were so in touch with their bodies. They were able to shift many of their debilitating symptoms merely by practicing the Three Steps with one another. Their stomach pains subsided, their constipation eased and their diarrhoea stopped. Their migraines disappeared, their anxiety diminished remarkably, and they were able to breathe again, to laugh and to rest. Many had suffered from insomnia since the cyclone; they could now sleep again. Phobias about the rain and fear of the returning cyclone vanished. I now knew that this simple technique could easily be taught across cultures.

It was no coincidence that events took me to Myanmar which is where S.N. Goenka learned and mastered the Vipassana meditation technique and which he has now spread worldwide. It was around this time, in India, that I participated in my first ten-day Vipassana retreat. My main motivation for attending the retreat was that some of my students had told me that the work I was teaching them was similar to Vipassana, and I wanted to be able to explain the difference between the two techniques.

To say that I was pleasantly surprised by the Vipassana retreat would be a gigantic understatement. For me, it was like going home. I loved everything about it. There was a structure and a space that supported everyone meditating, going inwards and, most of all, through the beautiful technique of Vipassana, investigating their bodily sensations. Goenkaji relates how the Buddha taught that if we want to clear out the impurities from our bodyminds we must explore our sensations; that through bodily sensations we can witness the deepest roots of our minds; and that this is the path towards transcending worldly conditioning and even towards, for lack of a better term, enlightenment. Because of the therapy sessions and trainings I was already giving I knew this to be true: by witnessing the body's workings we can release and change long-term, deep-seated patterns.

My sessions and trainings evolved into their present form—the Three Steps—a kind of synthesis between Somatic Experiencing and Vipassana meditation. Sitting through a ten-day meditation retreat can be very tough for people who are new to meditating. Those who have been through lots of trauma and are highly activated will probably be resistant to registering for a retreat in the first place. For them, sitting still, even for two minutes, is a ghastly prospect, and consciously exploring their bodily sensations at the same time only compounds the agony, at least initially. My experience is that working with the Three Steps is an easy, gentle way for people to explore the body's sensations, to release pent-up energy and to bring the body back into balance.

Education of how the body functions is an important part of the Three Steps, so that a person who is stuck in states of high arousal can consciously support his or her body to release and return to balance without interrupting the process. In this way, the Three Steps is a gentle approach that can be practiced at any time, and it assists people in working with movement towards stillness. Practicing the Three Steps naturally and eventually leads to a profound space of Vipassana, of watching the interrelationship between the mind and body at a very deep internal level. The Three Steps changes a person's perspective of their symptoms, and they realise that symptoms are just our bodies pointing the way towards our return to health.

S.N. Goenka tells how his severe migraines sent him in search of a cure via medicine, and when that failed, how he happened upon Vipassana meditation. After practicing Vipassana for some time his migraines fell away. Some of the most rewarding shifts I have had in my own health have come at times when I have applied the Three Steps during bouts of fever or flu and when my body has been in agony. At times of illness our deepest body-mind patterns come to the fore. By viewing sickness as a tide, and by sitting and watching symptoms rise and recede, I have been able to transform many of the deep-seated habit patterns of emoting, thinking and behaving that hitherto prevented me from achieving wellbeing.

My own healing and transformation has been astounding, and I am now a different person. Not only do I have greater emotional mastery, but I also perceive in wonder the stillness and silence out of which all creation comes forth. A Japanese master recently likened me to the Sherpa, Tensing Norgay, who led Edmund Hillary on their famous ascent of Mount Everest. The healing journey I gratefully share with you, the reader, is sometimes as perilous as climbing Mount Everest. To reach the summit, a guide along the way is often welcome company.

SECTION TWO

THE BODY AND ITS SENSATIONS

"If you have the willingness to accept the realities of life, you will live longer. It has allowed me to reach 93 years of age. I was raised to value the mind and intellect, not the body. Favoring the life of the mind went against my nature. Healing the splits between my mind and my body has been my life's challenge."

- Alexander Lowen, M.D. Honoring the Body,
one's home is one's body.

CHAPTER TWO

THE IMPORTANCE OF THE BODY

'The body' refers to our physical body, which contains our skeleton, joints, ligaments, muscles, organs, glands, the spinal column, the brain, nervous system, veins, blood, tissue and skin. As we explain throughout this book, there is really no separation between the body and the mind. Our thoughts, which we usually associate with the workings of the mind, have their deepest roots in the body. That is why we use the concept of the 'body-mind'.

Few of us have been properly educated about the real importance and value of the body. This section restores the body to its rightful place as the basis for all that we experience: our thoughts, feelings and actions; our behaviour and moods; and how we see the world and experience life. In fact, all elements of human experience occur within the theatre of the body.

As the book explains, in order to transform we need to make a conscious decision to enter the theatre of the body and watch the fantastic interplay between body and mind, with the main actors being our thoughts, emotions, feelings and bodily sensations. Fortunately, this particular theatre is never sold out. You can always get a seat. Plus, it is always close by. In fact, it goes everywhere you go, because it is your body.

This chapter familiarizes us with key concepts and various workings of the body which are crucial to understanding its interrelationship with thoughts, emotions and behaviour.

Survival and wellbeing

All elements of our experience are geared towards ensuring our survival with wellbeing. Every organism, from the amoeba to the human being, has evolved to maximize its chances of survival and wellbeing. These 'chances' are based on physiologies that have evolved over the course of many millions of years, starting with the amoeba and leading to increas-

Roots

ingly complex life forms: reptiles, mammals and humans. All mammals' nervous systems, including that of humans, are very similar.

Survival with wellbeing is based on homeostasis.

"All living organisms, from the humble amoeba to the human, are born with devices designed to solve automatically, no proper reasoning required, the basic problems of life. Those problems are: finding sources of energy; maintaining a chemical balance of the interior compatible with the life process; maintaining the organism's structure by repairing its wear and tear; and fending off external agents of disease and physical injury. The single word homeostasis is convenient shorthand for the ensemble of regulations and the resulting stage of regulated life.[1]"

In mammals, the life-regulating mechanisms that ensure homeostasis include various systems: circulatory, respiratory, immune, digestive, nervous, endocrine, musculoskeletal and reproductive. Maintaining homeostasis by means of these regulatory systems is the basis for our various drives, such as hunger, thirst, sex and territoriality. For example, when a mammal is active it expends energy in the form of sugar stored in the body. This causes its level of blood sugar to drop, which stimulates sensations of hunger and motivates the organism to search for food. Once the food has been ingested and digested, the blood sugar returns to balance and a sense of satiation occurs. The mammal's hunger drive has been sated.

Our drives and instincts are intrinsically linked to our bodies' physiological processes. In turn, our emotions are intrinsically linked to our drives and instincts. It follows that our emotions also have their basis in physiological processes. In other words, our body and its various processes are the building blocks of emotion. How quickly we breathe, the rhythm and rate at which our hearts pump, how resistant our bodies are to infection and disease, are all involved in emotion.

For example, two men have an argument. They start to get angry. Their faces become flushed, their jaws clench, they feel tightness and pressure in the chest, heat in their backs, their voices become louder, their tones more forceful, their hearts race and their breathing comes faster and shallower. At a physiological level, an incredible amount is happening within their bodies. Hormones, such as adrenalin, are being released, more blood is being channelled to their arms and legs, and digestion has momentarily stopped. Their muscles tense and ready for action, prepared for a fight. In fact, their whole bodies—all of their regulatory mechanisms—are organising themselves to fight, to ensure their survival and their wellbeing. There is a perceived threat and their bodies have prepared themselves to survive with wellbeing by thwarting the threat and then returning to equilibrium.

Elements of experience

Humans' experience of life is made up of different elements. One is behaviour. Some behaviour is voluntary, for example when we use our muscles to walk or talk or pick up something. There is also involuntary behaviour, for example habitual gestures, facial expressions and breathing. Voluntary and involuntary behaviour overlaps. Our constant breathing is essential to our survival, but we can also sometimes choose to control how quickly or deeply we breathe. Similarly, blinking is involuntary behaviour, but we can also choose to close our eyes and blink. Both involuntary and voluntary behaviour can be further classified as being either non-verbal or verbal. Verbally, we can talk and be conscious about what we're saying or, when we react instinctively to something, a slip of the tongue may occur and we may say something we later regret.

Another element of experience is impressions. Impressions are anything that arises through the five senses: sight, hearing, touch, smell and taste. There are external impressions (for example, when we see a friend) and internal impressions (when we remember seeing that friend).

Emotions (for example, anger, fear, sadness, shame, and happiness) are also elements of experience, as is intellect (thoughts, meanings and concepts). Sensations take place in the body and are felt physical experiences. They consist of all the biochemical and electromagnetic reactions occurring in the body.

Awareness is an overarching element of our experience. Awareness is the quality of being an observer or witness. It is that part of us which can observe all of these other elements, almost from an independent point of view. Part of the spiritual path is to develop and cultivate our capacity of awareness, of being a witness. Awareness has a strong physiological aspect because, as we shall see, we need to learn to tolerate a keen and regular awareness of these elements of experience in order to be in the present.

With each moment of our experience—every impression, emotion thought and action, whether voluntary or involuntary—sensations occur within our bodies. For example, a woman sees her daughter (impression) upon returning from a business trip. Her sense of joy and delight (emotion) arises, which displays on her face as she smiles (involuntary behaviour). She says, 'Oh, my darling!'—a (verbal) expression of her happiness—as she reaches out and opens her arms to embrace her daughter (non-verbal behavior).

At the same time that all these experiential elements are occurring within her body, there are millions of micro-processes taking place, which put this woman in a state of joy and delight and drive her to move, speak and express as she does. She might be able to feel these processes inside her body in various ways, including warmth and tingling or flowing sensations; a sense of expansion in her chest; and a general sense of openness and ease. As she moves to pick up her daughter her heart may pump faster to send blood rushing into her arms and legs. She might even experience an impulse to cry, and a tear may well up in her eye. The extent to which she has developed her capacity of awareness, of witnessing, will influence the degree to which she is aware of these various sensations.

States of being

At any given point in time each of us are in one sort of state of being or the other. A state of being (Bubble) includes all the elements of experience described above: emotions, thoughts, images, behaviour, sensations and awareness. These elements link together in certain patterns to create various states of being, which not only colour how we perceive and experience the present moment, but really is our experience of life in the present. A state of being can be thought of as a snapshot at any point in time of our experience in each moment.

Generally, most of the elements of experience—which are linked together based on previous experiences—occur without our conscious awareness. George Gurdjieff, an Armenian mystic, likened human beings to automatons, for the very reason that most of the time we are operating on automatic pilot.

Bubbles

In any given situation we are more or less thinking, feeling and acting in a pre-programmed manner, a phenomenon we shall explore more fully later in this section.

We can develop a sensitivity and awareness of the underlying implicit elements that constitute our experience of life. By doing so, changes and shifts in our experience can take place at a deep fundamental level. Not only will states of being that prevent us from maintaining wellbeing fall away, but we will also more regularly start to manifest states of being conducive to wellbeing—states of being that are, in and of themselves, wellbeing.

For example, a friend of mine ran his own business and was generally considered to be a successful, confident man. But whenever he was in the position of having to ask advice from someone in authority he choked up and entered a state of being dominated by feelings of fear. This would cause him to avoid asking for the advice or help he needed to run his business better. Through applying the Three Steps detailed in Section Three—which cultivated an awareness of sensations that made up his underlying physiological patterns—the intensity of fear my friend experienced decreased dramatically. He stopped choking up and found that he was able to ask for advice easily. Over time his state of being when asking for help went from one dominated by fear to one of confidence and expectation of success.

As with all of us, sometimes my friend received what he was asking for and sometimes his queries would be rejected. In the latter instance, he would apply the Three Steps to his 'rejected state of being'. And when successful, he would sit with the feelings of success and anchor them into his experience. He more regularly started to ask the right questions to the right people, thereby increasing his chances of obtaining the desired outcomes. His business became more successful and the positive ramifications rippled throughout his life. Even more important than the change in his outward behaviour were the shifts in his underlying emotions, which led his body to emit new frequencies and attract new people and positive circumstances into his life.

Most people try to manage their states of being by talking themselves into a different, more 'desirable' state. This works some of the time, but it is both exhausting and limited in its degree of success. As will be explained later in this section, our implicit elements—of which we are generally unaware—are always waiting around the corner, ready to hijack us . The most powerful way to change our experience of life is by going to its core, rooted in the sensations of the body.

The body as a biological musical instrument

Both nature and nurture determine how a person's physiology develops throughout his or her lifespan. As soon as we are conceived we are imparted with certain genes, certain DNA. This amounts to a hardwiring of the processes that ensure homeostasis.

While we are still in the womb, our mother's state of being strongly influences how our physiologies develop. For instance, a mother who is experiencing loneliness will transmit these feelings to her foetus. In response, the foetus might constrict and begin to develop a physiological pattern revolving around loneliness. This nurturing influence continues, of course, after we are born. The way our parents continue to nurture us—their actions and the environment they create—as well as our schooling and the surrounding social climate, impact the way our physiologies and brains develop.

Proceeding with the example of the lonely mother, a deep sense of loneliness may run like a background feeling throughout her child's life, but the child has no cognitive memory of why. This is because loneliness is a physiological pattern and not just a story, or a single event, which he can consciously recall. In an attempt to resolve this lonely feeling, the child develops strategies. Perhaps he reaches out for comfort, soothing, and love. Perhaps, due to his mother's own unresolved loneliness, she is unable to adequately nurture her child, to hold him and to comfort him. This establishes a precedent for his expectations, one informed by disappointment, and it reflects in his body. A solemn look might pervade his face. He might take on a drooped posture and a feeling of heaviness. Certain of his organs might become constricted and not function optimally. Together, a signature pattern for loneliness has been created in the boy, and every time loneliness is triggered this particular physiological pattern will be evoked and embedded more deeply.

According to Dr Candace Pert, who was chief of brain biochemistry at the National Institutes of Health and is the author of the book, molecules of emotion, "emotions are electrochemical signals that affect the chemistry and electricity of every cell in the body and orchestrate the interactions among all of the body's organs and systems. Plus, emotions not only modulate the body's electrical state, but also affect the world outside our bodies".[2] We each have our unique electrical states, which are continually emitting unique frequencies into the universe and attracting to us our life experiences. Our bodies can be likened to biological musical instruments constantly sending out vibrations, almost like tunes, to which the whole of existence responds.

We hug our child and feel contentment; our bodies organize into a pattern of contentment and send out one tune. We feel loneliness and disappointment; our bodies organize into a pattern representing loneliness and disappointment and send out another tune. We think about money and experience abundance; our bodies organize into a pattern representing abundance and send out yet another tune. All these tunes weave in and out of each other to compose the songs that we, our bodies, sing throughout the day, throughout our lives. And the universe responds in kind, magically attracting and creating our life experiences—from the people we meet and whom we choose as friends and lovers, to the kinds of jobs we have and the communities in which we live. Everything in our lives—including life's interconnectedness, its synchronicities—is a result of the notes, tunes and melodies we emit.

A musical instrument's vibrational frequencies create the sounds we identify as various musical notes. The piano for example is, a complex device with hundreds of separate parts. A keyboard has eighty-eight notes, ranging from high treble to low bass notes. When a key is pressed, a hammer strikes a specific string. Because it is strung with a particular tension, the string creates a specific musical sound. The strings, in turn, are connected to a large soundboard that amplifies the sound. By pushing down keys in different combinations we create music: melodies and songs which produce various atmospheres, moods and colours, all of which can be perceived by others.

Like pianos, our bodies also compose songs that contain complex vibrational patterns, frequencies and tones. Each and every physiological process within our bodies contributes to the note, tune or melody that the body is playing at any particular moment. These processes include the electromagnetic field exchanges and the hormonal, neurochemical, bioelectrical and chemical messages continuously moving through our bodies day and night, whether we are awake or asleep. These processes also include the quality of our blood and the tone and tension of our bodies—formed by the density of our bones and the tightness of our muscles, joints and ligaments, which create our posture and gestures.

Together, all these processes orchestrate the notes, vibrations and frequencies we send out to our surroundings. The body is an intricate interconnected web; pluck one strand and it reverberates throughout the whole. From the tip of our toes to the top of our heads, each cell, neuron and hormone, every bone, joint and ligament, and all of our organs and muscles are constantly shifting and changing in a dynamic interplay of biological patterns.

Whether we are aware of it or not, every single thing about our bodies contributes to our life melodies, from our physical features, the position of the tongue in the mouth, the quality and position of the teeth, the tone of the vocal chords, and the tension and health of the eyes; to the shallowness or depth of the breath, the pace of the digestive and elimination processes, the quantity of urine we store in the bladder, the quality and tone of our reproductive organs, and the state of our guts.

At the microscopic level, the vibrations created by our bodies as biological musical instruments are determined by metabolic processes, which are constantly working to maintain an internal chemical balance, or homeostasis. These metabolic processes affect the quality of the water within the trillions of cells of our bodies. Nearly two-thirds of the human body and one half of each of our organs by volume consist of water. Water within living cells is highly structured, and the structure of cellular water is critical to the healthy chemical functioning of the cell and, by extension, the organism as a whole. Water also functions as a conductor of energy patterns and information.[3]

Our cells are constantly transmitting and receiving messages which, together, ensure that our hearts beat at a rate necessary to circulate a sufficient amount of blood throughout our veins; that our blood is neither too acidic nor too alkaline; that our stomachs and small intestines release the correct enzymes at the right time to enable us to digest our food. When we cut one of our fingers the nearby cells emit chemical signals of pain. In response, the immune system creates more white blood cells to ward off any microbes that might invade via the open wound, in addition to fibrinogen and other types of cells that help to close the wound. Together, this 'alarm system' of cellular chemical signals and responses forms our experience of pain. In contrast, when we feel pleasure our bodies experience an expansive feeling and a sense of relaxation and wellbeing as certain chemicals—for example, endorphins—are released.

It is important for us to remember that any sensations we may experience in our bodies are biological processes promoting homeostasis. These sensations are our bodies, our emotions, our minds—at their deepest roots. In the same way we change a song by rearranging its notes, chords and melody, we shift our experience of life and re-tune our bodily instruments by returning to their roots: our physiologies.

In creating our life songs, everything in our bodies—from the smallest cells to the largest organs—plays an important role. Because the Three Steps leads us on an intuitive journey towards open-heartedness, the following two sub-sections focus on the heart and the gut. This is not to minimize the importance of any other bodily system or part. The body is simply too vast to cover all of its interconnections in this one section of the book, whose aim is to introduce us to the significance of the body in relation to our thoughts, emotions and actions.

The heart, our sun

The epicentre of our health, emotions, thinking and actions is the heart. The condition and wellbeing of the heart lie at the core of our experience of life. The heart is also an organ of perception, simultaneously receiving information from the surroundings and monitoring the body-mind's internal environment. The heart is ever active, but we are not usually aware of its important role because, due to our discomfort in experiencing emotions, we get stuck in survival modes of fight and flight in a bid to defend the heart. Thus, we have become numb to the heart's messages, creating a partial blindness in how we perceive the world. Through the Three Steps described in Section Three we can regain our perceptual faculties and reconnect with the essence of our beings.

In his book Stillness, Charles Ridley writes:

"The heart is many things: a pump; an endocrine gland that regulates bodily function; a neurological organ that releases neurotransmitters that syncronize all three nervous systems—the central, autonomic, and enteric; and a nonlinear electromagnetic field generator that emanates a holographic matrix to infinity and back. The heart is a nervous system in its own right. Over half of the heart's fibers are neural ones that, through ganglia, connect to the entire soma, and directly to the brain. Through these connections your heart senses electromagnetic waves that emanate from as far out as infinity, and from as infinitesimal as the molecules in each cell. The heart, therefore, is an organ of perception that is coherent with the universal holographic matrix, and with your personal bodily matrix. The heart receives, processes and generates a complex series of holographic electromagnetic patterns that both monitor and adjust physiological events to maintain coherence between all the cells and organs of the body, and it maintains synchrony between the body and the environment".[4]

In short, the heart is the axis that links and coordinates our bodies and our minds by means of electromagnetic field exchanges and hormonal, neurochemical, bioelectrical and chemical messages.

Scientists at the Institute of Heartmath in California have found that:

The heart generates the body's most powerful and most extensive rhythmic magnetic field. Compared to the electromagnetic field produced by the brain, the electrical component of the heart's field is about 60 times greater in amplitude, and permeates every cell in the body. The magnetic component is approximately 5000 times stronger than the brain's magnetic field and can be detected several feet away from the body with sensitive magnetometers. The heart generates a continuous series of electromagnetic impulses in which the time interval between each beat varies in a dynamic and complex manner. The heart's ever-present rhythmic field is a powerful influence on processes throughout the body. We have demonstrated, for example, that brain rhythms naturally synchronise to the heart's rhythmic activity, and also that during sustained feelings of love or appreciation, the blood pressure and respiratory rhythms, among other oscillatory systems, entrain to the heart's rhythm. We propose that the heart's field acts as a carrier wave for information that provides a global synchronising signal for the entire body.[5]

It is helpful to think of the heart as the sun of our body-minds. Many ancient cultures worshipped the sun as a god, as the source of life energy. Any change in the sun's energy impacts the entire Earth, including all its beings. Any change in our hearts greatly affects our body-minds. If the sun were to die, so would all of Earth's creatures, just as a person dies when his or her heart ceases to function. The entire human organism is designed to protect and preserve the heart. All our emotions and our corresponding learned behaviours, including our postures, are, in fact, strategies to safeguard our hearts—so that we may stay alive and enhance our wellbeing.

All of our other organs—for example, the stomach, lungs, liver and pancreas—and our skeletal muscles, as well as the myriad metabolic processes in our bodies, collaborate to protect the heart. They compensate for any lack of wellbeing felt by the heart. If the heart is in pain they will assume some of that pain in order to defend the heart.

When we attempt to reawaken our heart perception, it is difficult to delve directly into the inner workings of the heart. Precisely because the entire body is protecting the heart, healing must take place in a non-linear fashion, from the periphery towards the centre.

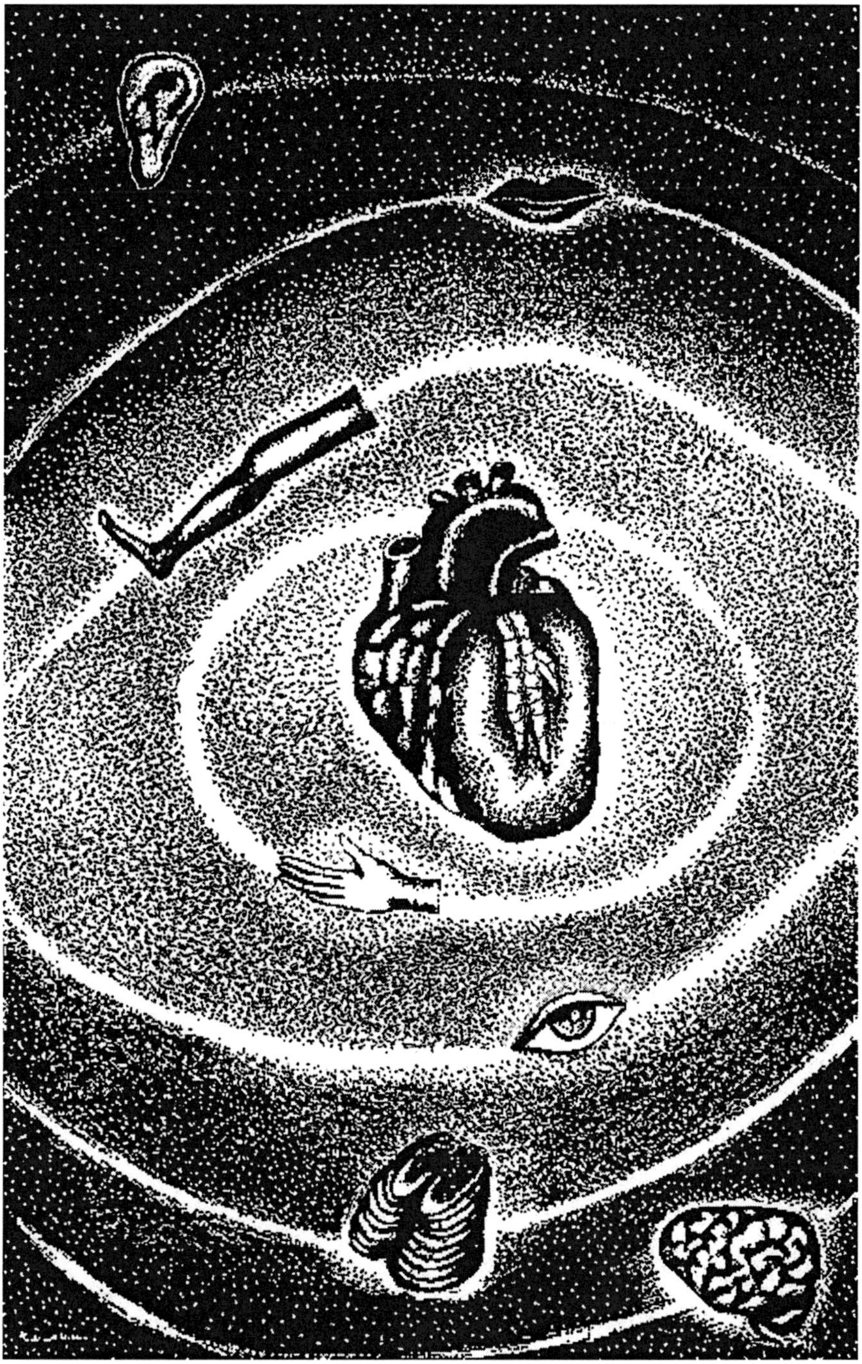

The Gut

We all know about 'gut instinct', which tells us when things feel right or when they don't. This instinct is something we cannot put into words; we just know. Dr. Michael Gershon, Professor of Anatomy and Cell Biology at Columbia-Presbyterian Medical Center in New York, has called the gut the 'second brain'.[6] It is fascinating that within our gastrointestinal tract—in the sheets of cells lining the oesophagus, stomach, small intestines and large intestines—is the enteric nervous system, which functions similarly to the brain in our heads. This 'second brain' is composed of a network of a hundred million neurons, which are constantly busy sensing, receiving and transmitting impulses.

Our 'gut-brains' are actually derived from the same embryonic tissue as our 'head-brains'. During early foetal development both the gut (oesophagus, stomach, small intestine and colon) and the primary brain develop from the same tissue. When this tissue divides, one piece grows into the central nervous system (our head-brain and cranial nerves), and the other becomes the enteric nervous system (the gut-brain). These two brains are connected via the autonomic nervous system.

Our gut-brain has a large role to play in our health and wellbeing. It literally has a mind of its own, recording and remembering experiences, responses and emotional reactions to whatever happens to us. It coordinates the metabolic and digestive processes, such as peristalsis and the release of hormones and enzymes to promote digestion, and it controls the immune cells in the gut. The gut is our primary source of pain relief, with the gut-brain arranging production of benzodiazepines, which can also be found in many pain relievers and anti-anxiety drugs, such as Valium. Ninety-five percent of our serotonin, the body's mood regulator, is produced in the gut.

The state of the gut has wide-ranging implications for the health of the entire body-mind. When the gut is overwhelmed it profoundly affects our comfort level and how we experience life. Various uncomfortable sensations emanate from the gut, such as the universal experience of 'butterflies' when we feel anxious. At other times, for example, when we are angry, the gut may constrict and feel like it is twisted into a knot. Other strong emotions may bring up a kind of gnawing or irritated feeling in the gut, and sometimes a burning sensation. It could indeed be 'burning up' from all the acid being generated within it. Growling, bloating, cramping and nausea are some other uncomfortable sensations felt in the gut. In contrast, in a state of ease and relaxation, the gut is balanced and feels soft, open, warm and at ease.

The gut comprises a large area of the body. The natural processes of digestion generate numerous sensations that form the basis of our instincts and emotions. The gut triggers emotions, and vice-versa: emotions trigger the gut. For example, a person may start to feel anxious about not having enough money. She feels 'butterflies' in the gut. At another time, due to particular digestive processes occurring within her gut, she may experience the same felt sensation of butterflies, and she then starts to dwell on thoughts of not having enough money, which escalate into feelings of anxiety.

Often, uncomfortable gut sensations are so constant and painful that we shut ourselves off from them and they are relegated to an unconscious level. In effect, we dissociate from the gut (dissociation is a process detailed in the next chapter) and lose our awareness of it. This may result in digestive imbalance and poor digestion, which causes a residue to accumulate in the body. Over time this residue blocks the ducts designed to absorb and transport the enzymes and other metabolic substances to the rest of the body.

The strength of our digestion and absorption is of utmost importance to our health and vitality—in my perspective, even more important than good nutrition. When our gut is compromised, no matter how well we eat, we cannot properly access the food's nutritional value. The vitamins and minerals so crucial to our health and wellbeing are not fully absorbed by the digestive tract, so they cannot be effectively metabolized and vital energy is lost.

Dissociating, or losing awareness, of our gut may offer us temporary relief from painful feelings, but it is ultimately detrimental to our health. Because the gut is such a vital organ of perception, losing awareness of the gut is as debilitating as losing one's eyesight. With practice, using the Three Steps, we can increase our level of awareness and regain consciousness of our gut-brain and all its vital messages that contribute to our survival and wellbeing.

The autonomic nervous system

A vital system in our bodies is the autonomic nervous system. It operates without us being aware of it, connecting the brain to all of the body's organs and helping to regulate all our basic bodily functions. The autonomic nervous system is involved in generating emotions and also our survival responses of fight, flight and freeze.

The autonomic nervous system has two main branches. One is 'the accelerator'. When we need energy for action, the accelerator is activated, just like when we want our car to go faster we press down on the gas pedal. This bodily accelerator is called the sympathetic nervous system. The other branch is 'the brake', or the parasympathetic nervous system. The brake allows the excess energy deployed while the accelerator has been active to release itself so that the body can return to a state of rest.

The autonomic nervous system is a reciprocal system. In a healthy, resilient nervous system, when the brake is released the accelerator activates, and when the brake is activated the accelerator releases. When our accelerators are activated—for example, in times of excitement, anger or stress, or when we need to exert ourselves physically—our entire bodies become prepared to meet these challenges. The heart rate, respiratory rate and blood pressure increase. The lungs dilate, the flow of saliva is inhibited, digestion slows down or even stops, the bladder contracts, and the pupils dilate and our eyes become more focused. The blood from our organs is directed into the skeletal muscles.

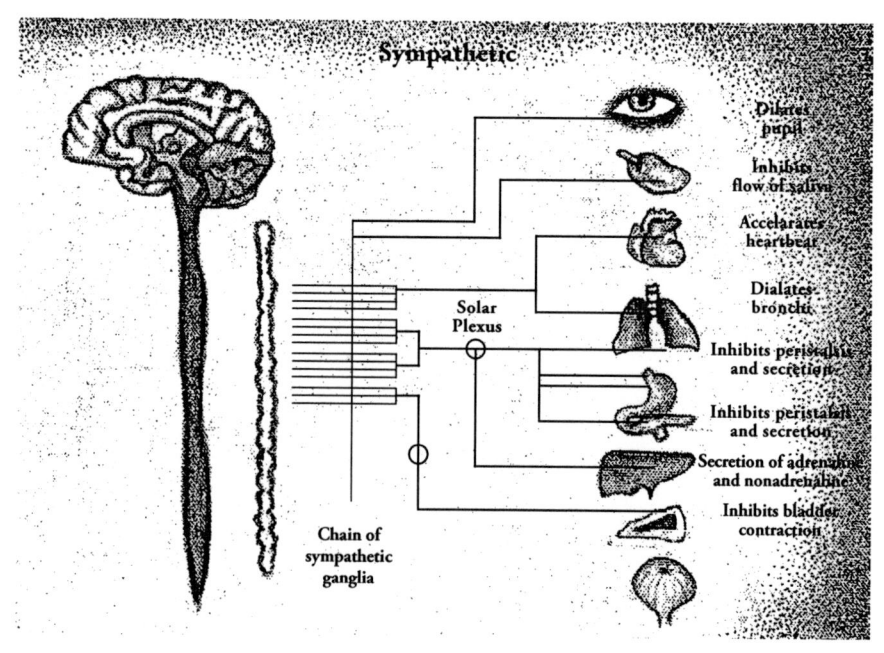

Accelerator

When the brake is activated to return us to a state of rest, the heart rate decreases and blood pressure drops; muscle tension relaxes; digestion resumes; and breathing becomes slower and deeper. The parasympathetic nervous system also promotes healthy functioning of the immune system, thereby allowing our bodies to regenerate as they rest. This seesaw process of accelerating and braking takes place throughout the day, even with simple actions like standing up (the accelerator activates to generate energy) and sitting back down (the brake is activated and we rest).

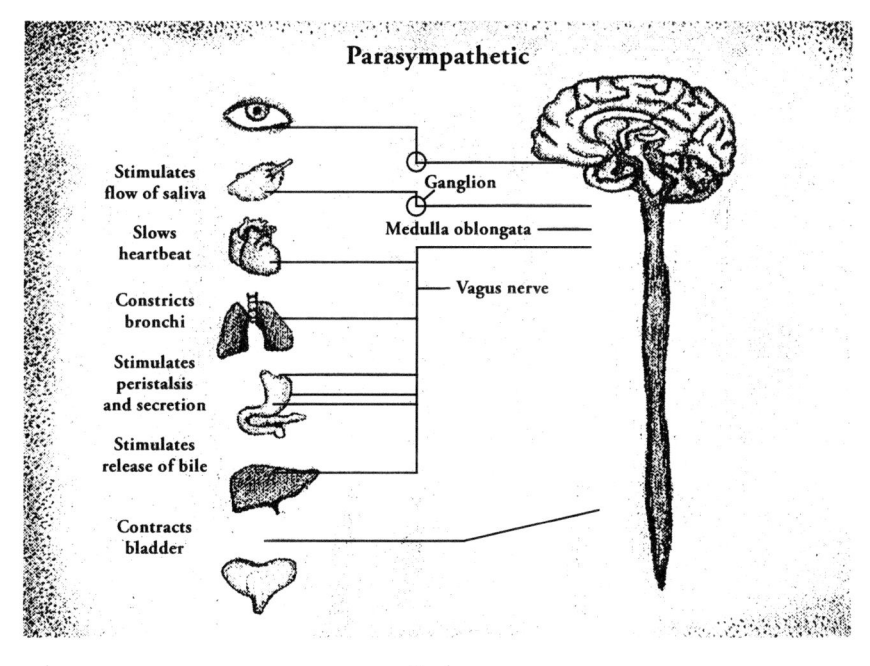

Brake

Thoughts alone can also activate the autonomic nervous system. Recalling an incident that made you angry will likely start up the accelerator, and your heart may start to beat faster, with a feeling of heat rising up through your body. On the other hand, relaxing thoughts—such as thinking about floating in a warm ocean beside a lovely beach—could well activate the brake and you could experience an enhanced feeling of relaxation.

The Three Steps increases the nervous system's resilience and helps us to master stress and all our emotions, and to shift habit patterns of behaviour, thinking and emoting.

In the next chapter we will look more closely at the relationship between the autonomic nervous system, the fight-flight-freeze response, and our self-regulatory mechanisms.

CHAPTER THREE

LOSING AND REGAINING THE BODY

Fight, flight and freeze

When we perceive an external threat our primitive survival mechanisms, which are hard-wired into our systems, kick in. In that moment, whatever our body-minds recognize as being the best of three different strategies will occur. We may fight the threat. If that is not a viable option we may flee. If neither fight nor flight is possible, another strategy, one that is not under our conscious or voluntary control, transpires: freeze.

In a time of freeze, both of the autonomic nervous system's pedals—the accelerator and the brake—are pushed down to the floor. This sudden, full acceleration creates a high state of activation within the body and the generation of a huge amount of energy. But the simultaneous hard braking prevents this energy from emerging as action. Instead, a state of freeze ensues.

When a cat corners a mouse, the mouse freezes and appears to be dead. A slow-moving animal like the possum may use freeze as its first line of defence. When a fox hunts a possum, the possum instinctively goes into a state of freeze. The fox may sniff the possum, use its jaws to pick it up and shake it, and then, believing the possum to be dead, drop it and move on. After the fox leaves and the threat is over the possum—whose successful freeze response adapted over the course of hundreds of thousands of years in conjunction with the fact that non-scavenging animals generally do not eat carrion—slowly revives and plods on with its day.

When wild animals come out of a freeze response their bodies start to shiver, shake and tremble, and their limbs may move about involuntarily. This is how the large amount of energy, which the freeze response suddenly shuts down, is released, allowing the animal to return to a restful and alert state, which is accompanied by deep abdominal breathing. A striking example of an animal emerging from a freeze response can be seen in the National Geographic video, Polar Bear Alert. A polar bear trembles and twitches and then enters a state of full-scale shaking, with its limbs flailing about wildly. This dramatic stage only lasts a short time before the polar bear calms down and resumes the deep belly-breathing characteristic of a state of relaxation.

Human beings have a very similar nervous system to other mammals. We also have the same need to discharge excessive energy and to complete defence-oriented movements associated with fight and flight so that our bodies may return to a restful, alert state. However, over time, humans have undermined the healing capacities that the possum and polar bear employ so naturally and successfully.

As humans have formed communities, societies and civilizations, certain norms have become established. We have internalized these norms, which, through successive generations, have become part of our genetic makeup or DNA. In most modern societies, people feel pressure to appear well-adjusted, strong and 'normal'. By and large, we do not feel it is acceptable for us—or others—to go into states of freeze and then thrash about like a polar bear while we release frozen energy. Even more subtle sensations of energy release, such as a slight trembling of the arms and legs, may cause us embarrassment, and we may repress any such movements.

Due to our inability or unwillingness to allow the release of energy to happen as a matter of course, we compromise our physiologies, emotions and minds. Peter Levine, who has done forty years of work in the field of trauma and has developed tremendous insight into its negative effects on our health and wellbeing and how we can heal it, says:

"Traumatic symptoms are not caused by the event itself. They arise when the residual energy from the experience is not discharged from the body. This energy remains trapped in the nervous system where it can wreak havoc on our bodies and minds".[7]

This trapped energy consists of all kinds of uncomfortable, horrible sensations, and our body-minds are protecting us from experiencing them. If a person were to feel all these sensations at once they could overwhelm him; and he could die. In an extreme example, shocked, after her hand became caught in a plane door, an air hostess felt such excruciating pain that she died on the spot. Normally, the body-mind defends against such a possibility—in the same way that a breaker switch operates in an electrical circuit. A house with a 240-

volt circuit suddenly hit with 500 volts would burn down, but a breaker switch shuts the house's power down and saves it from permanent damage.

Dissociation

When we experience states of freeze and are unable to release the horribly uncomfortable trapped energy sensations, they are placed in a kind of quarantine in our bodies—areas that become walled off from our awareness. We become disconnected from these parts of our bodies—numb to them—and, if we were to turn our attention inwards and scan our bodies, it would be difficult to perceive these regions. It may feel as if these parts were absent. This is known as somatic (bodily) dissociation, and it is the root cause of many physical, mental and emotional issues. Dissociation is the basic problem that needs to be remedied for us to return to wholeness. We need to become conscious of those parts of ourselves that we no longer feel.

An apt analogy for our healing process is the myth of Isis and Osiris, a story of death and resurrection. Isis is an Egyptian queen whose husband Osiris, the king, is killed by his brother, Seth. Seth dismembers Osiris into fourteen parts and scatters them across the land of Egypt. Isis goes in search of her husband's body parts, recovers them and puts them back together. By doing so, she helps to resurrect Osiris, who becomes the lord of the dead and the afterlife.

Similarly, when we dissociate in response to difficult events we may 'lose' parts of our bodies. Regaining awareness of the dissociated part is literally a re-membering, akin to being resurrected or reborn into a greater degree of consciousness. This is the primary aim of the Three Steps: to journey to wholeness through regaining the body and growing in awareness.

In the previous chapter, we discussed the negative ramifications for our wellbeing of becoming dissociated from the gut. Once we re-member the gut, digestion and elimination realign to their natural order and we regain health and vitality. We also ally with our gut instinct, and because this is such a centrepiece of our internal guidance system and our intuition, life becomes much easier for us.

Missing, Parts

Dissociation should not always be seen as a problem. In fact, dissociation is helpful when it is time-limited. It only becomes detrimental to our health when it persists. For example, a soldier in the heat of battle may only notice he has been wounded when the battle is over. If he has been shot—say, in his arm—it is helpful for his body to contain the pain by walling it off from his consciousness until he is out of the immediate danger of being fired upon. Furthermore, during dissociation his body's natural pain killers are released, which eases his suffering and delays his experience of pain so that he is not overwhelmed and faints, has a heart attack or even dies from shock—like the air hostess described above.

I remember the time a friend in South Africa had just received his handgun back from the shop, where it had been chromed. He was sitting a few metres away from me, testing the gun by cocking it, when it accidentally went off. There was a loud bang, which gave me a fright. There was momentary confusion, and then I asked him what had happened and if everything was okay.

'I think I shot myself in the foot,' he said.

Recalling the incident now, it is interesting that my friend wasn't sure whether or not he had shot himself. He took off his shoe and, yes, he had indeed shot himself in the foot. At that moment he was not experiencing any pain. His body's endorphins and painkillers were working their magic. As I drove him to the hospital, the excruciating pain of the open wound and the bullet in his foot began to break through into his awareness. But the process of dissociation had successfully supported him in not feeling all the pain at once, but rather gradually introducing to him, first, the fact that he was wounded and, second, that the wound was causing him great pain. In short, dissociation creates a gap during which we are temporarily saved from the experience of pain, and we can use that time to defend ourselves or to seek help and medical attention.

Ideally, when we are hurt or wounded, we receive the right kind of attention and nurturing. In addition, we receive the right kind of support, which allows the huge energy of high activation to leave our bodies, to discharge. Then, as the wound is healing, we continue to nurture it and maintain consciousness of it so that, over the long term, it does not become a dissociated area. Unfortunately, neither our caregivers nor most of us have been educated or trained in this healing process.

The majority of us have dissociated areas—blind spots—and many people cannot sense their bodies at all. When we lose parts of our body to conscious awareness, there is a corresponding loss in cognitive perception. Following high-impact accidents, for example, people often lose their abilities to prioritize and make lists, and they often are more prone to disorientation. If you ask someone who has lost awareness of parts of her body what she is feeling in her hand, she may say 'nothing'. Initially, we may find it difficult to locate and maintain attention on those parts of our bodies that are dissociated. Attempts to do so may even cause increased activation elsewhere in the body, resulting in restlessness and discomfort.

Paradoxically, chronic pain is also a sign of dissociation. In other words, areas of chronic pain are often dissociated areas. To focus our attention on these areas for any length of time and just be with the uncomfortable sensations is very difficult. Chronic pain is our bodies' way of alerting us that it is an area that needs attention and healing.

With practice, it becomes easier for us to observe any spot in our bodies and witness the sensations we are experiencing there—even the dissociated areas as they move from stuckness or fixity to flow. The Three Steps enables us to cultivate sensitivity to our inner bodies and to develop a great capacity to tolerate uncomfortable sensations. This allows our bodies' innate healing mechanisms to re-member our dissociated parts by releasing the stuck, pent-up energy, and to return us to a state of homeostasis based in wellbeing. Amazingly, when we regain our bodies, major cognitive shifts naturally follow. The way we process information is enhanced and we attain greater clarity and mastery over the mind and emotions. Essentially, we start to see, understand and experience life in fresh, new ways.

All the various elements of our experience— behaviour, sensory impressions, intellect and emotions—can become dissociated. We can dissociate from feelings of sadness or anger or even joy to as high a degree as we can dissociate from a bullet wound.

'Are you angry?' we might ask a friend.

'No, I'm not angry!' he shouts back.

Clearly, this person is dissociated from his feelings of anger. Similarly, when an event is highly distressing we can become walled off from our memory of it, so that, try as we might, we cannot remember that it ever happened.

To illustrate how dissociation may occur, let's examine an incident involving a boy named Peter. He is called in front of the class by the teacher to spell a word. He draws a blank, but tries anyway and misspells it. The teacher feels frustrated and makes a snide remark about the boy. The whole class laughs at him. Peter feels greatly embarrassed and ashamed and, in a split second, his body-mind perceives this event as a threat to his integrity, reputation and self-image. He begins to feel fearful and certain hormones are secreted in his body, which cause him, from a molecular level on up, to experience sensations of fear and shame.

Prior to this event, Peter already has his unique physiological patterns, shapes and tones of his 'fear and shame states of being'. These patterns are now triggered, but they are compounded by the extreme nature of this experience, creating a new pattern—one that is much more highly charged. His face becomes tight and flushed. His brain feels foggy and his eyes become a little blurred. His chest constricts and he feels breathless, almost winded. There is a pain in his heart as it pounds in fear. There are butterflies in his gut, plus a sensation of needing to pass his bowels. His digestion stops.

Because this combination of fear-shame sensations is so uncomfortable and scary to Peter, it compounds the fear he is already feeling. We can understand this phenomenon by imagining an adult sitting in an armchair in a room alone, reading a newspaper. Suddenly, his chest constricts and becomes tight. He becomes breathless and feels a tinge of pain in the heart. This will likely cause the man to panic. What to say of the effect of the same symptoms on a boy in an already frightening situation?

Peter enters a state of hyper-arousal. A tremendous amount of restless energy is shooting through his body. At the same time, parts of his body have constricted. More blood is being pumped into the muscles of his arms, legs and neck area to prepare them for action, to ward off the perceived threat. For a moment his body experiences a welling up of heat and a sense of power. He feels angry, even outraged, but he knows it is not acceptable for him to yell at or hit the teacher. He dares not escape by running out of the room. So he flees in a different sense. He goes into a state of collapse and dissociation. He loses a sense of his body and experiences a giddy feeling, becoming light-headed. He even puts on a smile for the class, but he is not even aware that he is smiling. He is no longer really present.

Symptoms

Later, whenever Peter needs to spell difficult words, the same scary sensations of—dissociation, bodily tightness, especially in the chest, together with blankness, confusion and giddiness—are triggered. They become an ingrained pattern and he becomes a terrible speller, negatively affecting his ability to learn new words and terms. This also affects his reading and comprehension. Because he has difficulty learning and absorbing information he is labelled 'stupid'. After being called stupid a few times he starts to believe that he is stupid. Each time he tries to sit down and learn, he is unable to concentrate and huge uncomfortable energy is activated within him. This energy is the engine that drives the restlessness and aggression that increasingly characterize his behaviour.

Peter's pattern is linked to context. Walking into a classroom full of students and a teacher evokes the same pattern of constriction in the chest, breathlessness, restlessness, and aggression. Over time even a more general context of places filled with people—such as the playground or the cafeteria—induces the same pattern. He complains to his parents about the regular pain in his chest and the breathlessness. They take him to a doctor, who diagnoses him as being asthmatic and gives him an asthma pump. The doctor also notices that Peter is having a difficult time concentrating on their conversation. He refers him to a psychiatrist, who gives Peter a second diagnosis—Attention Deficit Disorder—and more medicine: namely Ritalin.

Whenever Peter enters a place with lots of people he uses his asthma pump. It helps him to keep breathing somewhat normally, just as the Ritalin helps him to focus, but neither medicine cures the underlying causes of the symptoms.

In all of us, symptoms—physical, mental, emotional and behavioural—may arise that, in the long term, lead to chronic disease. There are countless combinations and permutations in the way that symptoms start to manifest. In Peter's case, the event that caused intense shame and fear and dissociation manifested as symptoms on all these levels: breathlessness, constriction in the chest and an inability to breathe in a normal, relaxed manner (physical symptoms); an inability to concentrate, racing thoughts, difficulty in absorbing new information (mental symptoms); anger, shame and anxiety (emotional symptoms); restlessness and aggression (behavioural symptoms).

These symptoms affect the various daily interactions Peter has with others. His pattern of symptoms lead to belief systems: not only that he is stupid, but also that it is dangerous for him to speak out and that places with many people are not safe. He develops a belief that there is something fundamentally wrong with him—that he is weak and not good enough. This belief is based in reality, because, at a physical level, he really does not feel alright. His body is constantly filled with sensations of fear, shame and aggression. His overall sense of self-worth diminishes further. Even hearing people in the background laughing as he passes by evokes shame and fear, and a kind of paranoia develops.

Peter's new 'fear and shame state of being' was at first triggered by being in a classroom. It then became generalized to a broader context of places filled with people. Now it has become even more generalized to include non-specific stimuli. Because this state of being is triggered so regularly, it has become a character trait.

Peter's symptoms start to define him. They affect his likes and dislikes, how he relates to people, his cognitive abilities and his ability to learn. Aggression, anxiety and shame become traits of his personality. Because his nervous system is always charged, his body is in a constant state of tension, and the cocktail of hormones and other chemicals that constitute these emotional states create a toxic environment in his body. Every single cell in his body is affected. His symptoms negatively impact his body and his overall state of health. If Peter's state of being continues, it will, over time, likely lead to chronic illness.

Like Peter, our bodies, minds, emotions and behavioural patterns have all been shaped in one way or another by our past experiences.

Uncomfortable sensations in our bodies are messages informing us that something is amiss and needs attention. If these messages go unanswered they may turn into symptoms, which are the body's way of managing excess energy that has not been discharged.

All symptoms of dis-ease—physical, emotional, mental or behavioural—derive from physiological processes in disarray. It is important to emphasize this fact: physical, emotional, mental and behavioural symptoms are all, at their root, physiological processes.

Medical intervention can be helpful, especially in cases of emergency. However, doctors often medicate to help a patient manage a symptom, but rarely does the medicine cure the symptom. There is a saying: if your only tool is a hammer, you will only see nails. In medical school, doctors are taught to identify diseases based on symptoms and then to treat them with medication. Many medical doctors know no other way. Due to doctors', and our own, misconceptions about the way the body-mind heals, when symptoms arise, as our bodies attempt to return themselves to balance, we inadvertently interrupt the process.

By using our understanding of the way symptoms develop as explained above, we can learn to treat many symptoms—and their underlying causes—in a different way. Then, when these symptoms arise, our first strategy will not be to try to fight them off with medication; but rather, to provide the right support and environment and allow the symptoms to run their course, together with the discharge of energy that wants to take place, but which we blocked off after the original event occurred. It is not always necessary to identify the original traumatic event; whenever a certain state is triggered in the present, the same unique pattern of bodily processes arises. Simply supporting discharge to occur is enough. Then the body can employ its self-regulating mechanisms according to its blueprint for returning to and maintaining wellbeing.

In times when we have the common flu or a fever our unique physiological stress patterns are activated. It is precisely at times like these that applying The Three Steps can produce wonderful, life-changing results. Chapter Eighteen discusses further how we can use the Three Steps to work with our habit patterns of illness.

Our quest for health is also a spiritual quest. Symptoms just point the way. The journey into the body not only leads us to health, but also into the mysteries and wonders of life.

CHAPTER FOUR

RE-MEMBERING OURSELVES

As noted in the previous chapter, our bodies, minds, emotions and behavioural patterns have all been shaped in one way or another by our past experiences. Knowledge of how memory works allows us to understand how states of being are formed and how elements of experience create our subjective sense of ourselves and formulate, at the level of the brain, our own particular 'truth' at any given moment.

Memory

The human brain has approximately one hundred billion neurons, with each neuron being connected to an average of ten thousand other neurons. These neural connections are called synapses, and there are more synapses in one brain than there are stars in the Milky Way, making the human brain one of the most complex structures in the universe.

The brain perceives the world—both the outer reality and the inner reality—through our senses. The outer reality consists of the events in our lives, including where and when they took place, their visual information, sounds, smells, tastes and tactile contacts with our bodies. The outer reality is both the content—for example, the people in the event and the things they said— and also the context, or the gist, of the event, such as where and when it occurred. The inner reality contains our internal processes, such as our emotions and thoughts (including our interpretations of events), as well as our body's internal regulatory mechanisms—such as heart beat and respiration, blood pressure, muscle tension, digestion, pupil dilation, and also our sense of balance.

Our brains store these perceptions, sensations, images, emotions, thoughts and behavioural impulses from our outer and inner realities. Memory is our ability to not only store these elements of experience, but also to recall and recollect them.

There are three steps for information to become a memory. The first step is encoding. This is the process of recording information, which is analogous to using a keyboard to type a word which then appears on a computer screen. When you see a horse, for example, your visual circuitry creates a representation in your mind and encodes an image of the horse.

The second step is storage, involving the recordaling of information. It is like saving the words that have appeared on the screen into a file—even though there is no filing cabinet, as such, in the brain. Hebb's Axiom elucidates the process of storage by stating that neurons that fire together, wire together. In other words, the neurons from different areas (such as visual, auditory, emotional, biological regulatory) of the brain that fire together during a particular event become wired together into a neural-net profile. This increases the likelihood that they will fire together in the future.

The third step of memory is recall, which is similar to retrieving information stored on a computer by reopening a file. Recall is the activation of the neural-net profile. When you intentionally try to remember an event an internal visual image may arise—for example, that of the horse. All elements of experience—images, emotions, thoughts and behavioural impulses—are stored in separate areas of the brain, and the brain 'brings them together' when a memory is recalled.

A common myth is that a memory is the exact replica of a past event. Memories are coloured and textured by many experiences, and storage is the neural-net profile, not the actual experience. What we recall is a representation of a past event, not the exact factual truth.

Both nature and nurture play a role in our memory. The particular manner in which neural connections occur is determined by both our genes and our life experiences, and these vary from individual to individual.

Another common misconception is that, as we age, the neural connections in our brain become fixed and not amenable to change. This is not so. It is important to understand that a neural-net profile is not a static arrangement, but rather it has a plasticity that allows for learning to occur and for neurons to change connections with each other—which enables it to change and be shaped and moulded in new ways.

Various changes can occur in neural connections: neurons can be strengthened by the repeated firing of a particular neural network; existing connections can be removed; and new connections can be added. Our life experiences are constantly altering our neural connections, which, in turn, are constantly transforming the structures of our brains. In this way our minds continue to develop throughout our lives. Reciprocally, as our brains continue to develop and change their individually unique structures, they influence our patterns of behaviour, perception and thought.

In the early 1960s, scientists speculated that we have both long-term and short-term memory. Long-term memory is the storage of information over a long period. We use our short-term memory to remember a list of items we need to buy at the supermarket, or to remember a telephone number long enough to dial it, or the name of someone we have to meet for the first time, say, for an interview. Items stored as short-term memory quickly leave our minds; in a way, this is a good thing, as it keeps the brain free from an overload of redundant information.

A concept related to short-term memory is that of working memory, which allows us to link various associated thoughts and representations and manipulate them in our minds. Today, many theorists use the concept of working memory to replace or include the older concept of short-term memory, but the two should not be confused. Working memory refers to structures and processes used for temporarily storing and manipulating information, and short-term memory involves short-term storage of information without the influence or manipulation of that material. For example, seeing the price of a camera involves short-term memory. When that price is mentally converted into a foreign currency, using knowledge garnered about the exchange rate from the morning newspaper—together with knowledge about how to multiply and divide as learned in school—working memory comes into play.

There is, however, much more to understand about memory than the length of time it is stored.

Implicit memory

There are two different—albeit interrelated—memory systems, which determine how different types of information are stored and how are they recalled: explicit memory and implicit memory. Explicit memory is what we commonly think of as 'memory'. This chapter, and indeed the entire book, focuses more on implicit memory due to its huge importance in charting the course of our lives.

Explicit memory depends on language, both oral and written. It is the ability to recollect the day's events, the time of an appointment or the sequence of events in which they happened. Explicit memory can be autobiographical, allowing us to tell the stories of our lives, along with a chronology of specific events, which includes interpreting the meanings of particular occurrences.

Explicit memory can also be factual. Factual memory involves the conscious recollection of factual information and general knowledge about the world, such as historic events or dates—information we have learned through reading, writing and the solving of equations in mathematics.

Explicit memory requires conscious focussed attention for encoding and retrieval to take place. For example, reciting everything you just read in the paragraph above would require focus and attention. Recollecting what you had for dinner last night, where you had it and at what time you had it would require focus on last night's activities centred on dinner.

An important factor regarding implicit memory is that there is no sense that we are remembering it. Conscious processing is not required during the encoding and retrieval of implicit memory. In contrast, when we have an explicit memory we have the internal sense of 'I am remembering'.

Implicit memory comprises implicit elements: emotions, behaviours, images, impulses, and bodily sensations. It constitutes the unconscious or subconscious parts of ourselves, of which we are not aware but which govern our beliefs, thoughts, and actions. Implicit memory shapes our deepest beliefs and charts our life journeys. It is the filter through which we anticipate the next moment in time, the indicator of what we expect to encounter. It is the glue that binds our limitations, habits and fears in place, and the force that drives our addictions. It is the part of us that we are usually in conflict with. It is the basis for our feelings of joy, love and gratitude. In sum, it is the true marker of our sense of wellbeing.

The brain structures that support explicit memory become functional around the age of eighteen months in infants, whereas the structures for implicit memory are functional at birth and even in utero. An infant can already take in visual, sound and touch patterns.

I remember when my daughter Sufia was born. I took her outside in the sun and gave her a gentle massage with calendula oil. According to our midwife, this was both a requirement for my daughter to bond with me as the father and also a measure to prevent yellow jaundice. Outside, a gentle breeze was blowing, hardly perceptible to me. Sufia, however, took a deep breath, a gasp, as she experienced the open air for the first time. When I softly touched the soles of her feet her whole body momentarily contracted and her toes curled.

It is obvious to anyone who has held a baby that babies are acutely sensitive to touch, just as they are to hunger, thirst and pain. They are delicate little beings, impressionable and fragile, and need to be handled with loving care. Every experience at this tender age, when their mental models are just forming, sets the stage for how they develop and how they will perceive life as adults.

From infancy we are able to make generalizations from repeated experiences or even from a single, highly emotional event. The fundamental aspect of learning is the ability to make generalizations from our experiences. Initial experiences are known as engrams, which are explained below. Generalizations from our initial and subsequent experiences form the basis of mental models, which, in turn, help us interpret the present and anticipate the future. Until very recently—in fact, right up to the end of the twentieth century—it was conventional wisdom among the western medical fraternity that babies are unfeeling beings with no sense of pain. This led doctors to routinely operate on babies without anaesthesia, a case in point being male circumcision—which can set in motion a fear-based mental model through which a man sees the world for the rest of his life.

Our mental models are being created all the time as we encounter the world, and are crucial to our survival. We only have to come across a dangerous animal once for us to learn that wild animals are dangerous and need to be avoided. Imagine the trouble if we had to learn anew with each and every experience. Our chances of survival would clearly diminish.

As Daniel Siegel has noted:

"The brain can be called an 'anticipation machine', constantly scanning the environment and trying to determine what will come next. Mental models of the world are what allow our minds to carry out this vital function which has enabled us as a species to survive. Prior experiences shape our anticipatory models, and thus the term 'prospective memory' has been used to describe how the mind attempts to 'remember the future' based on what has occurred in the past. Each moment the brain automatically tries to determine what is going on; it classifies an experience by activating a mental model, which helps bias present perceptions to allow for more rapid processing of the immediate environment. Readiness for response is enhanced by anticipating the next moment in time—what the world may offer next and what behavior to initiate in response".[8]

Think of a lemon and notice what happens. Did your mouth water? What else happens in your mouth, face and body? Do you like the taste or not? These are all implicit reactions based on your prior experiences of tasting lemons.

Implicit memory is a basis for our subjective sense of ourselves, for how we experience every living moment. Nonetheless, implicit memory is a much-missed phenomenon, and many of the implicit elements of our experience have been denied or even deemed taboo. The emotion of fear is a prime example. Many cultures teach their children to be strong, and that the feeling of fear is a trait of weakness. Just because we deny an element of experience does not mean that it ceases to exist; it may still have a profound impact on our lives. For example, no matter how much we pretend to be immune to fear, when we encounter a dangerous snake or a car hurtling towards us we will likely jump out of the way. This is fear working its magic, mobilizing our bodies to defend ourselves.

In short, implicit elements hold in place our mental models, which are the basis for how we experience ourselves and the world. Therefore, the key to happiness, empowerment and liberation all lie in an awareness of our implicit elements, and becoming conscious of our emotions, behaviour and sensations.

Engrams

An engram is the initial impact of an experience on the brain. It is a stored impression that, under certain circumstances, can be recalled. It includes various elements of experience and has both explicit and implicit elements wired together.

Each engram contains the following aspects: factual (the event itself), autobiographical (your sense of yourself at the time of the event), emotional (your mood at the time), behavioural (what you were doing with your body), sensation (what your body felt like at the time) and perceptual (images from the five senses, including what things looked like, how they smelled, and their taste). An engram also includes a snapshot of all the regulatory biological processes at any given time.

Engrams are not located in a specific 'memory bank' or in one special location in the brain; rather, they are spread throughout the brain. Each element of experience is stored in a particular region. A visual image is stored in the visual processing region, whereas a sound is stored in the auditory region, and an emotion in the emotional regions. When an engram is evoked all the elements that make up the experience are activated and seem as one whole.

For example, remembering my wedding day, I simultaneously recall various elements of experience. Factual: I remember the venue, which was a healing sanctuary in the countryside. The ceremony took place under a beautiful large tree next to a stream. Sergio, the pastor, who was also a healer, conducted the ceremony and blessed our union. My friends and family were present, as were my bride's parents, who had flown in from India for the wedding. Emotion: I was experiencing excitement, love, joy and nervousness. Autobiographical: I had a lot of energy and felt vibrant and hopeful for the future with my beautiful bride whom I had met only five weeks earlier. Behaviour: I remember how I held my body straight, in confidence, as I kissed my new wife. Sensation: As I recall the wedding I experience a similar sense of excitement and joy in my body as my belly tightens and my chest expands.

Engrams are operating all the time, usually without our conscious awareness, and they are retrieved according to cues, or triggers. Sometimes triggers are conscious. For example, a friend asks how you met your husband, which causes you to consciously recall your memory of how, where and when you first met. Triggers may also be unconscious. You find yourself remembering an old boyfriend and then wonder why you started thinking of him. Then you notice the background music in the coffee shop where you are sitting. It is a song that was popular during the time you were dating, and it triggered your memory of him without your conscious awareness. You are now in a nostalgic state of being.

Priming

In response to specific triggers, the brain readies itself for retrieval of certain memories. This is a key part of implicit memory and is called *priming*.[9] Priming is the implicit memory effect according to which exposure to a stimulus influences us—our thoughts, emotions, behaviours and perceptions—on a subconscious level; for example, background music conjuring up an image of a boyfriend.

Research shows that exposure to brief snippets of information measurably affects the way we think and act. Priming is used all the time in advertising. A beautiful woman is shown in an advert, selling something as mundane and unrelated as toilet and tap accessories. The attraction and desire we may feel for the woman becomes implicitly associated with the taps and basins being advertised, thereby impacting our behaviour—specifically, our decision-making process. We become primed to buy this particular brand of bathroom accessories.[10]

A further example of priming is described in Malcolm Gladwell's book, *Blink*:

In front of you is a sheet of paper with a list of five-word sets. I want you to make a grammatical four-word sentence as quickly as possible out of each set. It's called a scrambled-sentence test. Ready?

1. him was worried she always
2. are from Florida oranges temperature
3. ball the throw toss silently
4. shoes give replace old the
5. he observes occasionally people watches
6. be will sweat lonely they
7. sky the seamless gray is
8. should not withdraw forgetful we
9. us bingo sing play let
10. sunlight makes temperature wrinkle raisins

That seemed straightforward, right? Actually it wasn't. After you finished that test - believe it or not - you would have walked out of my office and back down the hall more slowly than you walked in. With that test, I affected the way you behaved. How? Well, look back at the list. Scattered throughout it are certain words, such as "worried," "Florida," "old," "lonely," "gray," "bingo," and "wrinkle." You thought that I was just making you take a language test. But, in fact, what I was also doing was making the big computer in your brain - your adaptive unconscious - think about the state of being old. It didn't inform the rest of your brain about its sudden obsession. But it took all this talk of old age so seriously that by the time you finished and walked down the corridor, you acted old. You walked slowly.[11]

You, the reader, have just experienced how priming, although it occurs without our conscious awareness, affects subsequent behaviour.

Mental models are continuously priming us to anticipate the future. Mental models are triggered by our environment through associations with elements from our five senses, and by the context in which we find ourselves. They may also be retrieved by explicit recall; that is, by thinking of something directly. For example, in one set of tests, researchers asked participants to recall an ethical or unethical act, and then asked them to fill in the missing letters in a series of incomplete words, like W_ _H and SH_ _ER. Those subjects who had recalled unethical acts mostly wrote WASH and SHOWER, while the others wrote a variety of words, like WISH and SHAKER.[12]

The wonderful advantage we humans have over animals is our capacity to be conscious of what we are doing, feeling, thinking and saying. When we develop a sensitivity and capacity to observe the implicit content of our mental models we are then able to effect change quickly. We are able to influence and shift the foundational aspects of our experience, thanks to the plasticity of the brain. As we do this we are creating new filters through which we live our lives. In effect, we retune our biological musical instruments so that the tunes they emit recalibrate our entire worlds.

Take the example of a woman in her thirties who came to me for a series of sessions. She was a partner in a firm of lawyers and, although she had a brilliant legal mind, she would not represent anyone in court. She had a mortal fear of standing up and arguing a case in front of a judge and a courtroom audience. Whenever one of her cases went to trial, one of her colleagues would represent the client in court. I learned that when she was twelve years old she had been humiliated in her classroom by her teacher as she was delivering a speech in front of the class. Similar to our previous example of Peter, the whole class had laughed at the teacher's insult. She had felt ashamed and belittled by this ridicule. Twenty-five years later, she still bore the expectation of being humiliated if she were to speak publically. Just the anticipation of doing so brought up intense feelings of fear and shame.

Through the Three Steps I taught her how to be with her body and how to tolerate and accept the debilitating sensations and processes within. She got in touch with how her patterns were affecting her; for example, how panic made her legs stiff with fear, to the point that she became unable to move, how her stomach churned to the point of nausea, and how her thinking became fuzzy.

With my support, she learned how to ride the wave of fear and shame and release its high charge. At the same time, she developed a capacity to be with all the uncomfortable sensations—both those associated with panic, fear and shame and also those of discharge, such as heat, tingling and trembling. She became progressively less fearful, more at ease in her body and clearer in her thinking. She gained strength and confidence, powerful feelings that she needed time to assimilate. Her posture straightened, her neck lengthened and her chest felt light and expansive. Her entire body danced in aliveness. She was an altogether different person.

After a short period of working with me, she noticed that in meetings where she used to mainly listen and occasionally speak with great trepidation, she was now fully participating. Before long, a colleague who was handling one of her court cases fell sick. She amazed herself by volunteering to handle the case. In the morning before her first court appearance she felt anxious, but it did not debilitate her, and she was able to distinguish the anxiety from the element of excitement which she also felt. As she stood to argue the case, she was able to tolerate the high charge within her body and even her shaking hands. When she began to speak the fear fell away. She won the case, and she had the presence of mind to sense how the success and excitement felt in her body. This helped her body-mind to record this new mental model of success, this new way of being. Now that her bodily patterns of fear had shifted, she was able to experience more empowered states of being more frequently, which created a new life melody that her body played to the universe.

CHAPTER FIVE

PATTERNS

Jennifer is a dancer, but she finds it difficult to move in both directions. Her movements to the left feel more fluid than those to the right. Whenever Sheila gets into an argument, her mind goes blank, she feels light-headed, her jaw clamps shut and, in frustration, she ends up swearing. Donald has to untangle his laptop cable several times a week, and each time he becomes irritated and short-tempered. Every time Priyanka leaves her apartment she has to return to collect something she has forgotten. Whenever Rose travels in a car she gets motion sickness, feels nauseous, her stomach churns and tightens, her vision blurs and she gets a headache. Joan flirts outrageously whenever she is in the presence of a man.

Habit Patterns

The above examples are instances of habit patterns, which are all driven by implicit elements. All of our behaviour, thoughts and emotions—from the way we get out of bed in the morning, how we brush our teeth and how we eat our food to how we deal with relationships, what we expect from life and everything else we do throughout the day—happen according to patterns. We are indeed creatures of habit. Habit patterns are based on our neural-net profiles. As soon as we enter a certain context, neurons that have been wired together fire again to conjure up a preconceived mental model, which shapes how we behave in that context.

Ivan Pavlov, the Russian psychologist, conducted seminal research on how associative learning takes place with implicit elements, and he coined the term classical conditioning. Pavlov's theory engages a known stimulus with a new conditioned stimulus to obtain a new behaviour called a conditioned response. In his famous experiment with a dog, Pavlov paired two natural stimuli (being fed and salivating) with an unrelated stimulus (ringing a bell). Before conditioning, the dog salivated every time it saw food, but had no reaction when it heard a ringing bell. Pavlov added the unrelated

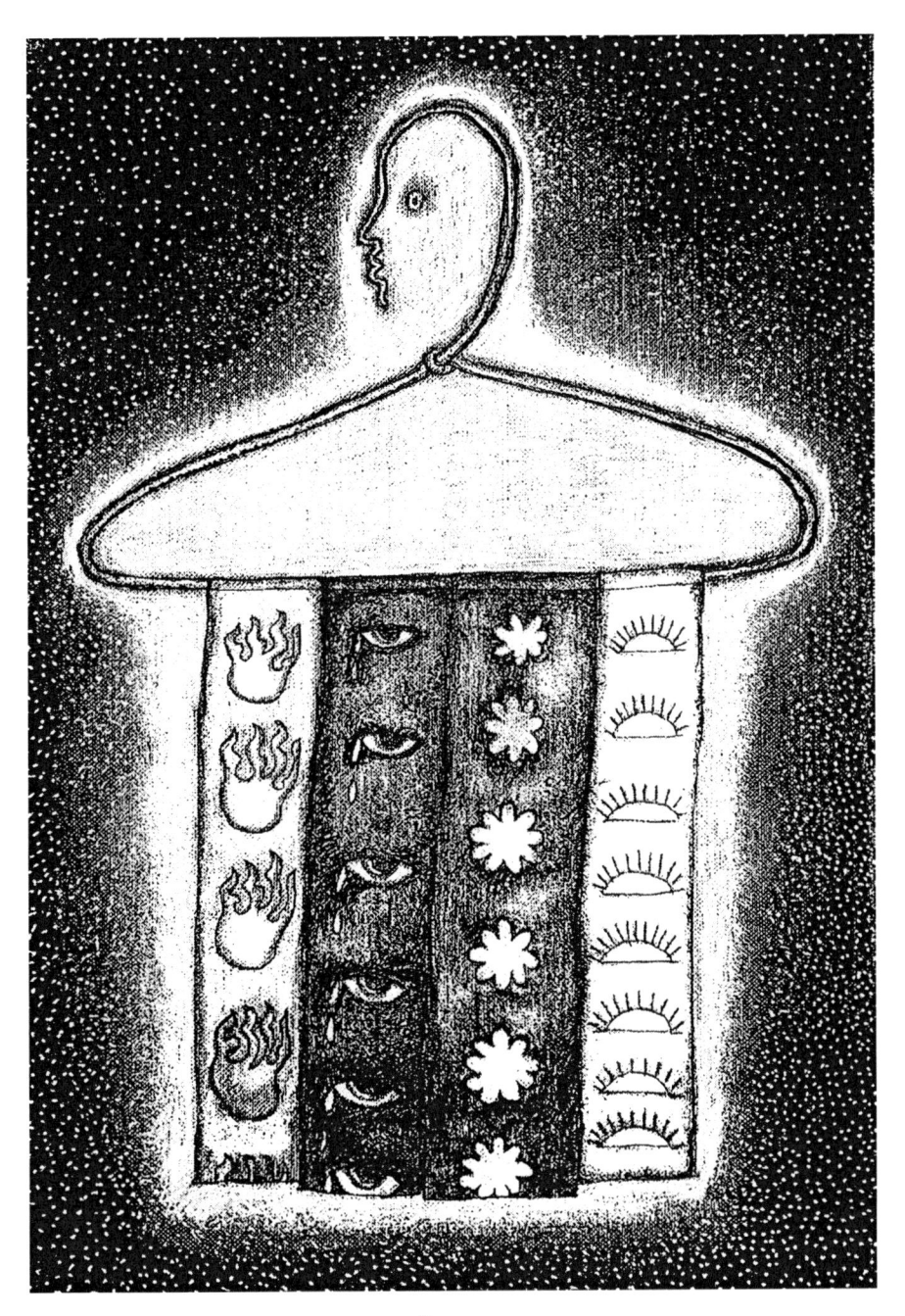

Patterns

stimulus of ringing a bell as he began feeding the dog. In time, the dog learned to associate the ringing of a bell with being fed. Merely hearing the bell—without even seeing or smelling food—caused the dog to salivate in anticipation of being fed. The conditioned stimulus of the bell became a trigger.

Interestingly, there can be many levels of conditioning, and of triggers. If we were to shine a bright light into the eyes of Pavlov's dog every time he heard a bell, eventually the bright light alone would also become a conditioned stimulus for it to start salivating. If we were to then cause the dog to smell perfume every time we shone the bright light into its eyes, the perfume would likewise become a conditioned stimulus for it to start salivating. This process could go on ad infinitum, and it explains why many triggers can evoke a response—in humans as well—that may be far removed from the original stimulus and therefore difficult to trace. Remember how, in Chapter Three, Peter's fear and shame state of being became generalized and, after being repeatedly triggered, became a character trait.

During an event, many triggers can become associated. When an event contains a high emotional charge, triggers may become instantly wired together, obviating the repetition Pavlov's dog needed to create the associations. Later, these same triggers will likely elicit a similar, charged response. For example, a woman slaps her young daughter hard and the girl feels very afraid. At the time of the slap, the mother happens to be wearing a blue dress. Later, when the girl sees the colour blue, fear arises in her. Most likely, she does not draw the link between her fear and the colour blue. Later still, she sees the colour blue, begins to feel fear and her brain starts to unconsciously scan her surroundings, seeking an explanation for the fear. There is a large man sitting opposite her, and now, in the girl's neural-net profile, large men become paired with the feeling of fear—even though, at the time she saw the man, he presented no actual danger to her.

It may well happen that the state of fear triggered when the girl sees a large man will evoke associated thoughts of fear, ones more relevant to the girl's present life circumstances. Fearful thoughts may start to arise, such as: 'Oh no! I may not have enough money to last me through to the end of the month'; or 'My boyfriend didn't phone me this evening. He's probably cheating on me'. These are all possible consequences of classically conditioned implicit memory: automatic reactions in the absence of cognitive or factual thought.

In order to change your habit patterns, it is necessary to become aware of your triggers. The simple act of brushing your teeth may be priming your body-mind with a mild sense of anxiety and tension. This could be because of a disturbing experience at the dentist, or because your mother always shouted at you when you didn't brush your teeth, or any number of other reasons. Now, when you brush your teeth, your anxiety and tension trigger, according to the laws of association, thoughts about things in your life that make you anxious. Fearful thoughts of being fired from your job or the possibility of your boyfriend leaving you start to race through your head. No longer are you simply brushing your teeth. Instead, you are absent and immersed in the past or future, or both. The fearful thoughts increase your anxiety, which then spirals upwards.

Which comes first, the chicken or the egg? It doesn't really matter. Sometimes brushing your teeth triggers anxious emotions and an anxious state of being which, in turn, triggers related anxious thoughts. Other times, your anxious thoughts trigger anxious emotions. In short, emotions trigger thoughts and thoughts trigger emotions in a Byzantine two-way network.

Neural constellations

Let us look at the hundred trillion connections and the hundred billion neurons that make up the brain in the same way that we would look up at the night sky. There are countless stars to be seen, but we only identify certain stars twinkling together as constellations. Not only are the stars in constellations linked together in certain patterns, but they also appear brighter than the surrounding stars. Although, to us, stars in a certain constellation may appear to be only inches apart, they may in fact be located in different galaxies. Similarly, recalling Hebb's Axiom—'neurons that fire together wire together'–although neurons may be firing from different regions of the brain, they are inextricably linked.

Using this metaphor of the brain as the night sky, different galaxies could represent some of the different regions of the brain related to various physiological processes, as follows:

Galaxy A – auditory
Galaxy B – visual
Galaxy C – gustatory

Galaxy D – olfactory

Galaxy E – gastrointestinal tract

Galaxy F – somatosensory

Galaxy G – respiratory system

Galaxy H – immune responses

Galaxy I – the heart

Galaxy J – reproductive processes

Galaxy K – speech

Galaxy L – autonomic nervous system processes

Let us now apply this galactic setup of the brain to the example of Pavlov's dog. As the dog gets hungry, stars in Galaxy E (the gastrointestinal tract and its related processes) twinkle. When food is presented to the dog it smells and sees the food, resulting in twinkling in both Galaxy D (olfactory) and Galaxy B (visual). The dog salivates and the stars in Galaxy C (gustatory) twinkle. At the same time, all the other stars—representing the state of all other bodily processes at this moment in time—are also twinkling. If we were to take a snapshot of the night sky at this moment, the stars would represent the dog's neuron-net profile of being hungry and receiving food, with the stars in Galaxies E, D, B and C forming a prominent constellation. Let us call it Constellation EDBoC in the night sky of the dog's 'hunger state of being'.

Each time the dog feels hungry and receives food, Constellation EDBoC is triggered and shines brightly, its stars becoming increasingly linked with every activation. What Pavlov did with his experiment is that he introduced Galaxy A (auditory) to the constellation by ringing the bell every time he fed the dog. By ringing the bell enough times, Galaxy A became an integral part of the constellation; it was now Constellation EDBoCA. Then he found that by activating the auditory area of Galaxy A by ringing the bell, the rest of the constellation lit up too and the dog salivated.

We could next replace the star in Galaxy B (food in the visual area) with a different star—for example, the colour red. Every time we ring the bell we show the dog the colour red. Eventually, the twinkling of this new red-colour star alone will also activate the constellation and the dog will salivate, because its 'hunger state of being' has been evoked. This works in the same way that the various physiological processes activated by brushing teeth could trigger a person's 'anxiety state of being'. The more intricate the 'anxiety constellation' becomes—the more it becomes linked to that person's thoughts, emotions, behaviour and so on—the more it will become one of his prominent character traits, a lens through which he views the world.

Our body-minds are constantly in states of being evoked through the activation of these complex constellations. In this way, we are operating according to set patterns, like the way a computer runs according to a program. This can be beneficial when the patterns promote our wellbeing. However, when, due to a highly charged event—like the boy Peter, whose asthma and Attention Deficit Disorder resulted directly from one experience in a classroom—the program develops a glitch, it is advisable to fix it.

Our patterned thinking, feeling and behaviour are our predicament, the sources of our misery we are seemingly unable to resolve. Our patterns keep us imprisoned, similar to the plot of the movie Groundhog's Day, in which the same sequence of events play out in the same town each and every day, starting at 6 a.m.—the same people relating to each other in the same way with the same results. If we were to keep track of how we play out the same relationships and the same social games, with very little scope for creating changes in our thoughts, feelings and behaviour, we would likely be shocked at the extent to which we live our lives like robots.

In desperation, we look for solutions to our problems on the outside: a new car, a new job, an ideal partner. What we fail to realize, however, is that all our problems originate from within us, from mental-emotional-behavioural patterns based on past experiences—often, difficult and highly emotional events involving fear and pain—and are mirrored in the outer physical world. Therefore, if we have not yet worked on the roots of our misery, our 'ideal partner' will likely reflect our misery. He or she will become yet another star in a constellation of misery. Then, in the same way that we buy another car or look for another job, there will be an urge to go in search of a new ideal partner.

As we shall see, by using the Three Steps and becoming aware of our patterns of thinking, feeling and behaving, we can use them as a guide to delve deeper into our bodies and uncover the implicit elements that constitute our states of being. Only then can we resolve our patterns—by dissolving the glue that binds them. In doing so, we free ourselves from limiting beliefs, judgments and principles and start to manifest aspects of life that promote our wellbeing.

Operant conditioning

Operant conditioning suggests that the frequency of certain behaviour will increase if it is followed by positive reinforcement, and will decrease if followed by negative reinforcement. Operant conditioning may be described as learning by consequence.

The classic example of operant conditioning is the carrot-and-stick method based on pleasure and pain. A child does something her parents consider desirable—like bringing home an excellent report card from school—so they praise her and give her a warm hug. Perhaps they even buy her a new toy. The child experiences pleasurable feelings. But when she does something they dislike, such as walking through the house with muddy shoes, they scold her. The child experiences painful feelings. In this way, working with reward and punishment, desire and fear, pleasure and pain, shame and praise, they encourage their daughter to get good grades and discourage her from leaving muddy footprints in the house.

The theory of operant conditioning was developed by B.F. Skinner, a behaviourist, to explain how we acquire the range of learned behaviours we exhibit each and every day. Skinner used the term operant to refer to any 'active behaviour that operates upon the environment to generate consequences'.[13] In one experiment, he put rats and pigeons in boxes containing a lever which, when pressed, led to food being dispensed. After accidentally knocking the lever and receiving food, the animals quickly learned to press it deliberately. Operant conditioning draws an association between behaviour (in this case, pressing a lever) and a consequence for that behaviour (receiving food). Most of our behaviour is linked to instincts like hunger, thirst and sex.

We humans regularly use operant conditioning as a mechanism for shaping the behaviour of our children, siblings, spouses, friends and co-workers—basically everyone. Unfortunately, negative reinforcement—using 'the stick' of verbal and even physical punishment—has been a preferred method of shaping behaviour. The reason this is unfortunate is that our behaviour, our everyday activities, often become implicitly motivated by fear and pain, which contributes to a life of stress. But, because the punitive conditioning process that shaped our behaviour has long since fallen away from our conscious memories, we have no idea why there is an underlying current of stress in our lives. And, like everything else that occurs in our body-minds, this stress has a physiological basis.

Take the example of George. As a young boy, his parents shouted at him or hit him when his room was messy, when his clothes got dirty, or when his shirt hung out from his trousers. George is now a perfectionist, always clean and neat. What drives his habit pattern of cleanliness, however, is fear and pain. The motivation for being neat and clean is based on uncomfortable sensations in his body—the same uncomfortable sensations he experienced every time his parents shouted or lashed out at him—whenever he perceives himself as being 'dirty'. For George—as for all of us—developing an awareness of his sensations holds the key to resolving stress and changing behaviour; in his case, the stress of always being 'clean'. Once he has resolved this stress, he can then freely choose whether to be clean or not.

Re-enactment

When our behaviour causes us a problem, re-enactment is often the phenomenon that drives us—in a seemingly compulsive manner—to repeat that behaviour over and over again. Because re-enactment especially causes us to replay events that contain emotional intensity, being conditioned by 'the stick' tends to set in motion a life of re-enacting behaviour that keeps us in a spiral of intensely charged, highly activated states of being.

Re-enactment is not just a challenge for us. It is also a wonderful opportunity for resolution and healing. Viewed from a spiritual perspective, re-enactment is life's way of offering us exactly what we need in order to evolve. There appear to be forces at play beyond our rational understanding; forces that recreate events, allowing us to re-experience them and thereby deepen our awareness and complete our karmic bonds. Re-enactment is the Law of Attraction's way of conspiring to reflect that which exists inside of us.

I once watched a documentary on BBC television about a porn star who held the record for sleeping with the most men at one time. She lay on a stage and two hundred men lined up to take their turn with her. In a subsequent interview she mentioned how, at the age of sixteen, she had been gang raped by six men. It was then obvious to me that, by re-enacting the gang rape, her body-mind was trying to resolve the chaos set in motion by this tragic event.

Often, people have recurring accidents or injuries. One trauma specialist ended up treating numerous clients who had been involved in a succession of multiple motor vehicle accidents—in one instance as many as eight such accidents over a twelve-year period. The frequency and cause of the accidents were sometimes inexplicable, as with the client who had six rear-end collisions in eighteen months.[14]

Repeatedly attracting the same situations to our lives not only perpetuates our habit patterns, but it also engrains them more deeply into our life experiences. No matter how much George, the perfectionist, cleans himself and his house, life will always conspire to bring mess his way. He may feel trapped inside a Catch-22 type of situation, one that keeps him locked into receiving exactly what he fears the most—until he starts to pay attention to the implicit elements inside of him that are demanding resolution.

Bessel Van Der Kolk, a psychiatric researcher, relates a story about a Vietnam veteran that illustrates re-enactment and what may be called the 'anniversary syndrome'. A man attempted to rob a store each year that he was not in jail, from 1969 to 1986. Every attempted robbery took place at exactly 6.30 a.m., always on the Fifth of July. On each occasion, he used his finger in his pocket to simulate a gun. He would then leave the store and wait in his car for the police to arrive. Once the police were on the scene, he would get out and, with his finger in his pocket, announce that he had a gun. Each time he was taken into custody without being shot. It transpired that while on a patrol in Vietnam in 1968 he had lit a match to light a cigarette. A Viet Cong sniper took the opportunity to fire a shot which killed the man's friend. His friend's death occurred at 6.30 a.m. on the Fifth of July.[15]

Many of us experience the anniversary syndrome in various ways, perhaps not in as extreme a manner as the Vietnam veteran. If we were to chart the course of our lives over many years, we might be surprised to find how certain times of the year present more difficulties for us.

Another common anniversary syndrome involves the beginning of the school/work week. For those of us who have grown up in countries where Monday marks the beginning of the school week, Sunday evenings may contain a particular emotional charge. Sunday evenings were when we may have realized that we still had lots of unfinished homework and, as a result, became nervous and edgy about the prospect of going to school the next day without completing it all. Later in life, we might have similar uncomfortable feelings about the beginning of the work week. Interestingly, we might find that at times when we are on holiday and Monday morning does not contain any special significance in terms of the progress of our week, we may still inexplicably become tense on Sunday evening. A mental model of Sunday evening—in anticipation of Monday—has become programmed, and it triggers various implicit elements in our body-minds.

Re-enactments do not have to involve dramatic, high profile events. They may involve everyday mundane events such as habitually forgetting where we left the car keys. Such mundane events prime our minds, creating low-level anxiety and confusion which, in turn, triggers associated anxious thoughts and perpetuates a state of stress. Using the Three Steps, my clients have been able to drop many of their behavioural patterns and, as if by magic, re-enactments stop occurring.

This has been my personal experience with the Three Steps, as well. Standing in queues always used to make me feel restless, defensive and even aggressive. 'This is my place in the queue. Don't you dare to jump in front of me!' was the attitude my body projected. In South Africa, where I used to live, people are not likely to jump a queue. Occasionally, however, someone would bypass the line of customers to 'ask a quick question', and this used to rile me.

Then I moved to India, where there is far less respect for the etiquette of lining up in a queue. Every time I went to the railway station, a fast food restaurant or the local supermarket, at least one person would inevitably jump the queue. This made me so angry that I felt like punching the interloper; but knowing that this was not a viable option, I would exercise great restraint and the aggression would come out verbally—I sometimes even swore. With my adrenalin pumping in high gear, my entire body-mind would be primed for a fight. Afterwards, the incident would play itself out repeatedly in my mind, and I would continue to swear at the idiot who had jumped the queue. Later, I would recount the episode to a friend, which would again fuel my aggression. I was continually priming myself to enter a fight.

After I started to work with the Three Steps, the intensity of my aggression lessened. Then, one day there was a breakthrough. It happened in a Kentucky Fried Chicken restaurant in Bombay, where I stood in the queue for ten minutes while the servers took forever to serve the customers ahead of me. As I neared the counter, a woman appeared from out of the blue, stood next to me and shouted out her order. As the server began to type her order into the computer, I said to him very pointedly, 'Excuse me, I was here first. Will you take my order?' The woman who had jumped the queue belligerently erupted at me. Because I had been working on my aggression, I did not immediately react to her outburst as I previously would have. Still, I felt anger well up inside of me. Then I turned to the manager, who was also behind the counter, and explained the situation, adding that it was not right for the woman to be served ahead of me. The manager defused the situation by instructing the server at the adjacent computer to take my order, so the woman and I were served at the same time.

I took the food upstairs to my mother, who was visiting from South Africa and who had already sat down at a table. As I sat down, I felt my whole body trembling. I told my mum that I needed some time to regulate. Being familiar with the Three Steps, she knew what I meant. For at least twenty minutes I sat in silence, observing my physiological sensations and allowing my body-mind to return to a more balanced state. I was astounded at how much charge this re-enactment had caused in my system. When I was ready I told my mother in a relaxed manner what had occurred downstairs.

The KFC incident, and how I dealt with it, led to a dramatic shift, not only in my behaviour, but also in my experience of life. The next few times people pushed in front of me, the huge charge inside of me was simply not there. Sometimes I let the person go ahead, other times I said in a very matter of fact manner, 'Excuse me, I'm here.' The person would generally acquiesce and move behind me. Then I noticed that the frequency of people jumping the queue ahead of me had decreased greatly. The re-enactments and their accompanying charged sensations inside of me had fallen away. Standing in queues, I am now relaxed and present, and even chat with the people waiting alongside me. I saw how life brought me these re-enactments as a way of helping me to resolve my pent-up aggression.

Importantly, I was able to resolve this particular habit pattern without linking it to any particular emotional event in my life. It could be that there was a highly charged emotional event that set these series of re-enactments in motion, but the Three Steps are able to work with current physiological sensations without tracing them back to a certain identifiable cause. It is evident that our stress lies in our nervous systems, not in outside events.

CHAPTER SIX

THE SOURCE OF OUR PATTERNS

The source of many of our patterns and re-enactments dates back to the very beginning of our lives: to the womb.

The womb: our initial, formative environment

As adults, we may still be reliving our earliest memories of what took place in the womb, but we lack the capacity to explain them at an explicit level. Our brain is always searching for a frame of reference to understand what is driving us in the present moment. For instance, a person may have a constant sense of anxiety and, not understanding why he is anxious, projects it onto his present circumstances.

'I don't have enough money,' he tells himself. 'That's why I'm anxious.'

In order to make more money he works even harder, which only compounds his stress and anxiety. What he doesn't realise is that the root cause of his anxiety lies deep within his body-mind and derives from his nervous system having being hyper-aroused because of the toxic environment created by his mother smoking cigarettes while he was in the womb.

The environment in the womb is so important that it is now being recognized that our physical, mental and emotional health is to a great extent shaped during those first nine months. Unfortunately, many pregnant women remain unaware of even the fact that intrauterine pollutants pose a major health hazard to the foetus. Toxic fumes from a recently painted house or insecticides used to eradicate termites or other insects not only affect the mother, but also find their way into the womb. A more direct threat to the foetus is too often posed by the mother smoking, drinking or ingesting various prescription drugs.

A foetus's most natural reaction to any threat is constriction and retreat. In this evasive action, the particular anatomy employed by the foetus will depend on its developmental stage. Early on in the term of pregnancy, perhaps all that is available is its central nervous system, which may constrict and, as it twists away from the threat, instigate a tension pattern in the spine. As other organs and bodily systems develop they too could develop defensive patterns. For example, pollutants could lead to the foetus's lungs feeling stuffy and congested and, to protect them, the bronchi constrict. As Fox et al have found:

> "Experiments measuring fetal reactions to mothers drinking one ounce of vodka in a glass of diet ginger ale show that breathing movements stop within three to thirty minutes. This hiatus in breathing lasts more than a half hour. Although the blood alcohol level of the mothers was low, as their blood alcohol level declined, the percentage of fetal breathing movements increased".[16]

Physiological processes such as constricted bronchi and a twisted spine lay foundations for physical, mental, emotional and behavioural patterns. After this hypothetical baby is born, any highly charged event—such as a fearful or exciting one—may elicit a similar pattern involving a twisted spine and sensations of congested bronchi. This could lead to spinal and breathing problems that persist throughout his or her lifetime, and could form the physiological core of the emotions that he unwittingly projects out towards his surroundings. Thankfully, the Three Steps is able to heal even the earliest of physiological patterns by working with the sensations that arise when the same patterns occur in the present moment.

Babies' reactions to threats in the womb show that our fight-flight reflexes are hardwired into our nervous systems and are already active in utero. A clear example of this is their reaction to amniocentesis:

> "Babies have been known to react to the experience of amniocentesis (usually done around 16 weeks g.a.) by shrinking away from the needle, or, if a needle nicks them, they may turn and attack it. Mothers and doctors who have watched this under ultrasound have been unnerved. Following amniocentesis, heart rates gyrate. Some babies remain motionless, and their breathing motions may not return to normal for several days".[17]

The heightened sensitivity of babies in the womb makes it clear that parenting starts at conception.

There is much evidence to show that as a foetus's senses develop, they are used immediately. Through the various stages of foetal development during our first nine months of life, our experience is solely at the implicit level of sensations. Remember that the implicit elements of our experience are the foundation of our beliefs, how we relate, our behaviour and our intellect. The structures supporting these elements are functional while we are still in the womb, but the structures that support cognition—such as the hippocampus—are only functional from approximately the age of eighteen months. Essentially, we are able to feel sensations and emotions way before we can describe them verbally.

Parental relationships during pregnancy greatly influence the future health and emotional life of their babies. When parents fight, their anger molecules and stress-response hormones become activated and affect the developing embryo—both through resonance with the mother and also because these bio-chemicals enter the womb and impact the embryo directly. These kinds of events shape a baby's neural architecture and even its genetic expression. Dowling et al's research indicates that 'maternal hormones regulate the expression of genes in the foetal brain, and that acute changes in maternal hormone induce changes in gene expression in the foetal brain that are retained when it reaches adulthood.'[18]

The particular body-mind nexus that develops through interaction with the environment in the womb is the template upon which all future development builds. Thomas Verny writes that

> "Every experience on the road of prenatal life alters the molecules of emotion, the autonomic and central nervous systems, and the architecture of the brain.... Before birth, experiences help to lay down the brain's primary circuits forming a foundation for development; after birth, the networking activity moves to increasingly higher levels of the cerebral cortex, fine-tuning sensory perception, emotional balance, cognitive skills, and interpersonal relationships".[19]

The miracle of birth

With birth, we each make the transition from a tiny protected environment into a much larger one. This transition is a highly charged experience and contains the potential for difficulties that can leave our nervous systems, bodies and brains indelibly scarred. A forceps birth, for example, can result in lifelong tension patterns in the head.

Birth can also be a wonderful nurturing and bonding experience for the entire family. The birth of my daughter Sufia, on the Ninth of January 2004, was a wonderful journey I shared with my wife Zia. Just remembering the event evokes in me an open heart and feelings of love.

With a certain sense of pride, I think of how I dove headlong into my role as father to be. I attended classes to learn how to support my wife through the birthing process, and I also arranged the first meeting with our midwife Sharon. After talking to her, Zia and I were confident that Sharon was the right person to assist us.

Zia and I were keen for Sufia to be born in a natural, supportive environment to make her entry into the world as soft as possible after her nine months in the safety of the womb. We had a home birth, with the intention of having a water birth. The home in which Sufia was born is located on a hill. While Zia was still pregnant, she and I would gently dance and whirl under the moonlight in front of a stunning view of Johannesburg.

I rented a pool for the bedroom and made many other preparations for the birth of my little princess. When we were certain that Zia was going into labour, I assembled the pool and filled it with warm water, making sure that its temperature was kept at 34° Celsius. Soft music and an inviting aroma wafted through the room, which was likewise regulated at 34 degrees so that our newborn's first exposure to the air would not come as a shock.

On the night of January 8th I called Sharon and told her that we suspected that Zia was in labour. Excitement coursed through my body as Zia climbed into the bedroom pool. The pool seemed the perfect environment for Zia, who is part mermaid, having been a scuba diving instructor for seven years. Water supports the mother and makes the birthing process much more comfortable for her. Nonetheless, with Sharon and me by her side, Zia pushed and breathed for many hours, but Sufia refused to come out.

Witnessing Zia giving birth gave me a newfound respect for her. Working solely with the assistance of her body's own analgesics and steroids, her bravery and stamina was truly inspiring. When, after some time, Sufia still didn't appear, Sharon suggested that Zia get out of the water and try squatting while I held her in my arms from behind. To squat holding Zia was a

Herculean task. My thighs were burning, my arms and shoulders ached; but I continued to hold her. It felt like an eternity, but at some point, Sufia crowned—the very top of her head appeared and I reached down and felt it. A few minutes later our daughter popped out so fast that Sharon had to catch her with the same urgency that a rugby player catches a ball in the heat of a championship game.

My little girl—'Little Lambrou'—was born. She was so beautiful, so small and delicate and, amazingly, so clean. I had the honour of cutting the umbilical cord as Zia held Sufia to her bosom. After some time I jumped into the warm water and Zia handed our daughter to me. I took Sufia for her first swimming lesson. For the next few years I was to take her swimming several times a week and would continue to hold a safe space for her to develop confidence in the water until she started swimming at her own pace. Today she loves swimming and is also part mermaid like her mother.

My life as Dad had begun. I emptied the pool and packed it away. Then I jumped into bed and fell asleep next to my family, a proud father.

My experience of having my daughter born in a natural way, without medication, in a nurturing environment that welcomed her into the world with as soft a landing as possible, is my wish for all babies. I would love to see every child born with loving care and for every husband to support his wife and witness the miracle of birth—not only of his child, but also the birth of his wife as a mother.

Early interactions with our parents

After we are born, our interactions with our mothers set the tone for all future relationships. Her emotional state and, in particular, how she handles stress is of the utmost importance. As our mothers relate to us, our homeostatic systems entrain to hers, and this allows for mutual regulation of the endocrine, autonomic, and central nervous systems.

A mother's eye contact, her touch, how much she smiles and laughs, and how she regulates emotion is the blueprint for her child's future emotional regulation and stress regulation capacities. It is not simply a case, however, of 'the more love the better'. The amount of love and attention a mother gives and how she gives it needs to allow for regulation according to the natural mechanisms of the body that, following activation, return it to a state of rest and equilibrium.

How a mother engages with her baby, and then disengages and reengages again, can be considered an art form that does much to shape her child's capacity to engage with the world in a healthy manner. When a mother plays with her baby he feels good and becomes excited. Like fear, excitement is a state with a high charge and needs time for soothing. It requires the time and space to regulate back to a baseline state of rest. Too much of a good thing is not a good thing anymore. When a mother grants her baby excessive attention he may feel like it is 'too much', as if he is being smothered. This could lead to the baby being overwhelmed by a state of stress—perhaps he cannot breathe as his chest constricts as a means of retreating from the smothering. This reaction could then develop into a lifelong pattern: whenever anyone gets close to him, his chest constricts and he retreats.

On the other hand, when a mother does not give enough loving care the baby will likely feel lonely and uncared for. As the little one's cries for attention—for his mother to take care of his thirst and hunger or his dirty nappies—go unanswered, the uncomfortable sensations associated with his unmet needs become linked to sensations of loneliness. These patterns of attachment from his early years, as discussed earlier, create the basis for his mental models, which, in turn, guide his feelings, thoughts, actions and expectations in his future relationships.

Although the brain retains its capacity to learn and rearrange its circuitry throughout the human lifespan, it is most malleable during its earliest years. This places more emphasis on the neural-net profiles formed during our early interactions.

To help understand this phenomenon, think of a pristine grassy hill leading down to a river. The grass is knee-high, and as the first person to appear on the hill makes her way down to the river, she steps on and bends the grass, creating a vague yet identifiable pathway. Each time she makes her way down she will most likely use the path she has already created. The next person on the hill looks down to the river, discerns the pathway and uses the same route to get to the river. As more people follow this pathway it becomes increasingly clear and easy to find, which increases the likelihood that even more people will use it in the future—rather than going to the trouble of creating a new one.

Similarly, our first walks down the hill of life pave the way for the same kinds of interactions later on. Our body-minds develop consistent with our elements of experience and the consequent mental models. Events, context and content mould us into who we are. Where did we live? What was the economic climate? Was it a time of peace or war? What was mom's relationship with dad like? What was dad like? What were his likes and dislikes? How did he discipline me? How did he show me he cared? How did mom take care of me? Did she enjoy breastfeeding me, or was she unable to? What was her emotional state? Did she feel supported and safe with dad? The answers to questions like these are the building blocks for the foundations of our lives. Everything else we experience is constructed on top of these original connections. It is important to remember that this development of our subjective sense of our selves happens at an implicit level.

Although the mother is the primary caregiver, all other caregivers—particularly the father, but also other significant family members, such as siblings and grandparents—are extremely important for a child's development. Creating a secure safe base for children is dependent on the caregivers' own capacities to self-regulate. Young children's nervous systems entrain to those of the adults around them; so the greater a caregiver's capacity to self-regulate, the greater the chance that the child will learn self-regulation.

As parents, what we do and how we do it—especially in stressful situations—has lifelong repercussions for our children. Monkey see, monkey do. I sit down on the sofa. Next to me is my daughter, and next to her is my mother. I witness three generations of Lambrous sitting in a similar manner, all of our legs crossed in the same way.

Our children become our greatest teachers, mirroring our beliefs and actions. How often have we heard parents shrug their shoulders and exclaim, 'Who knows where my child learned this from?' Such parents are generally unaware that they emote in a very similar way to their children, and how instrumental they have been in nurturing their children's personalities and beliefs.

Like begets like. An anxious mother will generally bring up an anxious child. If the mother does not know how to calm her own distress she will not be able to provide the child with support in his times of need. In contrast, a secure mother with a strong capacity to regulate is more likely to pick up her child and hold him lovingly, offering just the right amount of support. Such a mother has the patience to stop what she is doing and tend to her child, allowing the child's nervous system time to calm down. At the same time, the mother's own nervous system, activated by her child's distress, will self-regulate. This mutually reinforcing regulation is of great benefit to both mother and child.

A child who learns to regulate and calm early on has a good chance of developing a resilient nervous system which will support his health, emotional experience and vitality. A resilient nervous system helps to govern all the processes that keep us alive. It is central to the process of homeostasis, supporting our health and immunity to threat. It also determines how we deal with stress and challenge through our fight, flight, and freeze responses, and how fast we recover from these events and return to equilibrium. This, in turn, strongly influences our capacity for awareness of sensations in our bodies and the extent to which we dissociate and 'lose' parts of ourselves. It affects the patterns of emotions within our body and also the expression of them, including how much joy and happiness we can cope with. It affects our intellect and the beliefs we develop about ourselves and our world. In sum, a resilient nervous system is necessary for wellbeing.

We attach to our parents for safety and protection. As they nurture us we learn from them how to survive and respond to life. This attachment is based on trust. It is a learned ability whereby emotional connections between us and our parents are nurtured over time through mutual interaction. Our early relations with our parents shape not only our sense of them and the rest of the world around us, but also our sense of ourselves—and these mental models are the filters through which we interpret all subsequent experiences. Secure children tend to believe that others will be there for them because previous experiences have led to this conclusion. Once they have developed such expectations, they tend to seek out relational experiences consistent with these expectations.

Remember that our childhood is the source of many of the habit patterns we act out here and now. We learn through experience and adapt accordingly. If we are lucky we are born to parents who are sensitive and responsive to our needs, and who provide a safe environment for us to grow in. We cannot go back and choose new parents or change the way our parents have nurtured us. However, due to the phenomenal plasticity of the brain—its capacity to learn, shift and change, both through creating new neural connections and the dropping away of existing neural connections—we have the opportunity every day, moment by moment, to shift and change our mental models. In this way, we can create new filters through which to live and anticipate life.

It is important to build our houses on strong foundations. There is the potential for a strong foundation in each one of us. The Three Steps is a powerful technique to realize this potential—to build a resilient nervous system or to fortify an already resilient system. Because the Three Steps increases our awareness of the sensations representing the ensemble of processes that result from our initial experiences of life, it is the most substantial technique for effecting change at the foundational levels of our experience.

CHAPTER SEVEN

MIRROR MIRROR

As within so without. Our outer reality is a reflection of our inner world. Whatever is within us—the sum of all our experiences from conception to the present—reflects itself in our lives here and now. In this chapter we explore how the mirror of life happens through projections and how we can make use of our judgements of those projections as a means of self-discovery and transformation.

Projections

Through societal conditioning—from our parents, our schooling and society at large—we develop mental models of the world which inform us of what is 'bad' and what is 'good'. When we behave in accordance with the expectations of our parents and teachers they label us 'good' and we receive love and acceptance, which generates a sense of ease, expansion, pleasure and overall wellbeing inside of us. In this way, our notion of 'good' becomes associated with a pattern of biological processes.

When we do something that goes against the wishes of our parents and teachers, they may scold, shame or punish us, and this may include emotional and even physical abuse. This leads to sensations of constriction, tightness and pain, and of fear, anger, shame and sadness. These are the patterns of biological processes we associate with 'bad'.

Because we are hardwired to move towards pleasure and away from pain, we desire to be 'good' so that we remain safe, loved and accepted and, as far as possible, experience wellbeing. To maximize our chances of optimal survival with wellbeing, we are consistently monitoring and evaluating our environments. When we evaluate an environment as potentially 'bad' we employ strategies to protect ourselves by either moving away from it or acting to change the environment in a way that provides us safety or the possibility for enhanced wellbeing. When we see our environment as potentially 'good' we employ strategies to approach and engage with the environment. These various strategies—for 'bad' and 'good' environments—are motivated at the deepest levels by regulatory biological processes seeking to promote wellbeing.

In a bid to develop a perception of ourselves as 'good', which will optimize our chances of acceptance and love—and which, in turn, will help us to experience pleasurable sensations and avoid painful ones—we try to hide certain 'bad' parts of our personalities from ourselves as well as others. This is the phenomenon that Carl Jung has called the shadow.

The shadow consists of those parts of our personalities we choose not to see—those we do not like and therefore deny. Denial is a form of dissociation; therefore, the shadow can also be viewed as the dissociated parts of our body-minds. However, the shadow does not rest benignly within our dissociated parts; rather, it projects itself out onto the outside world. It becomes that hypocritical part of us pointing one finger outwards, with three fingers pointing back. For example, the phone rings and a mother tells her daughter to say that she is not home. But later that day the mother catches her daughter in a lie and punishes her heavily for it.

We sometimes act out our shadows in ways that are destructive to ourselves and others. Take the example of the priest who castigates 'sexual immorality' from the pulpit and, in public, cultivates a perfect image of propriety. It later emerges that he has a pattern of molesting altar boys.

We might relegate much of our wonderful creative energy to the shadow. For example, a child may have an incredible, natural dancing ability. But his father has been conditioned to believe that dancing is only for girls or 'sissies'. This leads the child to suppress his talent for dancing, and even his desire to dance. He banishes it to the realm of the shadow. The talent still exists, but it exists in the shadow. Through awareness practices such as the Three Steps, we can re-member our dissociated parts and uncover the gold that Jung tells us lies within the shadow.

Relationships as mirrors

In our journey to re-member ourselves, our relationships offer a wonderful reflection of those parts we have lost—those parts that are lying in the shadow. As a rule, we generally attract people into our lives who can display these lost parts and help us to find them again.

When we look at our friends, siblings, parents and all those with whom we interact, our perceptions of them are filtered by our projections. This bears repeating: what we see in another person is what we are projecting onto them. Therefore, our relationship with that person will play out according to the qualities we ascribe to him or her.

For example, John and Mary are both friends with Jane, who is an assertive, empowered individual. John and Mary separately see Jane filtered by their individual mental models and project different qualities on her. John finds Jane arrogant, while Mary considers her to be empowered and dynamic. John is assertive—like Jane—but he is arrogant in his assertion, and therefore he projects this arrogance onto Jane. Mary feels disempowered and weak, so Jane serves as a reflection of the gold within her that she is unable to access. Jane is the same person, but through John and Mary's eyes, it is almost as if she were two separate people. This underscores the fact that our reality is subjective.

The severity of our experiences during our youth—particularly the amount of punishment, shaming and threat—determines the extent to which we dissociate and hide various parts of our personalities. We have an almost unlimited capacity to hide or deny aspects of ourselves we are ashamed of and to dissociate from our corresponding behaviour, thoughts, emotions, sensations and impressions.

When we dissociate not only do we lose parts of ourselves, we also lose our capacity to be in the present moment and to witness the subtle perception of the ever-present now. This amounts to walling ourselves off from experiencing the divine presence. As long as parts of us are consigned to the unconscious, we cannot be still, silent, calm or present.

The journey of the body-mind on this earth is a spiritual one geared towards returning us to health and wholeness. Dissociation is dis-ease, the opposite of health. So life continually connives to present us with the events, people and circumstances that evoke that which we dare not see—in a bid for resolution and a return to health. This sets in place powerful processes of re-enactment: re-enacting behaviour and relationships seemingly against our will.

The Law of Attraction is working all the time. Our spouses, our children, our parents, our friends, our colleagues and even politicians are all reflections of ourselves. When we are confronted with terrorism we need to look inside and see how we terrorize ourselves, our families and our subordinates at work. We can then work at dismantling these habit patterns within ourselves and cultivating states of love, joy and gratitude. Life will reflect this too.

The most powerful way to effect change is to go inside. When we fight the outside it is like fighting our reflection in the mirror. It just reinforces our habit patterns and the wheel of life will again bring us exactly what we need to see in ourselves in order to resolve it and attain wellbeing. When an issue we have been working with repeats itself and we wonder why, the answer is that there are still lessons to be learned, another angle we have not yet made conscious, some more gold to uncover.

Judgments

Insofar as life has given us a way of seeing ourselves in others, our judgments are guides pointing the way to our projections. They are qualities of our personalities we need to own instead of deny. How we react to a particular quality we observe in someone else is a reflection of how we react to the same quality in ourselves. Understanding this dynamic presents us with a clear map of which aspects of ourselves we need to heal and integrate.

Pauline begins to notice that her friend Jackie sometimes lies. Pauline labels Jackie a 'liar'. There are three important lessons for Pauline. The first is for her to explore her reactions to someone lying. How does she feel about it? What states of being does someone who lies evoke in her? She may feel hurt, angry and betrayed. She may want to punish Jackie. The second lesson is that Pauline's reactions towards Jackie as a liar—her anger and desire to punish—are likely the same ones that her parents or teachers directed at her when they caught her in a lie. Furthermore, her reactions towards Jackie are the same reactions that Pauline directs against herself—usually unconsciously—when she herself lies.

Pauline's third lesson is to recognize and explore ways that she herself may lie, what motivates her to lie and how does she feel while she is telling a lie and immediately afterwards. Most likely, Pauline does not consider herself to be a liar, and she has various strategies for maintaining her self-image as an honest person. For example, out of fear of hurting her friends' feelings, Pauline has difficulty in turning down an invitation. 'Of course I'll come!' she always says, even when she has no intention of showing up for the occasion. She is afraid that if she were to be honest and say 'No, I don't want to come', her friends would reject and abandon her. Then she is forced to make an excuse for her absence, which invariably consists of some kind of lie. Similar to all of our behaviours, Pauline's lies, no matter how small or large, are motivated by survival with wellbeing—in the best way she knows how.

Once Pauline is able to recognize her own pattern of lying, she can mindfully apply the Three Steps to clear any knots that keep her tied to this habit pattern. Later, we will explore the process of the Three Steps in detail. For now, it is important to keep in mind that with any event there are various stages, which can be divided as follows: a time leading up to the event, the event itself, and the time after the event. During each of these stages, our states of being shift and morph into each other in a seamless manner. The shifting states of being are analogous to a movie, which consists of thousands of distinct frames. When the frames are rolled at speed they project the illusion of being one continuous, seamless flow of images. As with the movie's frames, our states of being project the illusion that they are seamlessly merged.

Just as we can pause a movie and freeze one of its frames, we have the option of pausing and exploring a particular state of being, in all its detail. So when Pauline catches Jackie in a lie, she can 'freeze the frame' and notice her judgments, observe her hurt, her anger and her desire to punish, as well as all the associated sensations in her body—possibly heat and tension. She can then notice her urge to take action, to punish Jackie. By watching these urges as she would watch a movie, there is no need for her to take action. She is able to watch the rising wave of anger and, instead of acting out in her habitual way, continue to watch as the wave peaks and then falls away.

The waves of our states of being, be they big or small, come and go just like waves in the ocean. They arise out of the ocean. They peak and fold and, as they break at the peak, their water spills forth onto the beach. Then it quietly and peacefully recedes once again into the ocean.

Observing the shadow

Identifying our shadow sides—our dissociated parts—through our patterns of judging, projecting and re-enactment is a wonderful opportunity to process and shift patterns and become empowered. Once we identify these parts of ourselves, we can accept, befriend and develop compassion for them. These parts contain all those sensations that have been too uncomfortable for us to tolerate. So, healing these patterns takes place at a deep biological level.

The most powerful form of acceptance is just to witness whatever state of being we happen to be in—at the level of the body in the form of sensations. Do not try to change the sensations; just be mindful of them. Awareness of sensations leads to being able to tolerate them, eventually with a sense of ease.

I have been observing my sensations for long enough that, even if there happens to be heat emanating from my heart or lungs, I usually have the capacity to sit with them, although there is always the possibility of being overwhelmed. As I watch these sensations, I do not feel like I am fighting with them or punishing myself. It is more as if I am watching as an interested observer: 'Ah, heat is there. I feel the heat.' I call this sitting in the fire of our experience.

Do not be misled by the term 'fire of experience'. It is not limited to hot, fiery feelings but can include the whole spectrum of sensations, including throbbing pain or numbness or coldness or expansion or effervescent aliveness. Over time, as we learn to observe our sensations with equanimity, the body can regulate naturally, releasing what it needs to, which creates space for body-mind reorganization.

When we shift our physiological patterns, our mental models transform, our sense of self changes, and we start to perceive life in new ways. I cannot repeat this enough times: by going into the body we can effect profound transformation—one that ripples through our being and affects the world at large.

CHAPTER EIGHT

SENSATIONS AND AWARENESS

This chapter explores how the sensory system is a conduit for our bodily sensations and how awareness of these sensations is the key to transformation and liberation.

The sensory system

At the core of implicit memory is the sensory system. The five senses—sight, hearing, touch, smell and taste—are how we perceive the outside world. Whether we are conscious of it or not, our body-minds are continually receiving, processing and encoding information. All memory begins with sensory input.

There are two main sensory systems: exteroceptive and interoceptive. The exteroceptive system includes the sensory nerves that receive and transmit information from the environment outside of the body, via our sense organs: our eyes, ears, skin, nose and tongue. The interoceptive system is comprised of sensory nerves that receive and transmit information emanating from inside the body.

There are two major types of interoception: proprioception and the vestibular sense. Proprioception provides feedback on the internal status of the body and comprises both our kinaesthetic sense and our internal sense. One example of proprioception is the fine adjustments and correction which the torso and legs make in order to balance on one leg with our eyes closed. The internal sense provides feedback on our internal biological regulatory mechanisms such as heart rate, respiration, internal temperature, muscular tension and the state of the internal organs.

The kinaesthetic sense indicates to us where the various parts of our bodies are located in relation to each other. The kinaesthetic sense is composed of nerves in our bodies' joints, tendons, ligaments and muscles, which tell us where our arms and legs are without having to look. It is your kinaesthetic sense that lets you know where your head is in relation to your hands, and enables you to touch your nose with the tip of your finger while your eyes are closed.

Try it. Take a moment to close your eyes and sense your body. Now bring your finger to the tip of your nose. This action relies on input from your muscles, joints and skeletal connective tissue indicating the height and angle of your arm, hand and finger. The internal sense also comes into play to inform you where your nose is in relation to all your other body parts.

The kinaesthetic sense helps us to learn and then remember how to perform all actions, like crawling, standing, walking, writing, typing, playing tennis, riding a bicycle and driving a car. It keeps track of where to put and how to move each part of our bodies when performing these actions. Postural and movement information are communicated by tension and compression of muscles in the body. The kinaesthetic sense even monitors the body's position when it remains stationary.

Many people are unconscious of the kinaesthetic sense, and this is often due to high-impact accidents—such as falls and motor vehicle accidents—or physical abuse. Even simple fender-benders or small falls from a bicycle can distort our kinaesthetic sense. When this happens our spatial perception and personal boundaries get ruptured, which can be a cause of much distress in our lives. An important part of our journey of awakening and becoming aware of ourselves involves cultivating our awareness of the kinaesthetic sense. The Three Steps facilitates this.

Feldenkrais movements and the Alexander Technique are two movement therapies which help to develop awareness of the kinaesthetic sense. They improve ease of movement and have been of great benefit to sportspeople, dancers, musicians and actors—in addition to anyone wanting to improve their posture or recover from physical injury. They are fun and safe ways of exploring our bodies and cultivating sensitivity to our kinaesthetic sense.

Our sense of balance is possible due to our vestibular sense. The vestibular system is a fluid-filled network of canals and chambers deep within our ears which helps us maintain our balance and our sense of 'which way is up'. The vestibular system is able to sense linear and angular accelerations or movements of the head, and its chief purpose is to keep our body balanced at all times, whether we are sitting, walking, running, doing cartwheels, or just standing still.

The vestibular system is the first sensory system to develop soon after conception. It is highly integrated with the motor system, as well as the auditory and visual systems and other brain systems that control the body and are responsible for gross and fine motor skills. Our facility to perform motor actions, control various parts of our bodies in space, and to project objects into visual and auditory space is possible because of the capabilities of the vestibular system.

Our vestibular sense is an integral part our experience of life and an important factor in the quality of our wellbeing. When the vestibular sense is disturbed we can suffer terribly. It can be the root of many symptoms, including vertigo, nausea and loss of balance.

Awareness: The secret key to freedom

Awareness. Mindfulness. Witnessing. Terms used by different teachers to refer to the same phenomenon: our capacity to observe, to focus our attention; more specifically, to enter a state of consciousness in which our awareness is directed towards experiencing the here-and-now, with the intention of simply observing rather than changing the experience.

To be mindful is simply to notice, to observe. When we say observe it is not necessarily a function of the eye. Becoming aware of the sensations in your hand happens through directing your attention to your hand, being mindful of it through your kinaesthetic sense. The active modality of perception required for awareness of sensations is your internal sense. As you become mindful of sounds—of a bird chirping or a dog barking in the distance—you can also become aware of the process of listening, sensing your ears and the rest of your body as you hear various sounds. When you touch an object you can simultaneously feel the object and sense the hand in contact with it. When you look at a flower you can also be aware of the eyes seeing the flower.

All of us already have a certain capacity to witness, a certain degree of awareness. When we see the moon, we are often aware of how beautiful and luminous it is. When we smell a flower we are often aware of its soft fragrance. When we hear a song we are often aware of its melody. When we feel the water on our body as we shower, we are often aware of whether it feels hot or cold and wet to us. When we feel sensations of joy we are often aware that we are smiling or generally feeling good.

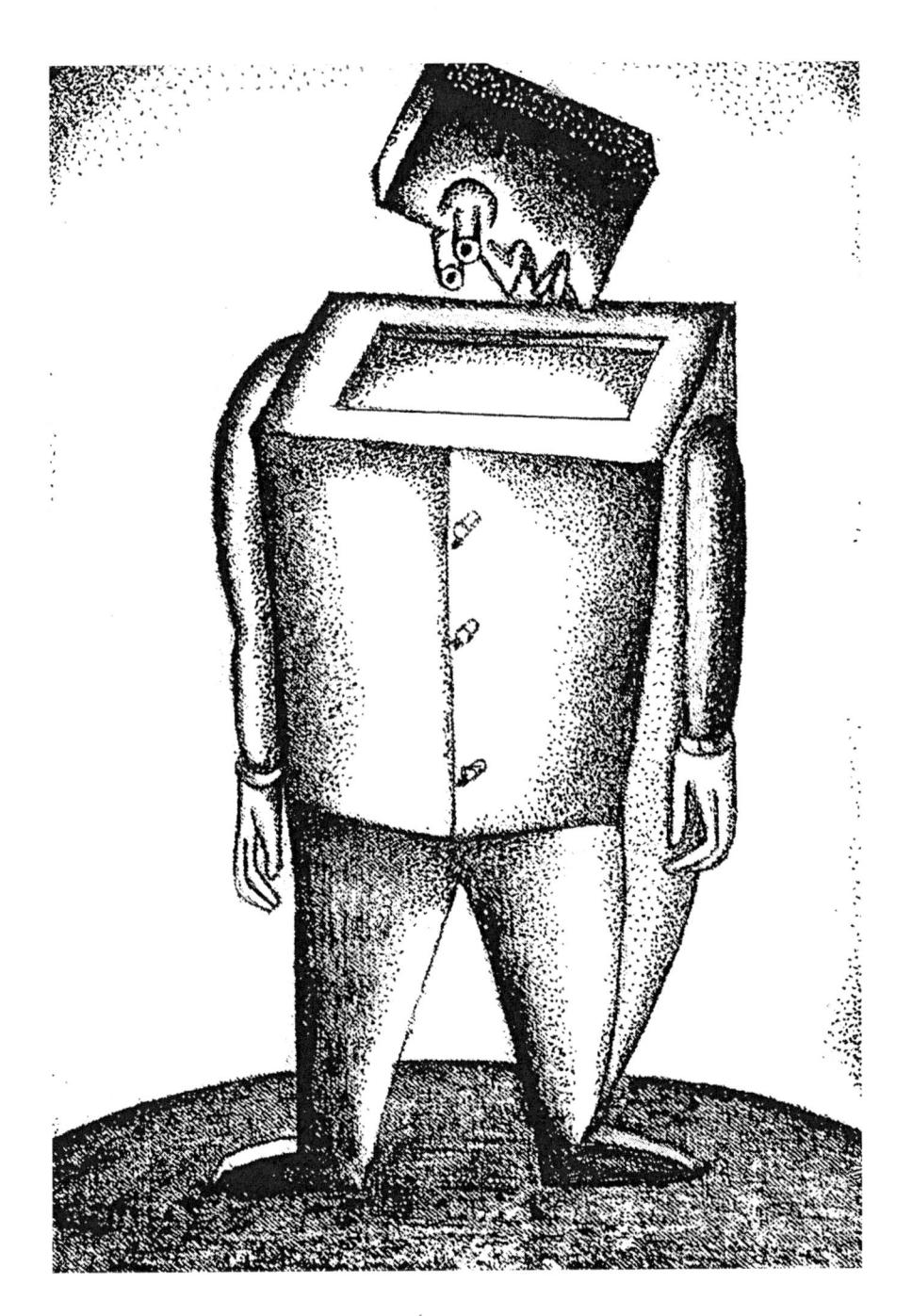

Awareness

We have the capacity to be mindful of all the different elements that constitute our experience of life. We can be mindful of what we see, hear, touch, smell and taste. We can shine the light of awareness on the internal processes of our body: on our sensations, our thoughts and our actions. We can witness our postures and our gestures, and how we are walking, eating and brushing our teeth. Our awareness can continue as we read a book, type a letter, watch TV or talk with a friend; as we walk along the beach and dance in the water. We can observe our emotions and moods as they rise and fall away, as our states of being morph into one another.

Awareness illuminates and transforms. When, for example, our sadness is the object of our awareness, it becomes conscious sadness. Awareness functions like a lamp shining its light on the process of sadness—together with all its associated behaviour, thought patterns and physiological sensations—within the theatre of our body-mind. Only through awareness can there be true acceptance, and acceptance is the cornerstone of transformation. When these conditions are met, it can be astonishing how quickly long-standing patterns are able to shift or simply fall away.

Beginning the process of awareness

Many of us live in a dissociated way, like automatons—'the lights are on but no one is home'. Dissociation is the opposite of awareness, and our dissociative conditioning is what prevents us from becoming more aware. In states of dissociation we are in dreamlike conditions—lost in thought, spaced out, daydreaming. Our attention is habitually centred on events of the past, or on our desires for, or fears of, the future.

Earlier in the book, we learned that dissociation is caused by a high charge and uncomfortable sensations in the body. To release the charge that keeps us dissociated we need to shine the light of awareness on it and help it to release in a slow and safe way. But how to practice awareness when we are constantly operating in a state of unawareness? We can only start where we are and proceed from there, so our limited capacity of awareness is where we must begin.

Just the first step of becoming aware of our unawareness—of when we are not being mindful of what is happening in the present moment—is difficult for most people. Know that the journey to awareness is a continual back-and-forth process between unawareness and awareness. One of the fastest and most effective ways of developing mindfulness is to keep orienting your awareness into your body, towards your sensations. Watch how your body—your muscles, your organs, your nervous system—organizes itself into patterns representing emotions, which orchestrate and direct your thinking processes. This is how you begin to see your self. It is how you develop the skill of awareness combined with equanimity, of observing your body-mind in a detached way, as a neutral witness. There is no need to label any sensation 'good' or 'bad'—just observe what is happening without judgement.

After focusing your awareness in the body, at some point your awareness will naturally move out again into your dominant pattern of thinking. When you notice this has happened simply and gently direct your attention back towards your bodily sensations. This will happen thousands of times. Just remember that with each pendulation you are strengthening your awareness. By and by, as you become more centred in awareness, you will stay longer and longer with the body.

Each time we make conscious any element of our experience, we are developing our capacity for awareness. Each time we become aware of the shift from a state of unawareness to that of awareness we increase our awareness. With each such pendulation we exercise our 'awareness muscle'. This faculty is likely quite weak because we have not been using it much, so the beginning of the journey towards mindfulness is the hardest part. As with any practice, however, the more we exercise the awareness muscle the stronger and more adept it becomes.

At first, as the flame of awareness is ignited, we may notice only a flicker. With time, the flicker grows into a steady flame and becomes a lantern lighting the way. The more we use the lantern of awareness the brighter and stronger it gets. Each increment of awareness becomes a tool with which to further expand our awareness and cultivate greater sensitivity to the subtler dimensions of life—both within ourselves and in the outer world.

By using the Three Steps, you can become familiar with all the states of being that come and go. You can get to know them intimately by experiencing them directly in the body through your kinaesthetic and internal sensory systems. You can observe how they arise in the body and can watch how you think when they arise, and how they compel you to act. By knowing them intimately and accepting them, you make space for them.

Awareness of sensations

Sensing your breathing is sensation—the rise and fall of your ribs, chest and belly is a felt sense. Feeling the air against your skin is sensation, and so is feeling pain, thirst and hunger. You know that you are feeling tired through your bodily sensations. When you burp or need to urinate or pass your bowels, these all become known to you through sensations. As you sit in a chair and notice you are feeling uncomfortable and need to readjust your posture, this happens through sensation.

The ever-changing sea of sensations within our bodies is the fundamental building block of our experience. Whatever our five senses and our minds experience evokes corresponding sensations. Furthermore, sensations are the 'glue that binds' elements of our experience together. Sensations link elements of our experience, just like Hebb's Axiom explains the parallel phenomenon at the level of the brain: 'Neurons that fire together wire together'. At the same time that our experiences are causing neurons in the brain to fire and wire together, thereby creating mental models and shaping our future, the elements of experience are likewise becoming wired together in the rest of our bodies via physiological sensations.

If the way our sensations are wired together is the 'glue that binds' us to our particular way of being in the world, we need a method to dissolve this particular glue in order for us to transform our patterns of thinking, emoting, behaving and relating. The Three Steps, which is based on close observation of the sensations, is one such method.

Recent research suggests that our bodily sensations are the basis for the brain's rational decision-making process. Science is slowly catching up with the spiritual masters of long ago. 2,500 years ago, the Buddha developed a meditation technique called Vipassana. He taught that if we want to free ourselves from the bondage of suffering and experience eternal freedom we must become conscious of the rising and falling of our bodies' inner sensations—and to develop equanimity towards them.

Today, scientists are beginning to suggest that sensations are at the core of both our mental and emotional lives. Therefore, it doesn't matter if you are a Buddhist or a scientist; to effect change quickly and efficiently in your life, it makes sense to go to the roots of your experience—to the sensations.

Sensations

As already mentioned, at first you may not find it easy to observe or keep attention on your sensations. This could be because you are often operating in a dissociated state of being. Dissociation can lead us to feel numb and to believe that we don't have any sensations at all. However, just because we are not aware of our sensations does not mean that they don't exist. A psychologist once told me that she could not feel any sensations in her body, and asked me if everybody has sensations. The answer is yes, everybody has sensations.

Twenty years ago I was one of these very same people. As I related in the first chapter, if you had asked me what I was feeling I would have had a difficult time answering your question. I was not in touch with my emotions, let alone their underlying sensations, and I didn't even possess the vocabulary to describe them. Today, it is a far different story. I have gained a sensitivity and capacity to observe the sensations in my body and, as a result, many of my long-standing difficult patterns have shifted. I have also helped many people to increase their capacity and sensitivity to explore their own interior landscape. When we have navigated our way to the top of the mountain we know the route and can lead others there too.

You may well say to yourself: 'I am already aware. I am aware that I get angry when someone talks to me in a certain way. I am even aware why I get angry: it's because my mother was always angry whenever someone spoke to her in the same way; I learned this pattern from her. I am also aware of what I say and do when I get angry. But still my patterns persist.' Yes, you have cultivated a certain degree of awareness of your emotions, your behavioural patterns and your personal history, but perhaps you have not yet explored your sensations in the way I suggest.

Linked to sensations are the other elements of experience: behaviour, emotions, images and mental interpretations. Certain sensations activate certain aspects of our implicit memory and our mental models, and they evoke particular learned behaviour and thinking patterns. For transformation to occur, we need to develop a capacity to make these connections conscious and to allow the innate wisdom of the body to complete stuck patterns of activation.

In our modern world, thinking is our focus. Learning in schools revolves around teaching at the explicit level—that is, the intellectual exercise of accumulating knowledge; knowing about things through reading, writing and arithmetic. However, schools largely ignore the implicit levels of our experience—the deeper processes that happen at an unconscious level, including our behaviour, emotions and sensations. What our body-minds are experiencing as we are learning is just as important—or even more important—than the actual information we are accumulating.

Once a pattern of ease of thinking is established, it will be easy to learn for the rest of our lives. Going back to the example of Peter from Chapter Three, the teacher's entire focus was on explicit learning, in this case correct spelling. He was not concerned about Peter's state of being and the related implicit processes, and the unfortunate incident in the classroom led to Peter's learning impairment. More of a focus on emotional and behavioural intelligence—and less on intellectual intelligence—would defuse much of the imbalance that has been created in our lives.

'Mind over matter' is a misleading axiom. Our understanding of mind as purely involving our thoughts is hopelessly limited. We have been misinformed and conditioned to exclude emotions and sensations as part of our minds. The result of this misunderstanding is that we try to change our experience solely through the power of thought. Then we become frustrated and start to believe we have weak minds when it doesn't work.

Deborah was bitten by a dog when she was five years old. For a long time, she was terrified of dogs; even cute cuddly puppies caused her to panic, squeal and run away. She had lived her life with the belief that dogs are dangerous. She was both afraid of dogs and had an intense dislike of them. To try and change this belief at a cognitive or verbal level—repeating an affirmation such as 'dogs are lovely and beautiful and fun to play with'—was impossible. Logically, Deborah could understand that small puppies are harmless, but as soon as she was in the same room with one her fear and dislike arose.

Contrary to popular belief, our fears—and all our other beliefs—are not just mental processes; rather, they are deeply rooted in our physiology. To rid herself of her intense fear of dogs, Deborah had to work with the implicit elements of experience that were associated in her body-mind with dogs—as represented by sensations.

The journey to wholeness and liberation from suffering involves ridding ourselves of the dual concept of the body and mind as two separate entities, and in cultivating a holistic awareness of the body-mind. It may be helpful to think of the body as the material manifestation of the mind. Therefore, if we want to become conscious of our minds at the deepest levels, we must witness the body. This is how we witness the mind in action.

In order for us to allow the body's innate wisdom to heal itself and return to balance, we need to get out of our bodies' own way. We need to re-learn how to listen to the messages that our bodies are continually sending us. Part of this is the process of de-conditioning many of the notions we have been taught about what particular bodily sensations imply; for example, that trembling and shaking are signs of weakness, or that tingling in the hands and feet is only a symptom of illness. Rather, trembling, shaking and tingling are signs that our bodies are releasing the excess energy in the body as a means of self-regulation.

An understanding about the importance of our bodies' sensations also helps us understand why behavioural reconditioning meets with limited success. Behavioural reconditioning amounts to altering behaviour through opting for a supposedly preferred form of behaviour: when you feel angry, for example, instead of hitting out, walk away. This may be temporarily helpful and more socially acceptable, but this alternative only impacts the behaviour resulting from anger, not the anger itself. You might still become angry as often as before—and with the same intensity—but you have learned not to hit out, just to walk away angry.

If, instead of hitting out or walking away, you start to watch and sense what happens in your body when you are angry, you will begin to discover the wonderful world inside of you. There is the rush of energy in the arms and legs, the pounding heart, the tightening of muscles, the heat in the back, the pressure in the chest and head, and the urge to protect yourself, to hit out, or push away. Can you stand in the fire of your experience and watch this wave of anger? Can you watch as the wave of anger grows, peaks and then dissipates in a cascade of rushing, tingling and trembling sensations throughout the body? If you can, you will start to notice that your body-mind responds to anger according to certain patterns. The pounding, tightening, pressure and whatever other sensations are present all occur in patterned ways unique to your body-mind.

With time, as you gain trust in your body's innate regulatory mechanisms and develop tolerance towards your particular patterns of sensations, you will 'befriend' your anger. You can now watch your anger in a similar way to how you watch a movie that you know and love. As you become intimate with your anger, you will notice that the pattern of anger starts to shift. The pressure in your chest might lessen and paradoxically, at the same time that your capacity to stay in the fire of anger increases, you might find that you do not get as hot as you used to. Your urge to hit out decreases and you are aware of finer nuances in your body-mind, such as when the initial angry impulse arises. You can follow the wave and trace its contours as it builds to a crescendo and then withers away.

By using the Three Steps and becoming intimately acquainted with your body-mind and its patterns, you also begin to detect what triggers your anger. Increasingly, you are able to defuse these triggers, or perhaps they simply stop bothering you at all. For example, maybe you are able to discern when your boundaries are being invaded and, because you now have more trust in yourself, you are able to say, 'No, I don't like that; don't do that.' The intensity of your anger is appropriate to the situation, whereas before, a tiny challenge to your integrity may have elicited a volcanic eruption.

You have now become an alchemist. Just as an alchemist changes base metal into gold, you are able to transmute—through shining the light of awareness on the sensations in the body—anger and violence into empowered assertion. Your 'base' emotions have become the foundation for opening your heart and your entire being to a life of untold possibilities.

How to observe sensations

When we understand how to look for sensations and what to look for, the uncharted territory of our sea of bodily sensations becomes less daunting. What follows is a brief introduction to observing sensations. Sections Three and Four take more in-depth approaches to using the Three Steps to observe sensations.

At any one time, there are a multitude of sensations coming and going inside of us. Some sensations are subtle and others gross. Some are pleasant and many are downright horrible. At the same time that we develop sensitivity to our sensations, we develop a capacity or tolerance to be with those sensations. Many times your sensations might overwhelm you. It takes time to build your capacity to allow powerful sensations to be present and to just observe them as if you were sitting beside a river and watching the water flow by. Your body-mind is the river and the water is the sensations. Observing sensations in this way, we learn to watch them with equanimity, without judgment.

Our body-mind systems become charged in states of activation, such as joy or anger. Observing the sensations that occur during activation, we will find sensations associated with arousal or others associated with constriction, or both. Arousal involves sensations like heat; a bubbling-like feeling; an electric type of feeling like a charged battery; edginess, similar to having drunk too much coffee; accelerated heartbeat; accelerated respiration, with the breath being focused more in the chest rather than the belly. Sensations associated with constriction are tightness; stuckness; feeling dense and heavy; contraction; congestion; and feeling knotted or blocked.

Following activation, the body starts to release the charge. This is called discharge, and it is the body's natural method of self-regulation, of bringing itself back to a state of restful alertness. It is like what happens to the body after running. As you sit or lie down, you can observe all the sensations of arousal—pounding heart, fast breath, heat—decrease and eventually fade away.

The body takes some time to return to rest. The arousal in the body starts to settle as the body releases the charge of energy still available for action. Discharge sensations can appear throughout the body and the main channels are in the arms and legs—warmth, tingling, shaking, flowing, vibrations, trembling and twitching.

Can you remember a time when you were leaning on your arm or leg for a long time and it went numb, or 'fell asleep'? As the arm awakens, there is an initial period of discomfort, a sensation of 'pins and needles'. These sensations can be intense and even painful. Discharge sensations can be similarly uncomfortable in the beginning. As we become more acquainted with discharge sensations and our tolerance for them increases—thereby assisting the body's self-regulatory mechanisms—they can be comfortable and even pleasant.

Often, people interrupt discharge sensations by tensing their muscles, crossing their legs, holding their hands tightly, and generally creating tension in the musculature. The muscles might be in a constant pattern of constriction, which impedes natural self-regulation from occurring efficiently.

Imagine that every time your body wants to release tension and arousal you impede it and stop the process from happening. This energy may remain stuck in your body, keeping certain symptoms in place, or compounding them. Also, the body will find it more difficult to return to a state of rest, with various unwanted effects on the body-mind. One person may find it difficult to sleep at night; another may tend towards anxiety or worry; another may keep cycling into anger and aggression.

Understanding that discharge sensations are a 'good sign'—a sign of healing—is great motivation for allowing them to occur without shutting them down. Allowing discharge sensations is to act as your own doctor. When someone breaks an arm his doctor applies a cast to the arm so that when his body's natural wisdom heals the bone it sets straight. The doctor does not heal the arm; she only provides a supportive function of protection and stability. This assists the body to heal itself correctly. Providing the right support and environment for discharge sensations to flow when, where and how they wish is similarly paving the way for our bodies to heal themselves naturally.

Awareness: the key to transformation

As you become more aware and learn to direct your awareness in the body, you build new connections between neurons that support this new sense of mindfulness. Your body-mind becomes wired to the regions in the brain that support awareness. Your nervous system becomes more resilient and you have a greater capacity to tolerate all the different sensations that the body has to offer. In this way you allow the body's innate regulating capacity to resolve the charge that has kept you in states of dissociation. As you regain the parts of your body that were dissociated, you increase your capacity to witness your patterned emotions, drives and instincts. You find that you are dissociating less and less, and concomitantly increasing your capacity to be aware more and more. You gradually transform the mechanism of dissociation into one of awareness.

Over time you notice that throughout the day, without any effort, you have at least some bodily awareness. Always in the background is an awareness of your body. Your actions become centred in the body, your listening happens through the body, your perceptions are sensed in the body. This is all part of becoming rooted in the body. When these roots take hold you can grow tall like a tree and spread your branches.

You are now aware that you are aware. Instead of being caught up in your mind—in the past or the future—you are grounded in an awareness of the present moment. We are usually grounded in our minds and it is from this vantage point that we view life. But, as a certain degree of detachment occurs, and as you observe your thought processes and the ever-changing sea of sensations within, you watch life happening through you. You watch the drama of life play out, yet remain stable and balanced. Some may ask: Is this kind of detachment not a deadening and numbing way to live life? On the contrary! You are now able to experience all that life has to offer—both the 'positive' and 'negative'—more consciously and fully. Yet you will remain untouched. You will live in this world but not be of it.

At some point in time the peace that passes all understanding becomes known to you. First you get glimpses of it, short moments. Then, through clearing away your perceptual blocks, the body becomes an organ of perception and you start to sense the sea of awareness that exists beyond the body-mind, and from which all life arises: the stillness underneath the movement, the silence that begets all sound.

Awareness is the key to transformation. When our awareness is anchored in the now we let go of old ways of being. We experience a paradigm shift in our consciousness and take a quantum leap into a new way of being in the world. Those emotions, thoughts and actions that do not support wellbeing will melt away in the light of awareness and those that do support wellbeing become stronger. Love, compassion, wisdom, friendliness and joy become the lenses through which we perceive life.

CHAPTER NINE

THE THREE-PART BRAIN

The intuitive mind is a sacred gift and the rational mind is a faithful servant. We have created a society that honours the servant and has forgotten the gift - Albert Einstein

The brain is integrated throughout the body via the nervous system. With advanced technology, such as Positron Emission Technology, a neuro-imagery technique, as well as Functional Magnetic Resonance, researchers can examine the brain in detail. These laboratory techniques have enabled scientists to further explore the concept of the triune, or three-part brain, which was first postulated in the 1960s. They are drawing the same conclusions about the interplay between physical, emotional and mental processes that Buddha did 2,500 years ago through meditation.

The 'first brain' is the lower part of the brain, which contains the structures representing basic regulatory mechanisms that ensure our homeostasis. These mechanisms include involuntary functions of the immune system and metabolic regulation, such as: respiration, heart rate, perspiration and temperature regulation; our basic pain and pleasure behavioural patterns of approach and withdrawal; our self-preservation responses of fight, flight and freeze; and our drives and motivations, for example, hunger, thirst, curiosity, exploration, sexual function and reproduction.

Our instinctual awareness of danger also comes from the level of the first brain, which is in charge of survival and automatically takes over in times of threat. Evolutionists refer to the first brain as the reptilian brain because amphibians (such as frogs and salamanders), reptiles (such as lizards, snakes and alligators) and birds of all kinds only have the first brain.

The 'second brain' contains many of the structures and circuits that support our experience of emotions: feelings such as fear, anger, sadness, joy, disgust, and surprise; the capacity to bond with others; and protection and territoriality. As with the mechanisms associated with the first brain, the purpose of those associated with the second brain are also life-regulation and survival with wellbeing. The second brain is crucial to our memory of past events, and it gives us the ability to remember and have hindsight. Other mammals, such as dogs, cats and elephants, also have this part of the brain.

The 'third brain' distinguishes human beings from the rest of the animal kingdom. The third brain is enormously more developed in humans than in other animals. Structures in the third brain support thinking and self-awareness, problem-solving, planning, language, self-reflection, and logic. This part of the brain provides for the ability to anticipate the future and consider the consequences of our present actions. It supports voluntary awareness and the possibility of being aware of being aware.

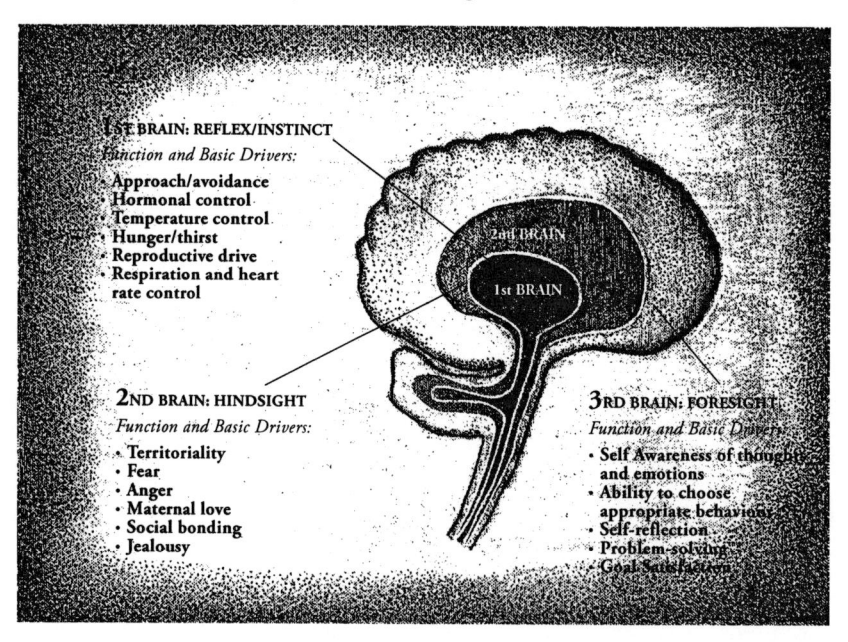

1ST BRAIN: REFLEX/INSTINCT
Function and Basic Drivers:
- Approach/avoidance
- Hormonal control
- Temperature control
- Hunger/thirst
- Reproductive drive
- Respiration and heart rate control

2ND BRAIN: HINDSIGHT
Function and Basic Drivers:
- Territoriality
- Fear
- Anger
- Maternal love
- Social bonding
- Jealousy

3RD BRAIN: FORESIGHT
Function and Basic Drivers:
- Self Awareness of thoughts and emotions
- Ability to choose appropriate behavior
- Self-reflection
- Problem-solving
- Goal Satisfaction

The 'three brains' each have their own dominant functions, yet they are interconnected and work in an integrated way. Looking at the above illustration of the triune brain, we can see how it corresponds with Antonio Damasio's nesting principle, in which parts of simpler reactions are incorporated as components of more elaborate ones—a nesting of the simple within the complex.[20] In *Looking for Spinoza: Joy, Sorrow, and the Feeling Brain*, Damasio discusses the nesting principle:

"Some of the machinery of the immune system and of the metabolic regulation is incorporated in the machinery of drives and motivations (most of which revolve around metabolic corrections and all of which involve pain or pleasure). Some of the machinery from all the prior levels—reflexes, immune responses, metabolic balancing, pain or pleasure behaviors, drives—is incorporated in the machinery of emotions-proper".[21]

Like a trio of Russian dolls, not only is all of the machinery of the first brain integrated into that of the second brain, but also all of the machinery of both the first and second brains—including emotions, drives, instincts, metabolic balancing and immune responses—is incorporated into the third brain's machinery of cognition and thinking. Damasio found that patients who had lost or damaged parts of the brain involved with emotions were unable to make reasonable decisions. This led to his theory of somatic markers that indicates rational thinking has its roots in biological regulation.

"The automated somatic marker device of most of us lucky enough to have been reared in a relatively healthy culture has been accommodated by education to the standards of rationality of that culture. In spite of its roots in biological regulation, the device has been tuned to a cultural prescription designed to ensure survival in a particular society. If we assume that the brain is normal and the culture in which it develops is healthy, the device has been made rational relative to social conventions and ethics. The action of biological drives, body states, and emotions may be an indispensable foundation for rationality. The lower levels in the neural edifice of reason are the same that regulate the processing of emotions and feelings, along with global functions of the body proper such that the organism can survive. These lower levels maintain direct and mutual relationships with the body proper, thus placing the body within the chain of operations that permit the highest reaches of reason and creativity. Rationality is probably shaped and modulated by body signals, even as it performs the most sublime distinctions and acts accordingly".[22]

Compared to humans, animals in the wild live in relative harmony, thanks to the fact that they do not possess the faculty of reason. Humans, however, rely far too much on the intellect, or the third brain. We have gone to the other extreme. As opposed to other animals, which live according to their bodily experience and instinct, we live according to our intellect. We are constantly trying to override our instincts and drives, and to control our emotions. This brings our three brains into conflict and creates confusion, stress, ill health and suffering inside of us and in the world at large.

Take the example of a man with a natural, instinctual drive to have sexual intercourse. He feels this drive as a sexual urge and is motivated to find a suitable partner with whom to have sex. But if his society has conditioned him to believe that sex is 'bad', he may employ his third brain to try and suppress his natural instincts. The conflict between the third and first brain begins, and the second brain—caught in the middle—retreats into uncomfortable emotions like lust, shame and fear of punishment. For a priest, who has taken a vow of celibacy, this could be a lifelong battle. Often, the instinctual brain wins out and the man either masturbates or has sex.

Another example is of a friend of mine who is a 35 year old virgin. She wishes with all her heart to be in a love relationship and to even get married. She confided in me that she feels she is technically not a virgin due to a surgical operation she underwent when she was ten years old. This invasive procedure left her body-mind scarred and she unconsciously avoids any type of sexual contact. Her brain is conflicted. She intellectually (third brain) and emotionally (second brain) wants one thing (a relationship), yet her instinct (first brain) defends against the very possibility. This is because her first brain deems sexual contact as a threat to its survival due to the invasive, fearful and painful experience she suffered as a young girl. Until now, the first brain is winning.

Our societal conditioning is at loggerheads with our instincts in so many ways. This creates much of our distress and is even the cause of rape, violence and war. When we are at war with ourselves, how can we expect to create peace in the outer world? To our detriment, we have separated, in a Cartesian way, the lower brains from the higher brain—the body from the mind—and have lost access to our true power as human beings.

Intuition

There is tragically little education about the implicit elements of experience orchestrated by our lower two brains, and how we can use them to live a powerful, peaceful and joyful life. Instead, most of our education is aimed at the third brain—at our intellect. Ironically, our educational systems place no emphasis on the key role played in inventiveness by intuition.

Intuition is widely regarded as a key source of inspiration in medical diagnosis, technological innovation, business decisions, artistic achievement and scientific discovery. Usually, however, we are unconscious of the mechanisms of thought and of the decision-making process—that part that 'just knows', the gut-feeling, the instinct that guides us towards a solution or to the right place at the right time. This unconsciousness is a result of having lost touch with our implicit levels of experience.

The greatest mathematicians and scientists assert that intuition plays a significant role in scientific thinking. Albert Einstein, writing in the early 1900s, described how emotion and his body in general were instrumental in his thinking process.

"The words or the language, as they are written or spoken, do not seem to play any role in my mechanism of thought. The psychical entities which seem to serve as elements in thought are certain signs and more or less clear images which can be "voluntarily" reproduced and combined. There is, of course, a certain connection between those elements and relevant logical concepts. It is also clear that the desire to arrive finally at logically connected concepts is the emotional basis of this rather vague play with the above mentioned elements".[23]

By exploring the body-mind—in fact, just by looking—we can discover the vast secrets that lie within. It is like the story of the beggar who found a wooden box. He didn't look inside the box. He just sat on it and begged for coins and scraps of food from passersby. When the beggar died someone opened the box to find that it was filled with gold. Similarly, our bodies are boxes waiting for us to open them up, look inside and find the gold.

In learning to live in an alternative, more empowering way, we have only to look for guidance from our spiritual masters who, for centuries, have pointed the way home. The Armenian mystic George Gurdjieff said that the spiritual journey involves bringing our three brains into sync through awareness; in other words, integrating the gut-brain (instinct), the heart (emotions) and the head (intellect). When this happens, a 'fourth way' of being is created. Similarly, Buddha's sutra on the four establishments of mindfulness teaches the importance of witnessing the processes of the first and second brain at the level of sensations in order to attain liberation. Living in a fourth way means mastering the emotions and instincts and integrating them with

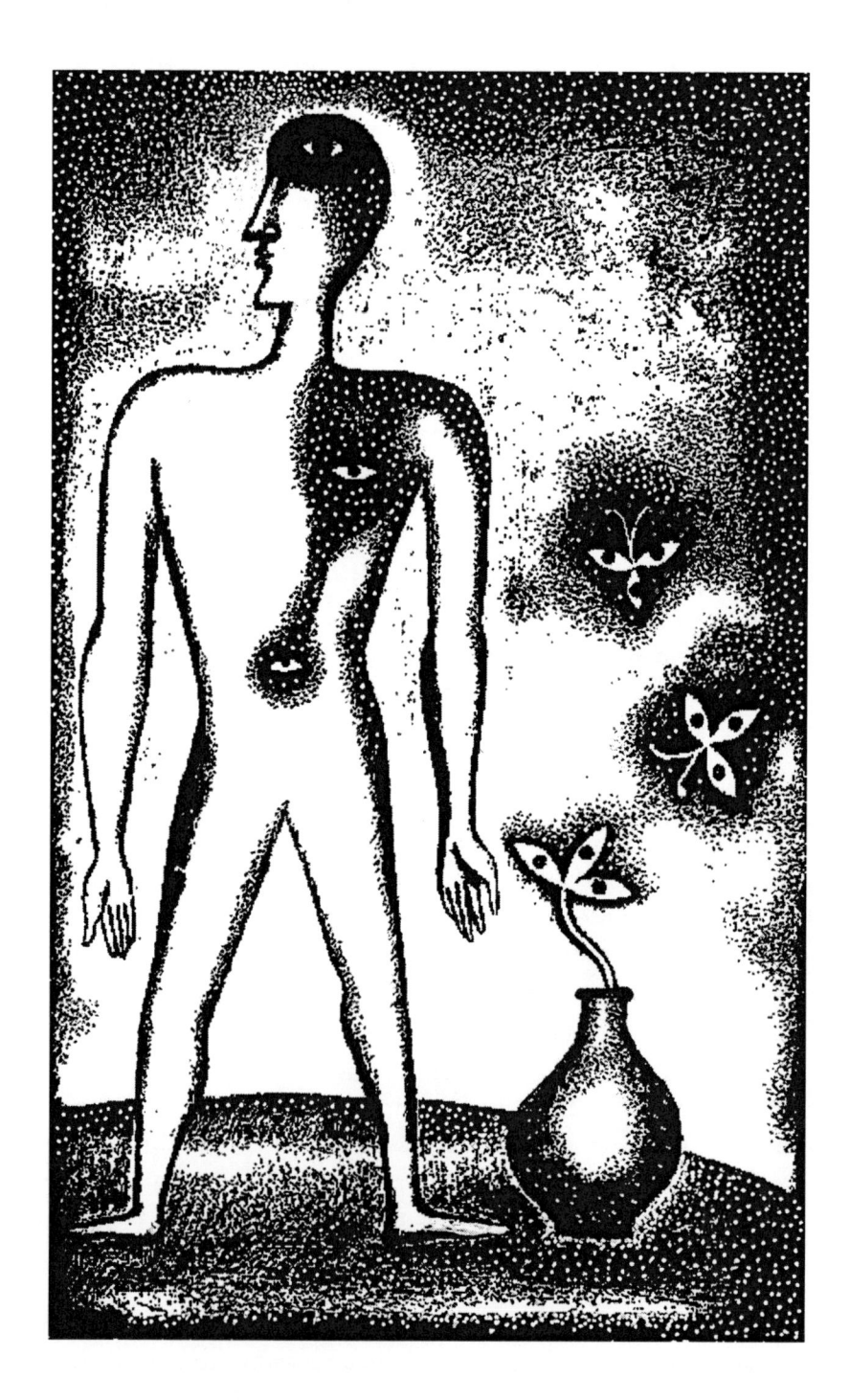

Perception

the intellect, making the whole greater than the sum of parts.

By merely reading about a 'fourth way' we cannot actually know the fourth way. It is not yet our experience. We may realize, 'Oh, wow! Our heart is actually more than a pump; it's also an organ of perception, integral in the heart states of sadness, joy and love.' The key question is: what do we do with this knowledge? Do we just continue to read about the theatre of the body, or do we buy a ticket, enter the theatre and watch the main performance?

The value of the body cannot be underestimated. Whether our interest is to master our emotions or to dispel physical symptoms like migraine, chronic pain, insomnia, or any one of the hundreds of other ailments that exist, the most powerful way is by observing our bodily sensations with mindfulness. When we are suffering the only solution is to go inside. This is the opposite of what most of us do, which is to look for answers outside. In looking for happiness, joy and love outside, we all too often get caught up in addictive behaviour.

In this section, you have learned how the mind and body are parts of a single body-mind, and that the mind's deepest roots are in the processes of biological regulation. Through being mindful of the body at the level of sensations you can develop sensitivity to the perceptions of the gut and the heart, thereby learning to perceive life in new ways. This will lead to fundamental shifts in perception that will alter how you view and interact with yourself and the world around you.

By being mindful of the body you are actually fine-tuning your awareness to the subtler dimensions of life. This will enable you to quickly shift long-standing patterns that don't serve you any longer, to develop greater capacity to handle stress, and to think more clearly and work more efficiently. Intuition becomes a way of life, and we become creators of our universe. If you want to master life, learn how to explore your body with the technique described in the next chapter: the Three Steps.

SECTION THREE

ALCHEMY IN ACTION

"If you want to reach your being, begin with the body."

"The body is the outer side of the being and your being is the inner side of your body."

"The body should be accepted lovingly, thankfully, gracefully and it can become a stepping stone to your being."

- Osho

Alchemy: The Three Steps

CHAPTER TEN

PREPARING TO PRACTICE THE THREE STEPS

As we have seen in the previous chapters, our instincts, emotions, thoughts and behaviour all involve bodily patterns. Often times, these patterns become dysfunctional due to past experiences that have overwhelmed the body. The body manages this state of overwhelm by developing symptoms and becoming dissociated in various regions. This dissociation, this loss of awareness of parts of our bodies, enables us to continue life in as 'normal' away as possible.

By strengthening the body's self-regulating mechanisms through supporting discharge and allowing involuntary movements to occur, the body is able to release the energy that has bound the symptoms and dissociation in place. Now, the body has a chance to smooth the rough edges, to thaw the 'frozen' energy and begin to flow again. Because our instincts, emotions and thoughts are grounded in biological processes, it follows that once bodily patterns change, so too will our mental, emotional and behavioural patterns.

The body is like a spider web. Touch one strand and the entire web quivers. Alter one area in the body and there is a knock-on effect throughout the entire body-mind. So, as we regain 'lost' body parts and energy, vitality and aliveness begin to flow again, the body needs some time to reorganize itself and accommodate the change. As old patterns are dissolved new ones promoting wellbeing are created, and immense transformation can quickly occur.

This reorganization continues as the changes start to manifest not only inside the body-mind, but outside as well. This requires more time still. New patterns generate a new sense of ourselves, allowing us to perceive the world in new ways, change our behaviour and attract new life circumstances. It is important that we allow time for this rejuvenation to take place and to integrate this new way of being into our life experience.

Just as the body-mind needs time to adjust, so does the world. All life is interconnected, creating the 'butterfly effect'. When a butterfly flaps its wings in China, it affects the weather in America. Our shifts reverberate throughout the world and change the whole of existence. Insofar as we are all biological musical instruments, when our body-minds play a new tune, it affects the entire symphony of the universe.

Remember the concept of a state of being from Chapter Two. It includes your thoughts and emotions, and more importantly your bodily awareness of a situation, person or event. We can think of a state of being as a physical experience with an accompanying mental commentary.

A state of being includes all the elements, both implicit and explicit, of any given mental model activated beneath your conscious awareness. Because mental models are generalizations of all our past experiences regarding the present, they encompass everything we feel and know about a particular situation at any moment in time. Our job is to bring our mental models to the surface—to make conscious that which is unconscious.

The Three Steps focuses our attention on our body-mind experiences at the level of sensations. In this way, we are able to develop our internal and kinaesthetic senses and become aware of the sea of sensations drifting through the body according to our particular state of being in any given moment.

A state of being is a bodily response to both our internal and external environments. It is a product of the pattern that the body's biological regulatory processes are creating in that situation. These patterns include:

- Bodily postures and gestures, including the tension and position of the spine, neck, shoulders, arms, hands, pelvis, legs and feet, and the tension in the joints, ligaments and muscles.
- The tension, of the jaw, the tongue and the upper palette in the mouth.
- The density of the bones throughout the skeleton.
- The vestibular sense, which determines our sense of balance and our relationship to gravity.
- The quality and pressure of the blood.
- The 'molecules of emotion', i.e. the various cocktails of hormones, chemicals, neurotransmitters.
- All the organs in their different states of processing at any moment in time.
- The temperature changes in the different regions of the body.

PREPARING TO PRACTICE THE THREE STEPS

- The tension and quality of the eyes.
- The nasal passages and the constricting or expansion of the bronchi in the lungs.
- The tone of the autonomic nervous system.
- The state of the heart, including the heart rate, and its tone and tension.
- The state of the head and brain.

Together, these regulatory processes are the charge and discharge that naturally occur in our bodies as we move through life. We are usually not aware of our bodies becoming charged, or when they discharge. Our bodies have natural rhythms of charging and discharging, although we are not usually aware of them. The following two exercises will help you to start tracing the process of your body becoming charged.

Exercise 1

The body responds to thoughts, so even when we think about taking action, it enters a state of arousal. The objective of this exercise is to introduce you to the practice of exploring your body through an imagined situation.

Sit comfortably, with your arms and legs uncrossed. After you read the following instructions, put down this book. If you need a reminder of the instructions while you are doing the exercise, feel free to refer to them again.

Check in with your body. Notice:

- Your breathing
- Your heart rate
- Your body temperature
- Your energy level

Now imagine you are late for work and have to catch the bus. As you approach the bus stop the bus is already there. To catch it, you have to run and jump on. Imagine yourself running to catch that bus. You have to run a bit faster than that....

Ah, great! You made it! You jump on the bus and find a seat to sit down.

Again, check in with your body in the here and now:

- Notice your breathing. Is it fast or slow? Can you breathe easily or is the chest a little tight?
- Notice your heart rate. Is it fast or slow? If you cannot sense your heart rate, you might want to place your hand on your chest.
- Check your body temperature. Are you feeling warmer or cooler than before you started?
- Check for any tightness in the body. Notice where you feel uncomfortable and become aware of where you are comfortable.
- Can you feel whether there is more energy in your body than before?

The language of sensation

Using the Three Steps means noticing sensations as physical experiences. Since we do not usually pay attention to the sensations in our bodies, we may not be familiar with the language used to describe them. Below is a list of words to describe some of the sensations you may experience when trying these exercises and using the Three Steps.

metallic,	disconnected,	wobbly,	streaming,
tight,	dull,	weak,	sweaty,
loose,	dizzy,	strong,	dry,
constricted,	itchy,	heavy,	moist,
expansive,	hot,	thick,	breathless,
open,	warm,	dense,	queasy,
stuck,	cold,	knotted,	numb,
flowing,	frozen,	wooden,	full,
trembling,	light,	nervous,	empty,
twitching	airy,	irritable,	smooth,
tingling,	floating,	calm,	rough
spacey,	bubbling,	suffocating,	
crisp,	buzzy,	congested,	
clear,	electric,	blocked,	
foggy,	shaky,	energized,	

Remember that all states of being have a particular constellation of sensations which constitute what we are actually feeling. Take the example of 'feeling good'—the body organizes itself into a particular pattern we interpret as feeling good. When we become aware of the sensations that underlie this state of feeling good, we may find that the breathing is regular, easy and centred in the belly, which feels softer, more open and alive with tingling. The chest may also feel light and open, with the overall musculature relaxed. Our thinking and sense of vision may feel clearer.

In the same way, 'feeling bad' also encompasses a body-mind pattern. It may include a stomach-ache, a stiff and painful neck, a constricted chest and laboured breathing. There may be a general tightening of muscles in the legs and arms, with the body temperature feeling too warm, which may lead to a feeling of irritability.

Applying this new vocabulary to the observations of our bodily sensations allows us to label and become more consciously aware of the particular constellations that make up our various states of being.

Exercise 2

Now we will try Exercise 1 again, but instead of imagining a situation, you will actually run on the spot.

While still seated, check in with your body. Notice:

- Your breathing
- Your heart rate
- Your body temperature
- Your energy level

Now stand up. What changes have occurred in your body just by standing? Can you notice that the act of standing has generated more energy in your body? What has happened to your breathing and your heart rate?

Run on the spot for twenty seconds and then sit down.

Monitor your body again.

- Notice your breathing. Is it fast or slow? Can you breathe easily or is the chest a little tight?
- Notice your heart rate. Is it fast or slow? If you cannot sense your heart

rate, you might want to place your hand on your chest.

- Check your body temperature. Are you feeling warmer or cooler than before you started?

- Check for any tightness in the body. Notice where you feel uncomfortable and become aware of where you are comfortable.

Overall, do you notice how running has put your body in a state of arousal?

Try exploring Exercise 2 once again, this time noticing more specific details of what is happening in your body.

Run on the spot for twenty seconds and then sit down.

Scan your body from the top of your head down to your toes.

- Where do you feel uncomfortable and where do you feel comfortable?

- Do you feel tight or heavy anywhere?

- Is there a sense of constriction or tightness anywhere in your body?

- Does your head feel tight or loose?

- Is your throat tight or loose?

- Is your chest tight or loose?

- Is your belly tight or loose?

- Is there any tightness in your neck or back?

- Do your arms feel tight or loose? How about your legs?

- How do your feet feel?

- Is your heart beating fast or slowly?

- Is your breathing fast or slow? Is it concentrated in your belly or your chest?

- Overall, is your body in a state of arousal? Do you feel a charge in your body? Perhaps it feels as if you have drunk too much coffee?

- Do you feel pain anywhere?

Experiment with Exercise 2 numerous times so that you become accustomed to internal inquiry. Remember, practice makes perfect. In the beginning, scanning the body may feel foreign and difficult to do. Persevere and repeat often. It will become easier, I promise.

Now apply Exercise 2 throughout the day to your daily life. When you stand up, check in with your body. As you sit down, take a few minutes to scan your internal landscape. Practice whenever you remember. Over time, this simple exercise will provide you with great dividends.

Because the body-mind has, as its blueprint, a tendency towards equilibrium and a desire for homeostasis, nature has endowed us with innate mechanisms of self-regulation. These are the means that allow us to descend from a charged state to a baseline state of rest—a phenomenon sometimes referred to as down-regulating. We can observe down-regulation by noticing discharge sensations, such as tingling, warmth, trembling, twitching, flowing sensations, and vibrations.

Discharge sensations can be witnessed throughout the body, but they also have some main 'channels'—namely, the arms, legs, neck and head. The lower part of the body, including the abdomen, discharges through the legs. The upper part of the body discharges through the arms. For a further reminder about discharge sensations and the importance of assisting and supporting the body's process of down-regulation, refer to Chapter Three.

Exercise 3

The objective of this exercise is to identify discharge sensations in the body.

While still seated, check in with your body. Notice:

- Your breathing
- Your heart rate
- Your body temperature
- Your energy level

Stand up and run on the spot for thirty seconds.

Now stop running. In the same manner as the previous exercises, monitor your body.

- Notice your breathing. Is it fast or slow? Can you breathe easily or is the chest a little tight?
- Notice your heart rate. Is it fast or slow? If you cannot sense your heart

rate, you might want to place your hand on your chest.

- Check your body temperature. Are you feeling warmer or cooler than before you started? -- Check for any tightness in the body. Notice where you feel uncomfortable and become aware of where you are comfortable.

- Overall, do you notice how running has put your body in a state of arousal?

Now look for discharge sensations in your arms. Are there sensations like warmth, tingling, shaking, flowing, vibrations, or trembling?

Focus your awareness on your left arm and hand. Take as much time as you need to observe:

- Does your arm or hand feel light or heavy, warm or cold, tight or loose?

- Does the arm or hand contain any sensations, such as tingling or vibrations or maybe flowing sensations?

Now focus your awareness on your right arm and hand. Again, take as much time as you need to observe:

- Does your arm or hand feel light or heavy, warm or cold, tight or loose?

- Does the arm or hand contain any sensations, such as tingling or vibrations or maybe flowing sensations?

- Does your right arm and hand feel the same as your left arm and hand? What, if any, differences are there between the two arms?

Just watch whatever sensations you perceive and allow them to occur.

As you did with your arms, systematically look for discharge sensations in your legs. Remember to take as much time as you need.

- Start with your upper left leg, proceed to the knee and then the foot and toes.

- Now shift your attention to your right leg: your upper leg, then your knee, and then your foot and toes.

- Does your right leg feel the same as your left leg? What, if any, differences are there between the two legs?

Again, check your body.

- Notice your breathing. Is it fast or slow? Is your breath flowing more easily in some way, or is it the same as before? Is your breathing more open and in your belly or is it more shallow and higher up in your chest?

- Notice your heart rate? Has it slowed down or is it the same as before?

- What is the temperature of your body? Are you feeling warmer or cooler than after you ran on the spot?

Overall, are you feeling more comfortable or uncomfortable?

Remember that when we experience a greater sense of comfort, there may still be uncomfortable parts of the body. It is perfectly fine to have an overall sense of wellbeing and at the same time feel aches and pains along the way.

Once the body has released its excess charge, it is possible to notice that we are calm and that the body is experiencing greater comfort. This represents another state of being.

Each state of being has a signature tune, a particular pattern into which the body organizes. One state morphs seamlessly into the next, and the body moves through an ever-changing landscape. Because a state of being may have many subtle, complex and even conflicting aspects, it is often difficult for us to verbalize how we feel at any moment in time.

Before a person begins to practice the Three Steps, his or her body-mind is generally activated—to the extent that he or she may have become numb to the highly charged, uncomfortable sensations just to get through the day. When you begin to experience your body, you will probably feel these uncomfortable—even horrible—sensations to which you were hitherto numb. Feeling these sensations is likely to catapult your attention right out of the body again. The rule of thumb is to go slowly and, step-by-step, you will cultivate greater tolerance and sensitivity towards your bodily sensations.

CHAPTER ELEVEN

PRACTICING THE THREE STEPS

Most people are caught in habitual internal dialogue, going over events that have just occurred. They either berate themselves for their actions or stand steadfast and justify their positions. This internal dialogue rarely changes their habit patterns. Practicing the Three Steps—stopping and going into the body—shifts your thinking, emoting and behavioural patterns. Once healing has occurred, there is no struggle to try and refrain from compulsive habit patterns—they simply no longer occur. You naturally do not do things the way you formerly did. You start thinking in new ways. There is no need to exhaustively talk yourself into being a better person. The Three Steps may seem slow in the short term, but in the long run it is fast, effective and the way of true change.

Through the three exercises above, you have already practiced the essence of The Three Steps. The steps are as follows:

Step 1

- Become aware of your state of being.
- Check out the internal landscape.

Stop! Just stop whatever you are doing. Stop talking, stop thinking and turn your awareness towards what is happening in your body in this moment—just as you did in Exercises 1 and 2.

Take a few minutes to scan your body and notice how it is doing. At any moment in time many biological processes are occurring, and these processes constitute your state of being. Are there any particular emotions you are experiencing?

When we are, for example, in a state of being of excitement and we examine this state at the level of sensations we discover our particular bodily pattern of an 'excited state of being'. There may be a feeling of high energy, as if we have drunk a few cups of coffee. The belly may feel tighter, and so may the chest, arms and legs. The heart may be beating faster, and the breath may be faster and shallower. It may be difficult to sit still because we want to move.

Observe signs of constriction and arousal, as well as places of comfort and discomfort in your body as you did in Exercises 1 and 2 above. Perhaps you have some pain. Regularly taking a few moments to perceive what is happening inside you at the level of sensations will lead you to recognize your various patterns. You will see, for example, that each time you get angry your chest tightens and heats up like a furnace; or, whenever you have to pay a large bill your entire body contracts and you get a headache.

All states of being may include uncomfortable bodily sensations. A state of sadness may trigger your symptoms—such as a headache or backache or fuzziness in your thinking—but so may a state of excitement, and so may a state of joy.

Before you stopped to apply Step 1, your mind may have been preoccupied with the past, or perhaps with the future. By paying attention to your bodily sensations, you have returned to the present moment in an immediate way. The body is always present, it is always here now, responding to the present environment and to your thoughts.

Scan your body from the top of your head down to your toes.
- Where do you feel uncomfortable and where do you feel comfortable?
- Do you feel tight or heavy anywhere?
- Is there a sense of constriction or tightness anywhere in your body?
- Does your head feel tight or loose?
- Is your throat tight or loose?
- Is your chest tight or loose?
- Is your belly tight or loose?
- Is there any tightness in your neck or back?
- Do your arms feel tight or loose? How about your legs?
- How do your feet feel?

- Is your heart beating fast or slowly?

- Is your breathing fast or slow? Is it concentrated in your belly or your chest?

- Overall, is your body in a state of arousal? Do you feel a charge in your body as if you have drunk too much coffee?

- Do you feel pain anywhere?

Step 2

- Look for how the body is regulating (discharging).

- If you cannot sense the body regulating, encourage this to happen through movement and touch.

Discharge is the release of energy throughout the body, analogous to steam releasing through the valve of a pressure cooker. When you support your body's natural self-regulating mechanisms of discharge the body can regulate and return to balance much faster.

After Step 1—after you have stopped and observed your state of being, including its signs of arousal, constriction and emotion—proceed to Step 2, as described in Exercise 3 above. Systematically look for signs of discharge.

By switching the focus from activation sensations—such as emotion, arousal and constriction—to discharge sensations, the body regulates and moves to a more resourceful and comfortable state of being. We can therefore think of discharge sensations as healing sensations.

The brain often places emphasis on bodily difficulties. When we have a headache our attention keeps returning to the pain in our head. When our awareness is narrowly focused on the pain, it can become unbearable and we may become overwhelmed. In this case, a natural response is to constrict, which impedes the discharge process and keeps the activation locked within the body, and in an attempt to not feel the pain and discomfort, we may dissociate.

By directing our focus towards discharge or healing sensations, pains like headaches will become more tolerable. Also, your attention will include more of your body and not be narrowly focused on difficult sensations—which usually happens in activated states. Pain can be a magnet that keeps our awareness captive.

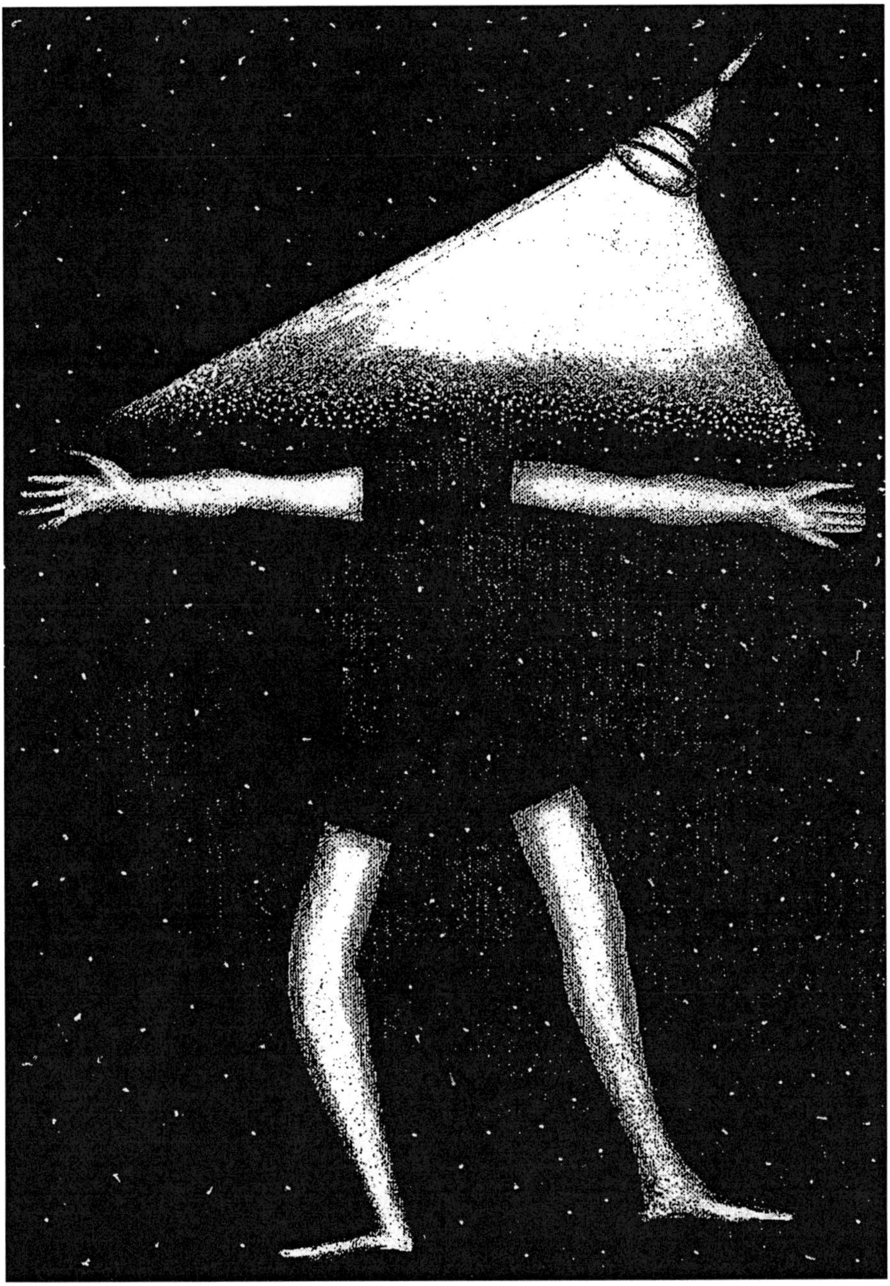

We can become fixated on what's wrong with the body. When we limit our attention to what is wrong, to the exclusion of the rest of the body, we may become overwhelmed and the body may constrict further, impeding a return to equilibrium.

Spreading awareness to other areas of the body helps us to 'dilute' difficulty with the help of a much larger container. Think of what happens when you mix deep red ink in a small glass of water. You will have a dark red solution. If you then pour the dark red water into a large jug of clear water, the solution will dilute and become lighter, more pink than red. Now, imagining the dark red ink to be pain or discomfort in an activated state, the Second Step is like pouring the dark red solution into the jug. Opening up to the rest of your body, the pain becomes diluted and more manageable. The body does not brace as much, allowing discharge and regulation to take place more easily.

The more of our bodies we 'regain', the easier it is to spread our awareness and dilute difficulties, and discharge and regulation can occur more easily and quickly.

Our arms and legs are the central channels for discharge. As you become aware of discharge sensations—such as warmth, tingling, flowing sensations, vibrations, twitching and trembling—and allow them to occur, you are supporting your body's regulation. You are training your brain to notice and support self-healing sensations.

You may already have acquired the habit of impeding discharge by clasping your hands together, balling them into a fist, crossing your legs and tightening your pelvis. By consciously opening your hands, uncrossing your legs and allowing discharge sensations to flow, you are creating a new, supportive habit pattern. Each time you observe and allow the discharge process you are helping to rewire your mental model of activation, regulation and return to equilibrium and wellbeing.

Because many people have a limited capacity to witness their bodies and observe and tolerate uncomfortable feelings, they are at first resistant to the Three Steps. They prefer to rely on old habits such as self-medicating or other ways of distracting themselves from the reality of their body-minds. Addictions and most of our suffering are because of our intolerance to bodily sensations. But after they have been through many cycles of charge and discharge, their doubts vanish. By developing trust in our bodies' capacity for self-regulation, we positively impact our health and take a crucial step towards mastering our emotions.

Discharge sensations not only can be uncomfortable, they can also be scary. Trembling, for example, is a sign of release of high arousal energy. Most of us, however, associate trembling with fear and weakness, so we try to hide these healing sensations by tensing our muscles and otherwise constricting. Also, because trembling occurs at an involuntary level, it can lead to a person feeling out of control, which makes the sensation even scarier.

Remember that trembling sensations are healing sensations; if you watch them and allow them to continue you will notice how your body starts to feel better.

You now possess a mental understanding of how important it is to allow trembling to occur, but you will need to allow the experience of trembling to happen in order to truly understand its positive effect towards your well-being.

Discharging

The body takes much longer to down-regulate than it does to charge. In order to defend itself or take action like jumping out of the way of a speeding car, the body needs to be able to charge in a split second. When the threat is over the body can then start to down–regulate.

Patience is required as you allow discharge to happen. In our busy, action-packed lives we need to find short pockets of time to sit and regulate. The more we do this throughout the day, the more energy and power we will have.

How long it takes for the body to return to balance depends on the intensity of our activation. It can take anywhere from one to thirty minutes, or even more, to down-regulate. As our resilience increases, the time it takes to regulate decreases. We also find that coming to balance takes less and less effort on our part. It just happens naturally.

Practicing self-regulation and discharge is like doing nervous system aerobics. 'Repeated activation of the relaxation response can reverse sustained problems in the body and mend the internal wear and tear brought on by stress,' Dr Herbert Benson author of the bestselling book, The Relaxation Response, tells us.[24] Furthermore:

> Just as we have the 'stress reaction' as one of the body's built-in response systems, so there is an innate relaxation response. The relaxation response brings about decreased muscle tension, lowered heart rate and blood pressure, a deeper breathing pattern, calming of the belly, and a peaceful, pleasant mood. The problem we face in managing stress is that the stress reaction is more easily elicited than the relaxation response. The stress reaction happens immediately without any effort on your part. A loud noise at this moment would startle you, and the stress reaction would speed through your body. A stress reaction happens automatically, while the relaxation response must be purposefully sought and brought under control. While the relaxation response will occur naturally, as when you sit on the beach watching the ocean, hectic modern society does not give us many chances for such natural elicitation. To control our stress we must engage in an intentional practice of creating the relaxation response.[25]

What if discharge is not occurring?

Many people's self-regulating mechanisms have been overwhelmed and thwarted. When this happens the body may require some extra support to prompt down-regulation. We can easily provide this support through simple movements and self-touch.

When you notice that there are no discharge sensations, check that your legs are uncrossed, your feet are resting comfortably on the ground, and your hands are unclasped and placed comfortably on your lap. Merely opening the channels of discharge of your arms and legs may be enough for discharge sensations to start flowing.

If there is still no discharge you can rotate your wrists and open and close your fingers a few times. It is best to do these movements slowly and with awareness. The same can be done with your feet. Rotate one foot at a time while keeping the other on the ground. Flex and contract your toes a few times.

Another helpful movement is to look around. Slowly turn your head from one side to the other. Take in what you see. Don't just look with your eyes, but rather move your whole head.

It is important that you do all these movements slowly. Moving too fast may activate your system further instead of supporting discharge.

After practicing these supportive movements, return to the process of looking for discharge sensations and observing how the body is regulating:

- Observe your arms, hands and fingers. What do you notice?

- Do you feel any sensations like tingling, trembling, flowing sensations, vibrations or warmth? Stay with any sensations you observe for a few moments.

- Alternate your attention between the left arm and the right arm. Is there any difference in the sensations you are sensing in the arms or are they the same? (Often one arm or leg may be more responsive than the other. This is okay. Just notice it). Now observe your legs, ankles and feet. What do you notice?

You can also support regulation through self-touch.

It is natural for us to support ourselves through touch. When we have a stomach ache we often place a hand on the stomach, or when we have a headache we may place a hand on the temple or the forehead. Placing our hands gently on an area that is tight or in pain is very helpful in helping the pain or the constriction to open up and discharge.

If you notice that there are uncomfortable sensations or pain in, for example, your abdomen, gently place your hand on that area. Just let your hand remain there, comforting the abdomen. Do not massage or press down. Support it like your hand is a band-aid. While keeping your hand on the area, return to the process of looking for discharge sensations and observing how the body is regulating

Whenever you catch yourself thinking about something else, gently bring your attention back to the body and continue the process.

Remember to give yourself plenty of time. It takes time for the body to discharge and regulate. Part of being activated is being in a restless and impatient state. This can become a Catch-22 situation: to regulate you need to slow down; meanwhile, your whole body has sped up and readied itself for action. It requires practice and perseverance to sit through activation and watch the discharge. Once we do this, the body releases the charge and we calm down and are able to sit with greater ease.

Some important reminders to facilitate self-regulation:
- Discharge sensations are healing sensations.
- It takes time for discharge to work its magic.
- When you constrict you keep the charge inside your body.
- Feel your feet on the ground and feel the support of the chair you are sitting on.

Step 3

- Watch how the body changes for the better.
- Look for signs of the body improving and opening up.

By giving yourself time to support the body it can release its charge. The body starts to feel easier and less constricted, and the breath and heart rate return to a more regulated state. The body feels less tight, yet more expansive, in a softer way.

Often, we are not aware of our state of being when we are doing well. Identifying states of wellbeing and their accompanying sensations can serve as useful markers in the cycle towards health.

Sensations of wellbeing may feel foreign and hence a little uncomfortable. Stress, and even difficult symptoms, may arise because some states of wellbeing are high-energy states and, without capacity, your body may not be able to contain them. Your pains, headaches, digestive disorders and so on may well get triggered. This is a major reason that we do not feel happy or joyful for long periods: we do not yet have the capacity to tolerate these states. On the journey towards greater health, love and joy you will need to develop tolerance and capacity for sensations that you may now find uncomfortable so that they can course through your body without stressing you out.

Step 3 involves tracking the small, often subtle bodily changes for the better that occur following discharge. These include the changes that you looked for in Exercise 3 above:

- A slower heart rate.
- Breathing more evenly and deeper in the belly.
- An easing of tightness and constriction.

- More comfortable body temperature.

Notice any changes that have occurred so that you have a sense of how the body has shifted towards a relative state of wellbeing. If you notice that the constriction in the stomach has released by even five percent, this will pave the way for further discharge and wellbeing. Ask yourself: 'How is my body doing better, even if just a little?' All the incremental changes for the better combine to move the body towards a more regulated state. For example, your breathing gets easier and deeper as your heart rate slows down and you notice the heat in your back is turning into a slightly cooler, more manageable temperature. All these changes combined are like a snowball gathering more snow and speed as it rolls down the hill. The positive changes combine as the body gathers momentum towards regulation.

When you have an overall sense of wellbeing, slowly look around the room. How is it to perceive your surroundings when you are feeling good?

Recap of the Three Steps

Step 1: Identify your state of being.

In an example used above, you may notice that you are in a state of excitement. By watching, you will observe the combination of bodily sensations you have labelled 'excitement'. There is likely high energy, as if you have just drunk a few cups of coffee. Your heart is beating faster and your breath is both faster and shallower. Your belly may be tighter, and so may your chest, arms and legs. It may be difficult to sit still because your body wants to move.

Step 2: Sit comfortably, uncross your arms and legs. Place your feet flat on the floor and allow your hands to be open and relaxed.

This opens the channels for discharge. You may notice tingling and warmth in your hands and feet. Keep exploring both arms and both hands and notice any differences between the two. Continue to pay attention to the discharge sensations in the arms and legs for a few minutes.

Step 3: Become aware of how your body is doing better in some way.

Perhaps the tension in the arms and legs is less, the belly is softer, the chest feels more open, your heart rate has reduced and your breath is coming more easily and smoothly. Pendulate your attention between discharge sensations in the arms and legs and the enhanced wellbeing in the body, allowing yourself a few more minutes to stabilize in this more resourceful and comfortable state. Then take some time to slowly look around the room. Remember to move your head, not just your eyes. Take in what you see.

Guided Instructions for the Three Steps

Step 1

Stop! Just stop whatever you are doing. Stop talking, stop thinking and turn your awareness towards what is happening in your body in this moment:

Scan your body from the top of your head down to your toes.

- Where do you feel uncomfortable and where do you feel comfortable?

- Do you feel pain anywhere?

- Do you feel tight or heavy anywhere?

- Is there a sense of constriction or tightness anywhere in your body?

- Does your head feel tight or loose?

- Is your throat tight or loose?

- Is your chest tight or loose?

- Is your belly tight or loose?

- Is there any tightness in your neck or back?

- Do your arms feel tight or loose? How about your legs?

- How do your feet feel?

- Is your heart beating fast or slowly?

- Is your breathing fast or slow? Is it concentrated in your belly or your chest?

- Overall, is your body in a state of arousal? Do you feel a charge in your body as if you have drunk too much coffee?

Step 2

- Look for how the body is regulating (discharging).

- If you cannot sense the body regulating, encourage this to happen through movement and touch.

Look for discharge sensations in your arms. Are there sensations like warmth, tingling, shaking, flowing, vibrations, or trembling?

Focus your awareness on your left arm and hand. Take as much time as you need to observe:

- Does your arm or hand feel light or heavy, warm or cold, tight or loose?

- Does the arm or hand contain any sensations, such as trembling or tingling or vibrations or maybe flowing sensations? Scan from the shoulder down to the elbow, from the elbow down to the wrist, now sense the palm, and then the back of the hand.

Now focus your awareness on your right arm and hand. Again, take as much time as you need to observe:

- Does your arm or hand feel light or heavy, warm or cold, tight or loose?

- Does the arm or hand contain any sensations, such as trembling or tingling or vibrations or maybe flowing sensations? Scan from the shoulder down to the elbow, from the elbow down to the wrist, now sense the palm, and then the back of the hand.

- Does your right arm and hand feel the same as your left arm and hand? What, if any, differences are there between the two arms?

Just watch whatever sensations you perceive and allow them to occur spend a few minutes exploring these sensations.

As you did with your arms, systematically look for discharge sensations in your legs. Remember to take as much time as you need.

Start with your upper left leg, proceed to the knee and then the foot and toes.

- What sensations are you experiencing? Does the leg or foot contain any sensations, such as trembling or tingling or vibrations or maybe flowing sensations? Is there tightness or heaviness?

Now shift your attention to your right leg: your upper leg, then your knee, and then your foot and toes.

- What sensations are you experiencing? Does the leg or foot contain any sensations, such as trembling or tingling or vibrations or maybe flowing sensations? Is there tightness or heaviness?

- Does your right leg feel the same as your left leg? What, if any, differences are there between the two legs?

Movement to encourage discharge to occur

When you notice that there are no discharge sensations, check that your legs are uncrossed, your feet are resting comfortably on the ground, and your hands are unclasped and placed comfortably on your lap. Merely opening the channels of discharge of your arms and legs may be enough for discharge sensations to start flowing.

If there is still no discharge you can rotate your wrists and open and close your fingers a few times. It is best to do these movements slowly and with awareness. The same can be done with your feet. Rotate one foot at a time while keeping the other on the ground. Flex and contract your toes a few times.

Another helpful movement is to look around. Slowly turn your head from one side to the other. Take in what you see. Don't just look with your eyes, but rather move your whole head. Try slowly looking up and down too.

Step 3

- Become aware of how your body is doing better in some way.

Scan your body from the top of your head down to your toes.

Where do you feel most comfortable?

Perhaps the tension in the arms and legs is less, the belly is softer, the chest feels more open, your heart rate has reduced and your breath is coming more easily and smoothly.

Pendulate your attention between discharge sensations in the arms and legs and the enhanced wellbeing in the body, allowing yourself a few more minutes to stabilize in this more resourceful and comfortable state. Then take some time to slowly look around the room. Remember to move your head, not just your eyes. Take in what you see.

CHAPTER TWELVE

HOW TO START WITH THE THREE STEPS

When you go to the gym for the first time you begin by exercising with a weight you can manage. You don't pick up a 40 kilogram weight; rather, you start with 5 kg or 7.5 kg. This much you can handle, and slowly, over the weeks and months, you increase your capacity as your muscles adjust and strengthen.

There are a hundred opportunities every day for us to practice the Three Steps. The best way to begin is to choose small events when the intensity of activation is mild. This will provide a good 'weight' with which to start exercising your regulation machinery.

When we repeatedly practice the Three Steps, using the small habits or quirks of our personalities, we find our way with the technique. These small steps are important in building confidence in our bodies and the process. By establishing the right foundation we can proceed with confidence.

As well as practicing throughout the day, I recommend that at the end of the day, when you are home, sit down either on a sofa or chair and practice the Three Steps. Simply focus your attention on your body. You have been on the go the whole day and your system is charged.

I remember how tempted I was, when I sat down to regulate, to turn on the television or talk with my family. This is not advisable. TV stimulates us too much, often sending us into a state of dissociation—a spacey, daydream-like condition. It is better to sit and practice without external stimuli, especially in the beginning.

By giving ourselves time to regulate, we are then better able to connect with others. I remember returning after work, tired, and my family wanting my attention. I made a habit of greeting them, giving them a hug and a kiss, and then taking twenty minutes alone to regulate. It was a beneficial means of going from 'work-mode' to 'home-mode'. Through experimenting, you will find the right place and time to regulate that works best for you.

Working alone is always more difficult than working with the help of a trained practitioner. You may feel restless, suddenly becoming interested in tending to some chore or other. You may simply feel bored or tired or sleepy. These are all part of your habit patterns of dealing with activation. Be patient. It is part of your process. Follow the steps and remember: This too shall pass. As the body regulates, you will enter a more comfortable state.

Small steps at a time

The Three Steps are designed to slow down our experience and allow us to handle activation in manageable amounts. This is the key to success. Working with small amounts builds resilience in the nervous system and enables the body to deal with activation in new ways, thereby resolving our symptoms in the process.

Titration is used in chemistry to combine two potentially explosive elements by adding them one drop at a time, creating a compound without an explosion. Similarly, practicing the Three Steps in small increments is a safe and gentle way to heal. By taking small pockets of activation (charge) and supporting regulation, we provide the body with the support it needs to re-integrate lost aspects into our experience. When we take small steps and slow things down, we can become aware of our emotions, feelings and activation through bodily sensations. The Three Steps helps us to manage activation by slowing the process down, and allowing time for the wave to arise, peak and fall away.

Observing the 'lost' body

When we first start to observe the body, our eyes will naturally want to move to the areas to which we are directing our attention—even when our eyes are closed. Our eyes have a deeply ingrained habit of following wherever the mind focuses. By and by, with practice we can maintain a perception of the body—as if the body is 'looking out at us'—and our eyes no longer need to move up and down or from side to side. When we focus our attention on the foot, for example, the foot sends messages to the brain: 'Hello! I am here, connected to the earth.'

It may be, however, that you find it difficult to sense certain parts of your body because they have become dissociated (see Chapter Three). Dissociation kicks off a 'domino effect' throughout the body-mind. Because we do not feel parts of the body we cannot allow the charge that may be stored there to regulate. Failure to regulate means staying in a state of activation, being stuck in either 'on' mode or 'off' mode. With our mental models constantly spiralling us into the vortexes of past experiences and anticipation of the future, it is difficult to rest and recuperate, and to have an internal sense of safety. We may become disoriented in time and space, leading to a sense of lack of control, emotional outbursts, and even depression. There is a loss of connection to self, to others, to nature, and to existence.

Dissociated body parts are not just reflections of whatever 'issues' we may have in our lives. Dissociated body parts are, in and of themselves, our issues. Regaining our bodies in wholeness is the sine qua non in our return to wellbeing.

Everyone is located at some point along the continuum of sensitivity towards bodily sensations. Some people have cultivated their sensitivity and are in touch with nuanced feelings. They can feel sensations of arousal and discharge. They can feel sensations deep within the bellies, hearts, livers and spines. Others may find it difficult to feel their buttocks connected to the chair. They may be sceptical that sensations even exist.

Whatever our degree of awareness towards our bodily sensations, developing this awareness further is the key to health, happiness and well being. It is the key to establishing a deep connection to ourselves and to the world in which we live.

In observing our bodily sensations, there are certain qualities that greatly assist us: namely curiosity, patience, tolerance and equanimity.

Curiosity

Curiosity as applied to the Three Steps means exploring your life like a research scientist, asking yourself: Which activities cause me stress? Which ones excite me or activate me in other ways?

Curiosity means exploring your life patterns, being open enough to recognize, for example: 'Aha! It's actually this particular behaviour of mine that gets me stuck in these situations over and over again. It's not because of those people I keep blaming.'

Curiosity means perceiving your various states of being, including the elements of behaviour, emotions, thoughts and bodily sensations. How does your body organize itself in this particular moment? Where do I feel activated or constricted?

Just like a scientist observing the reactions to an experiment, you need add no judgment to your observations. Nothing is good, nothing is bad, it is just what is happening right now. Maybe you are feeling hot, maybe tense, maybe there is a buzzing in your head—just notice it. Maybe there is tightness in your gut. What else is happening in your body? Ah, your neck feels stiff, and, oh, there is heat in your chest. When this happens I feel angry.

Being curious about the sensations of the body in the present moment allows openness to whatever happens next. In this way you can observe the ever-changing flow of bodily phenomena, the 'waves of being' passing through your body-mind. You begin to trust that your body keeps shifting, and that no matter how stuck it may seem, your body will regulate.

Be curious about all phenomena. Be curious about comfortable sensations, such as warmth, ease, expansion, flowing, opening, softening, relaxation, connection, aliveness and pleasure. Also be curious about uncomfortable sensations, such as constriction, pain, numbness, cold, heat, disconnection, spaciness, disorientation, fogginess, shakiness and arousal. Be curious about your body's discharge sensations, including tingling, warmth, flowing sensations and vibrations. And finally be curious about involuntary movements such as trembling and twitching.

Patience and tolerance

As tolerance of our bodily sensations increases we begin to trust in the innate wisdom of the body. This requires patience because it can take time to work through things. Nature has its own way of unfolding, its own time schedule.

To honour nature's way we need to tolerate our sensations; the greater our tolerance, the greater our patience. Patience is merely a function of tolerance. Through repetition of the Three Steps our capacity for awareness increases, and so does our tolerance of our bodily sensations.

Tolerating sensations does not mean becoming like a soldier undergoing basic training. It does not mean just gritting your teeth and bearing the pain. By doing so, you will be merely ingraining the habit pattern of gritting your teeth and bearing pain. This is the opposite of what we need to do to achieve wellbeing.

Tolerance as applied to the Three Steps means gently accepting whatever is happening in the moment. It means patiently watching things unfold, no matter how long they take, without reacting according to habitual responses. Habit patterns usually short-circuit our experiences by not giving the body the time it needs to move through events and situations in a new way.

There is no need to urgently seek inner or outer harmony. Just allow the present moment to unfold, allow the wave to complete itself by rising, peaking and falling away. With patience, you will learn to not let your habitual patterns make you jump quickly into reactions. Until then, sometimes you will jump too fast. When this happens, watch yourself jumping and be as present as possible with your habitual patterns. Be curious. Don't judge. And even if you do judge, observe your judgments. Everything is a chance to watch, an opportunity for awareness.

What is sometimes most challenging is that patience is only learned in times of difficulty, because this is when difficult patterns arise. This is when we have the opportunity to apply all our learning, to put into practice all the hours we have spent practicing the Three Steps with smaller, less intense states. Difficult, charged states are our litmus tests.

My experience has been that the more patience and tolerance I develop the more conscious I become, and the more fully I feel. I have become more sensitive to my internal and external environments, yet I possess greater tolerance to contain them with equanimity. I don't suffer as much as I used to, but I still suffer. A big difference is that I now suffer consciously and use it as an opportunity for growth.

We also need patience when practicing the Three Steps to repeatedly return our attention to our bodily sensations. Hundreds, if not thousands of times, you will find yourself lost in thought, daydreaming. Be patient with yourself. This is normal. When you notice that you are in 'thinking land', gently shift your focus back to the body. Because thinking has become the predominant human modality of functioning, it takes time to become centred in observing bodily sensations.

Part of the reason we become lost in thought is to distract ourselves from the stimulation inside our bodies. Each time we shift our attention towards our bodily sensations we increase our capacity to be in the present moment.

Practicing the Three Steps patiently requires a certain degree of aloneness. When we are constantly busy with everyday life it may be difficult to begin observing bodily sensations. We often get swept up in what we are doing and become distracted when relating to others. When we are distracted it is too easy for our deeply entrenched habit of being lost in thought to take over. So take some time each day to be in solitude.

Equanimity

Observing bodily sensations with equanimity means to just notice them without trying to get rid of them and without holding onto them. We are hardwired to move towards pleasure and away from pain, so with the Three Steps we are rewiring our neural-net profiles. We are learning to allow whatever is happening to unfold without aversion or clinging.

As our tolerance increases, equanimity becomes easier. For example, when trembling happens it can be quite scary. We do not like to feel scared, so most people shut this sensation off by clenching their musculature. After educating ourselves about the Three Steps, we know that trembling is beneficial, a sign of discharge, so we allow it. For some time, however, we may still shut down the trembling. But the more we watch the trembling in a conscious manner, the more we allow it to happen without impeding it. Now we have a new tolerance for trembling sensations. Later still, trembling occurs and we notice it with the attitude of a research scientist: 'Ah, trembling is happening.' This attitude is equanimity.

Equanimity goes hand in hand with curiosity, patience and tolerance in observing our states of being without reacting according to old habit patterns. Once equanimity becomes a character trait, it underlies our experience of life, which becomes more supportive and nourishing.

Pendulation and cycles

Pendulation is the movement from one side to the other, like the swinging pendulum of a grandfather clock. When practicing the Three Steps pendulation happens when the body moves from an uncomfortable state to one of comfort, from activation to restfulness. It is the rhythm of the nervous system shifting between expansion and contraction, charge and discharge.

In this work, the transition from a charged state to a restful one may take some time. The journey of the body from arousal and constriction, through discharge, and on to restfulness and comfort happens in little, almost imperceptible steps. The pendulum starts on one side, that of arousal, constriction and discomfort. As the body discharges, arousal gradually lessens, constriction slowly opens and the pendulum begins its swing to the other side. The more discharge there is the more the pendulum is able to complete its swing to the other side, where the body feels relaxed, soft and expansive. However, just one anxiety-provoking thought can send the body into action, propelling the pendulum back to a state of constriction and arousal.

The body-mind is a dynamic system. Whenever we stop and apply the Three Steps mindfully, we start from where we are—in whatever state of being we find ourselves. We then look for signs of regulation, if need be assisting the body to regulate. The next step is to notice how the body is feeling better, even in tiny amounts, and how it is in a more comfortable and easy state. This is one cycle of the Three Steps. When we remember something distressing our body-mind takes on a new, activated state of being. Then we can work through another cycle back to comfort.

Slowing down and allowing time for self-regulation is an essential skill in enjoying health and wellbeing.

Inclusion

When our bodies are stable and we feel safe, we naturally return to a state of being of curiosity and engagement. We can simultaneously explore and include both our external surroundings and our internal environments without becoming overwhelmed by either one.

In Step Three, as you slowly look around, maintain a sense of your overall bodily environment while extending your awareness to the external surroundings. Notice how it feels to perceive your surroundings when you are feeling good and whether you are able to include more of the environment in your vision. As you are observing the surroundings there is a simultaneous remembering—via sensations—of yourself.

This remembering will begin to seep into your everyday actions. As you listen, you start to listen with your whole body. As you eat you will become less caught up in extraneous thoughts and maintain an awareness of your body eating. The quality of awareness will permeate all mental models and all states of being. Awareness will become easy and life beautiful.

Resilience

Resilience is a material's ability to return to its original shape or position after being bent, stretched, compressed or otherwise deformed. Resilience is determined by the material's elasticity, buoyancy, flexibility and tonicity.

When the body-mind has been activated its regulatory mechanisms, centred around the autonomic nervous system, can return it to a state of equilibrium. Resilience is the capacity of an individual's regulatory system to right itself after being 'bent out of shape'.

Successfully negotiating challenging events allows our resilience to increase. The body-mind has a chance to set new precedents by being 'bowled over' and coming back. We sense that, next time, we can go a little bit further and still come back. It is like a long-distance runner who is comfortable running a half marathon but has never ventured to attempt a full marathon. One day he enters a full marathon, completes it and recovers well. From then on, he runs full marathons, and now he even focuses on improving his time.

We can gauge our resilience according to two major factors. The first is the capacity of charge the body-mind can experience without becoming overwhelmed and symptoms being triggered.

For example, a certain level of stress always causes Christine to have headaches. This stress can be both 'good' and 'bad'—it could come from excitement after concluding a deal she has been working on, or from an argument with her lover. In both cases, the high level of activation in her body-mind leads to a headache. Christine can gauge her resilience by being aware of the intensity of the highly charged experiences she can tolerate without becoming symptomatic—in other words, without getting a headache.

The second factor in determining resilience is the ability to bounce back. When I have been overwhelmed by an experience, how quickly can I return to a state of relative wellbeing? This is a function of the strength of my self-regulating mechanisms. For example, I have had a heated argument with my friend whom I feel has betrayed me. I feel hurt and angry. How long do I stay in this angry and hurt state? How much do I play this scene over in my mind, reactivating the feelings of hurt and anger? Am I able to put this issue aside and deal with the next person I encounter in a fresh way? Or, because I am primed with anger from the previous incident with my friend, do I take this anger out on my subordinate at work, on a taxi driver, or on anyone else who may cross my path?

As our range of resilience increases we can experience a greater degree of charge and still experience a sense of wellbeing and feel that life is manageable. With resilience, the body-mind is confident that it can return to equilibrium and a baseline state of rest that supports rejuvenation. We can fluidly transition from a charged state in order to take care of life circumstances and then back to a state of rest. The Three Steps—which we have already likened to doing nervous system aerobics—is an excellent way to increase resilience by strengthening our capacity to cycle through charged states to restful ones.

Resilience is our greatest resource in life. When we are resilient we feel confident, creative and curious to explore life. We are generally more playful and assertive, and it is easy for us to connect with others, both in friendship and in intimacy. Resilience is a key factor in the quality of wellbeing that we experience.

Resources

Ultimately, our bodies are our main resource. In the journey of regaining the body we may sometimes need to rely on other devices. A resource is anything that helps us to maintain a sense of ourselves and manage excitation and activation. It is a supportive device that helps us to regulate in times of stress. Resources help in balancing the nervous system and supporting self-regulation, so consciously developing resources can be of great assistance on the path to wholeness.

For me, a strong resource is remembering my daughter, which always spreads feelings of love throughout my body. In a loving state of being I can more easily discharge and return to a baseline state of rest. In this case, my memory is acting like a mother who comforts her toddler when he falls and hurts himself. In the safety and support of his mother, the toddler can relax.

The greater we feel resourced, the more we can face in life. Resources may include: getting a good night's sleep, taking rest in the afternoon, going for a walk, some form of exercise, socializing with friends, listening to your favourite music, and going to see a movie. These are all examples of external resources because they are activities and people that nourish us. When we remember external sources they become internal resources. Remembering my daughter's birth is an example of an internal resource. Another internal resource is to remember our strengths, such as: intelligence, perseverance, a healthy body, and patience.

At the same time that external and internal resources can assist us, by working with the Three Steps we can increasingly rely on our bodies. Building resilience and having confidence in the body-mind's capacity to self-regulate allows us to firmly ensconce our bodies in their rightful place as our number one resource.

A new way

It is important to know that catching ourselves in the midst of activated states of being and providing the time and support for the body to down-regulate allows the body to do something new with this activation. Because the body has the time and space needed to release its charge, it moves towards healthy homeostasis, which is indicative of wellbeing. In this way, stuck bodily patterns are transmuted into natural vitality.

For a new way to happen, slowing down, awareness, support, patience and tolerance are crucial. Failure to stop and provide support keeps the body-mind stuck in the same patterns, and symptoms are not shifted and released. The more we support the innate mechanisms of the body the stronger they become. Then, the body naturally follows this new way more of the time. At some point, this 'new' body, functioning in this new way, is constantly supporting us from behind the scenes.

An apt analogy is a toy train that has fallen off the tracks. Once we return it to the tracks, off it goes. Nature has given us powerful mechanisms of regulation, but somewhere along the way they have become derailed. The Three Steps returns them to the tracks, and after that they will operate healthily without much active participation.

Slowing down is speeding up

To effectively heal and transform ourselves we need to follow the laws of the body. Otherwise it is like swimming upstream against a strong current; exhaustion quickly sets in and we may drown.

The way we often live our modern lives is like swimming against the flow. Busy trying to survive, we feel compelled to keep swimming just to keep our heads above water. Being 'on' all the time, our nervous systems become overwhelmed and we develop symptoms that reduce our sense of wellbeing.

Humans have a well-developed 'third brain'. Animals in the wild don't. As animals move from charge to restful alertness, their bodies allow nature to take its course unimpeded by bringing them back to a baseline state of rest. To return to wholeness, our job as humans is to undo habit patterns that impede the natural workings of the body and support our bodies in carrying out their natural flow. By slowing down we support our natural rhythms of regulation.

Proactively taking short moments throughout the day to self-regulate, we allow the body to recharge. Then we can get up and go, go, go once again.

Slowing down is of utmost importance in practicing the Three Steps. I like to see slowing down as speeding up. When our body's regulatory mechanisms are working optimally, our physical, emotional, interpersonal and work-related issues shift for the better. Our overall sense of wellbeing improves. We can literally make quantum leaps in our life experience. By stopping our swim against the flow, we follow the river's natural course and end up where we wanted to be all along: in the sea—the sea of life.

By slowing down we are able to perceive the building blocks of both our integrity and our woes. This allows us to rebuild the foundation of our experience. For a house or a building, this is impossible to do. Once its foundations are set, that's it. In the past, most scientists and doctors have followed this same logic regarding humans: once our brain connections are set, they say, it is impossible to change them. However, as we saw in Chapter Four, the brain's plasticity lasts throughout our lifespan, so we have the possibility of altering our neural connections and networks. The most powerful way to do this is through the Three Steps, with the body and its sensations.

By slowing down and changing the biological patterns of our states of being, we create new mental models for the context, events and even specific situations that we repeatedly play out. This is what happened to me as I worked with my anger, and specifically with the anger that manifested with the frustrations of queuing up in India (described in Chapter Five).

With the Three Steps I was able to change my body-mind patterns, so that my body was better prepared for stress. When angry my chest used to burn and huge pressure would build up in the area. Gradually, this pattern released, and now, when angry, my chest no longer burns and I feel only a mild sensation of pressure there. This leads to a completely different experience of anger, and consequently very different behaviour. When anger arises, there is greater comfort and wellbeing in my body. Difficult patterns like a burning chest with huge pressure in it are the kinds of sensations that drive peoples' violence, rage and addictions. By shifting these bodily patterns, the body becomes a safer, more comfortable and more enjoyable place to inhabit, and behaviour easily yet dramatically shifts.

When to process

The heat of the moment, as the intensity of a state of being is evoked, is the ideal time to shift longstanding patterns dramatically. Remaining aware as we abide in the fire of our experience with equanimity will dramatically shift our body-mind patterning and alter the course of our lives.

But even if we are still unable to do this and, due to habit, we act out, all is not lost. It is always of great benefit, after an event, to take some time to process, allowing the body to regulate and return to balance. This very act shifts some of the charge, it may start to shift physiological patterns, and it is helpful in developing our capacity and resilience.

Rest assured that with time you will have the inner strength, tolerance and resilience to be mindful even in the heat of the moment. Maybe it will be next time. Or the time after that. Or a hundred times from now. Persevere, knowing that everybody faces powerful patterns of compelling re-enactments and addictions of all kinds. Sometimes it may feel like you are trying to swim against a tsunami. My experience is that as I persevere, I may not manage the 'heat' this time or the next, but maybe a hundred times down the line I do manage; then, all the effort is worth it.

With each act of mindfulness, mental-emotional charges in the body begin to dissipate and disappear. Even if you become aware of a state of being as you replay an incident in your mind several days after it occurred, it is still a great time to do the processing. As soon as you become mindful, it is time to process. By processing, you shift the physiological patterning of the mental model and change how you will perceive and act in the future.

The spiral effect

It may happen that you are working with a particular emotion, such as anger, or a certain region of the body, such as the belly. You may be working with them for a few days or perhaps for a few months. You find yourself gaining sensitivity and tolerance, patterns begin to shift and life feels better than when you started processing. Then you move to another area or issue, for example brushing your teeth or claustrophobia, and you work on this for some time. Six months later you find that you are again working with anger or the belly. This is normal.

You may return many times to work with some aspect of the body-mind you have already processed. Usually, with every return you will work at a deeper level. Perhaps you need to regain awareness of your belly before mastering your anger. Now that you are experiencing the sensations in your belly, you have a fuller bodily experience of emotions, including anger. So you will naturally return to process your anger. This I call the spiral effect. We keep spiralling back to process areas, issues, emotions and patterns of behaviour. Be patient. Keep going. The journey is long and rigorous.

Catching the wave

As our resilience, tolerance and sensitivity to sensations increases we become aware more of the time. We are able to sense the initial swell, the first rising of an emotion or state of being. In that split-second, we are able to choose to 'catch the wave', to watch the body with equanimity as the wave rises, peaks and falls away. We are able to observe without getting sucked into the story and our accompanying habit patterns. These are the moments in which we are alchemists, changing the course of the future through the present moment. Realizing this, every single moment becomes an opportunity for transmutation and magic.

Slowing down allows us to become keen observers of the interrelations between the body and the mind, and we can notice how our nervous systems and the rest of our bodies respond to various thoughts. Slowing down the speed with which the frames of our states of being unfold, we can take general snapshots of them. Then we can go a step deeper and observe details: the sea of sensations; the increase in activation; our posture, our gestures and vocal tones; the constriction and arousal in different regions of our bodies. Following this, we look for signs of regulation and settling, for sensations of discharge: tingling, warmth, vibrations, flowing sensations and even trembling.

As we maintain awareness of our bodies through the cycles of charge, discharge and rest, we re-establish the self-regulating mechanisms of the nervous system and re-member the body parts we have 'lost'. Most importantly, we regain the heart and the gut, so that our actions no longer emanate from just the head and its intellect. With our gut instincts and heart perception reinstated, our experience of life automatically transforms.

Re-membering our bodies grants us access to long-lost vital energy, and a fresh sense of aliveness springs forth. We gain newfound confidence and feel safe and curious to venture out and explore life. Feeling connected from within, we gain a new sense of ourselves, empowered and open, and our interpersonal relationships become easier and more fulfilling.

Then we become aware, almost by accident, of one of the most beautiful experiences in life: the stillness and silence from which all life emerges. We become acquainted with who we are beyond words.

Integrating the Three Steps into daily life

The more we increase our capacity to be in the 'fire' of a state of being the less effort we need to make in order to regulate. Slowly, the mysterious art of doing nothing starts to become apparent. You develop a sense of the observer, watching over all that is taking place, and how life introduces experiences that evoke different states of being. It is now possible to include everything that life brings, and to let go of the need to control events. You watch it all happening in an embodied way and are able to decide when, where and how to respond, instead of unconsciously reacting from old dysfunctional habit patterns.

As our capacity to be present in our various states of being increases, we can apply the Three Steps during our daily activities. With a healthily functioning regulatory system, self-regulation requires less assistance. All we need is awareness and minimal support, as when we are standing comfortably in a queue or sitting relaxedly in a waiting room chair. Instead of reading a newspaper to distract yourself from the fact that you are waiting for your appointment, take the opportunity to allow your nervous system to regulate and settle.

It is both interesting and wonderful to observe ourselves doing things in a new way, noticing that we less often become entangled in situations that used to make us 'boil-over' or collapse. This is Step Three in action—watching new states of being and supporting our lives in new ways. For example, Jim never ventured to meet women. Just the thought of approaching a woman would send him into states of fear, panic and freeze. After working with the Three Steps, he was able to initiate conversation not only with women whom he was interested in dating, but also with many other people whom, in the past, he would have shied away from.

Catching ourselves in action anchors new supportive ways of being into our nervous systems: 'See? I am doing it—doing what used to make me freeze—and I feel good.' Then we can notice how it feels to feel good. In this way awareness builds exponentially upon awareness.

The paradoxical theory of change

Paradoxically, the more we attempt to change, the more we remain the same. Whatever we resist persists. Conversely, when we witness ourselves with equanimity, the innate wisdom of the universe supports whatever changes need to take place in order for us to return to wholeness. Change comes about as a result of accepting what is, rather than striving to be different. The deepest form of acceptance is to watch the sensations of the body with equanimity and curiosity.

'Changing myself' used to be a deep-seated pattern of mine. It was the driving force that led me to explore my inner world. I wanted to 'better myself' and change all the patterns that were hurting me and others. I am thankful for this great fire that fuelled my spiritual evolution. I am also thankful that, at some point, I realized that the more I was able to observe those patterns—and their associated bodily sensations—the faster they transformed. That is when a new way of being in the world surfaced for me.

But before that, I had to work even with the subtleties of my way of observing. My habit pattern of striving for change had entered my intention of mindfulness. There was an almost imperceptible pressure in the way I watched my bodily sensations. So I had to go a level deeper and observe the way I was observing—and to accept it.

This was not easy for me. The outer world kept demanding my attention. I felt caught in between my new, still fragile attitude of 'let's see what life brings' and the need to make money, work and be successful. I often doubted if practicing the Three Steps was just another elaborate scheme to avoid the realities of the world. But when I started to notice tangible changes in my behavioural patterns, I realized that my doubts were, in and of themselves, habit patterns—and these too fell away the more I observed them.

Intention

It is important to make a commitment to your health and wellbeing. Give yourself an ample 'window' of time to experiment and see if the Three Steps works for you. Give yourself at least six months. Remember, slowing down is speeding up, and patience is needed; but the rewards are priceless.

Resolving your intention to 'work'—to process and use the Three Steps—is necessary because there will be times when you feel you have 'got it', only to feel lost the very next moment. This is a natural flow and rhythm we all experience. Having made a commitment to health, all our experiences—every emotion and state of being, both 'positive' and 'negative' ones—become valuable opportunities for growth.

Within six months of regularly practicing the Three Steps, you will have enough confidence in the technique to continue using it—or not. Give yourself this gift. You will be happy you did.

As you continue to practice the Three Steps, you will greatly increase your sensitivity towards your bodily sensations and regain various 'lost' parts of your body—regions that were dissociated because they had a lot of uncomfortable, even horrible, sensations. After opening up each of these areas, a period of time is needed during which you can become accustomed to feeling these once-hidden sensations and for them to dissipate. You need to get used to feeling those parts of the body again.

When we regain parts of our body a period of heightened activation—in just those specific parts, or perhaps throughout the whole body—might ensue. This activation might have a strong effect on your emotions, and you may temporarily experience more anger or sadness or other strong feelings. Being more activated may also make it harder to sit still and observe your bodily sensations. At times it may feel like you are not making progress, or even as if you are regressing. Just remember that you are going through this difficult period precisely because you have made progress and now have more tolerance and capacity to contain your bodily sensations. We can view these periods as tests of our resolve and intention to achieve wellbeing.

As we become much more adept with the Three Steps, the secrets of the body unfold by themselves. These secrets are about how we are shifted and shaped, at very deep, subtle, energetic levels. One reason that these are 'secrets' is because they cannot be explained. They have to be experienced. Then there is also the experience of the beyond.

The body is like the layers of an onion. Beneath each layer there is always another. The deepest of layers is the heart, brain and nervous system, which were the first to develop in the womb and were affected by our earliest experiences. However, it is not usually advisable to dive headlong into these deepest layers. Opening all of our dissociated parts at once is an overwhelming shock. In order to resolve our deepest dysfunctional body-mind patterns, we have to patiently prepare the entire body to be able to contain heightened activation.

Approach the Three Steps like a slow dance: two steps forward, one step back. It is not a catharsis. After catharsis, people often experience a temporary surge of energy, and then their bodies either shut down or they become addicted to the rush of catharsis. In many cases, catharsis is similar to going to a chiropractor who does a magnificent job of manipulating and freeing the locked energy in your back. Afterwards, you feel wonderful as the energy flows through your spine. But if you have not developed your capacity to contain this energy, your spine may soon restrict into the same old painful pattern in order to manage the activation.

I don't advise approaching spiritual growth through catharsis, like a raging bull. When we run full steam ahead shouting wildly we are more likely to run straight off a cliff. Be patient and gentle with yourself. Two steps forward, one step back…two steps forward, one step back. Enjoy the dance.

"In the pursuit of learning one knows more every day.
In the pursuit of the way, one does less every day.
Less and less until one does nothing at all.
And when one does nothing
There is nothing that's left undone."

- Tao-Te Ching

SECTION FOUR

WORKING WITH EMOTIONS, STATES OF BEING AND BEHAVIOUR PATTERNS

The Guest House

*This being human is a guest house.
Every morning a new arrival.*

*A joy, a depression, a meanness, some momentary
awareness comes as an unexpected visitor.*

*Welcome and entertain them all!
Even if they're a crowd of sorrows, who violently sweep your
house empty of its furniture, still, treat each guest honorably.
He may be clearing you out for some new delight.*

*The dark thought, the shame, the malice, meet them
at the door laughing, and invite them in.*

*Be grateful for whoever comes, because each has
been sent as a guide from beyond.*

*~ Rumi ~
(The Essential Rumi, versions by Coleman Barks)*

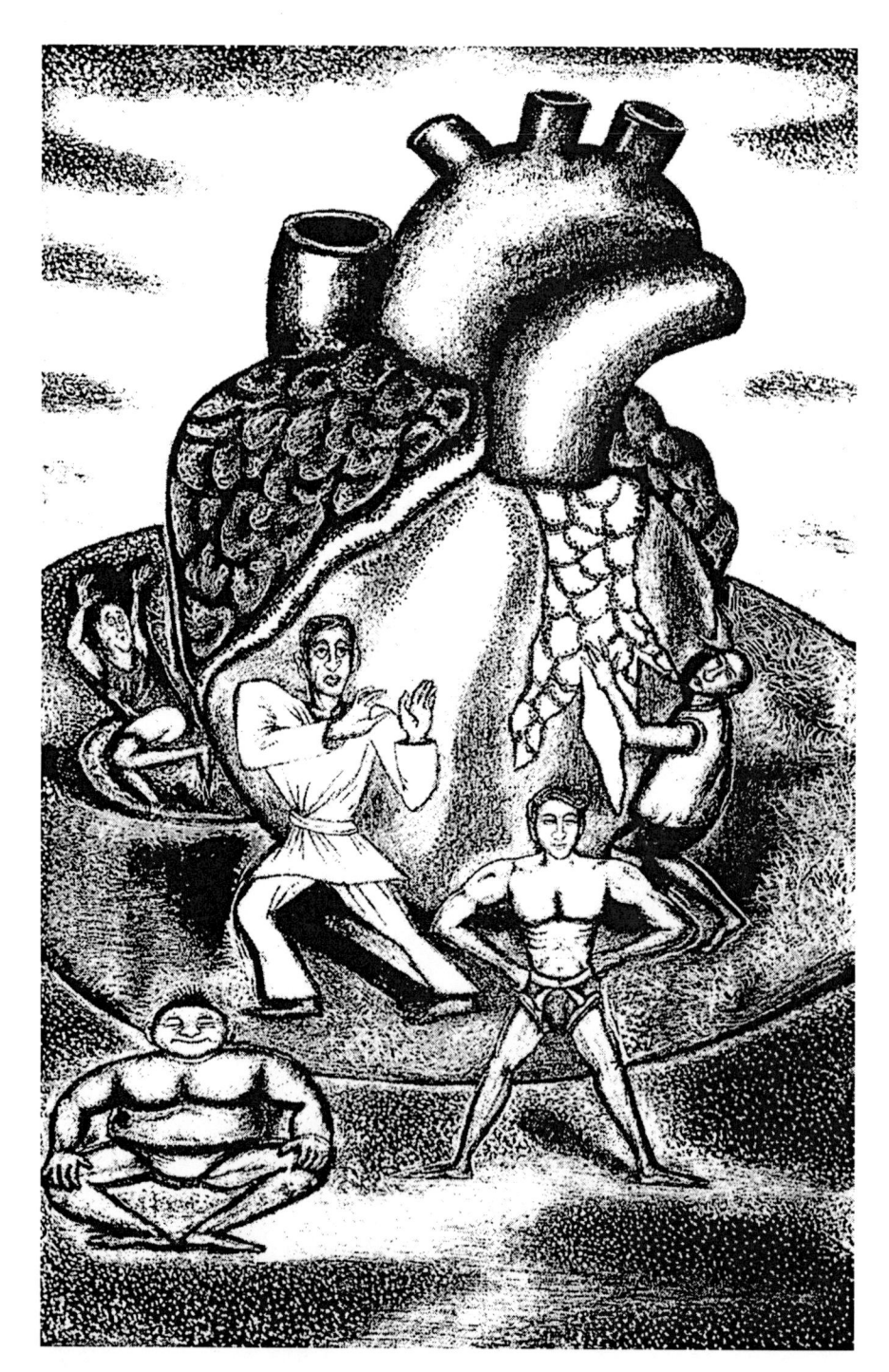

Protection

CHAPTER THIRTEEN

THE ALCHEMY OF EMOTIONS

Know thyself
- The Delphie Oracle

Humans, like other creatures, are geared for survival. In human survival, emotions play a key role, providing the basis for appraising situations and responding accordingly. Fear sets in motion our flight, fight and freeze responses. Anger and rage are the backbone of our protective responses and gear up our bodies to fight. Disgust initiates the avoidance of toxic substances. Sorrow signals the need for support and comfort. Love and joy bring us together.

Our emotions are the generating energies for what we attract into our lives, and are vital elements of our states of being. They are the basis for our sense of self—our self-image and self-esteem—and how we connect and relate to one another.

When an emotion is triggered it evokes a particular 'signature pattern' in the body. For instance, sadness may make our eyes burn. This burning sensation may lead us to feel that sadness is an intolerable emotion. The Three Steps can shift signature patterns to make the experience of emotions more manageable and wholesome. Then, when sadness arises and our eyes do not burn, we can tolerate sadness longer and explore the emotion at a deeper level. This is emotional alchemy, which has many steps and many levels. Each increment opens the way for deeper insights and more profound changes.

Our signature patterns are the glue that binds a particular emotion so that it keeps being triggered. The body wants to resolve the bound energy and return us to a state of wholeness. It can only do this when the state of the body is activated according to a particular signature pattern. From there, we can regulate in a new way, as long as we give the body the time and support it needs.

Each time a signature pattern is evoked, our organs release a specific cocktail of hormones and chemicals according to the emotion. These cocktails of emotions, together with the activation of the autonomic nervous system and skeletal muscles, prepare us for appropriate responses. In the face alone there are forty-four facial muscles, which organize themselves into specific patterns. These facial patterns represent our emotional state to the outside world, and communicate signals to others—for example, to warn them off (anger), or to attract them to us either for comforting (sadness) or socializing (happiness). The ensemble of bodily responses constitutes our emotions.

Working with emotions through the body

Certain molecules of emotion, such as the cocktail of chemicals continuously released into the bloodstream of a person who regularly cycles into fear and anger will, over a period of time, have a negative impact on bodily health. Our bodies can manage constant internally generated chemical bombardments for some time, but eventually chronic disease is likely to develop.

Dr. John E. Sarno, Professor of Clinical Rehabilitation Medicine at New York University School of Medicine, believes that emotions lie at the heart of most chronic pain disorders and 'syndromes'.[26] Dr Hans Seyle conducted more than fifty years of research on the impact emotions have on the body and mind. Seyle coined the term 'stress' and defined it as 'the non-specific response of the body to any demand for change'.[27] In numerous experiments he subjected laboratory animals to acute but different physical and emotional stimuli. They all exhibited the same pathological changes of enlargement of the adrenals, stomach ulcerations, and shrinkage of lymphoid tissue. Continued exposure to these stressful conditions was likely to cause these animals to develop various diseases similar to those seen in humans, such as kidney disease, diabetes, heart attacks, and rheumatoid arthritis.

For eons, people have tried to control their emotions through reason, but have failed. Just try asking someone in the deep throes of sadness to reason her way into happiness. It is unlikely that she will be able to.

Our conditioning of prioritizing the mind and denying our bodies has reduced our sensitivity and tolerance to our feelings. This is the source of most of our problems—most mental illness is because of emotions gone awry. In this section, I show you a new way of working with your emotions: the way of the body.

When we honour the body and acknowledge our emotions through perceiving our bodily patterns, only then can we find harmony. This work is a journey of intimacy with ourselves, and the end product is friendliness with all emotions. Whichever emotion comes to say hello, you will be able to greet it, invite it into your home and get to know it deeply like you would your best friend. Many of our strategies to defend ourselves are not necessary. If we can sit with sensations of loneliness as our friend, there is no longer a need to cling to our partners or constantly seek entertainment. If we can sit with sadness we don't have to fear losing again. If we can watch our anger we don't need to project it outwards in destructive ways.

We also need to work with those emotions that we usually consider to be 'positive feelings'. Interestingly, we will find that excitement generates a bodily expression similar to that of fear. In order for our hearts to be open and breathe, we need to be able to sit with our sadness and hurt. Having open hearts makes us more vulnerable and allows love to be with us for longer periods. These states of being also generate their signature patterns and cocktails of hormones and chemicals—'love chemicals' and 'joy chemicals'—and we have to learn to tolerate them as well. Our entire body configurations—our muscles, faces, postures and organs—all change. We have to slowly adjust to this new way of being.

Emotional alchemy via the Three Steps

We are constantly tuning into our environment through our perceptual systems of sight, sound, touch, smell, taste, our vestibular sense of gravity and balance, our kinaesthetic and proprioceptive senses, as well as our heart perceptions. We are scanning the environment to determine whether conditions are favourable or dangerous.

These initial appraisals are done by the amygdala, an almond-shaped structure situated in the 'second brain', which non-consciously assigns significance to stimuli.[28] The amygdala can send the body and mind into a flurry of activity to react to the situation. Memories of how we have felt in the past are processed in the amygdala, and these emotional memories can cause us to react automatically—even if these reactions are not appropriate to the current situation. This is how emotions keep 'hijacking' us, and why—even when we vow to act differently in the same circumstances—we react exactly the same way.

When we tell ourselves not to be anxious, angry, embarrassed or depressed, we have little chance of success. This is because emotions have a greater influence on our thoughts than thoughts do on our emotions—due to there being more pathways in the brain from the amygdala to the cortex than the other way around. Therefore, emotional arousal dominates and controls our thinking.[29] In other words, whether we are aware of it or not, emotions are integral to our reasoning process. Kenneth Dodge writes that 'all information processing is emotional, in that the emotion is the energy that drives, organizes, amplifies, and attunes cognitive activity and in turn is the experience and expression of this activity.'[30]

Emotions are essentially bodily processes accompanied by mental narrative. Emotions play a key role in our survival with wellbeing, generating the internal conditions to take action and solve our immediate problems. The autonomic nervous system, as well as the endocrine and immune systems, all become involved in a maelstrom of internal biological activity that produces our emotional experience and motivates our behavioural responses.

Everyone experiences each emotion in a unique way, but there are certain processes that occur within the body which are similar across the board. In fear, for example, the body is hardwired to activate the autonomic nervous system's accelerator, sending adrenaline rushing into the bloodstream, along with myriad other responses. When someone feels fear, due to her particular conditioning she may experience a surge of energy and a sense of clarity. Her body feels strong as it prepares for fight or flight. However, when another person is fearful he may experience fogginess in the head, confusion and a weak and collapsed body.

Challenging experiences while we were growing up left their marks on our body-minds. Past experiences, right up to what happened yesterday, can impact us—for better or worse. Because our body-minds contain a blueprint for a return to health, we can, through the Three Steps, shift debilitating

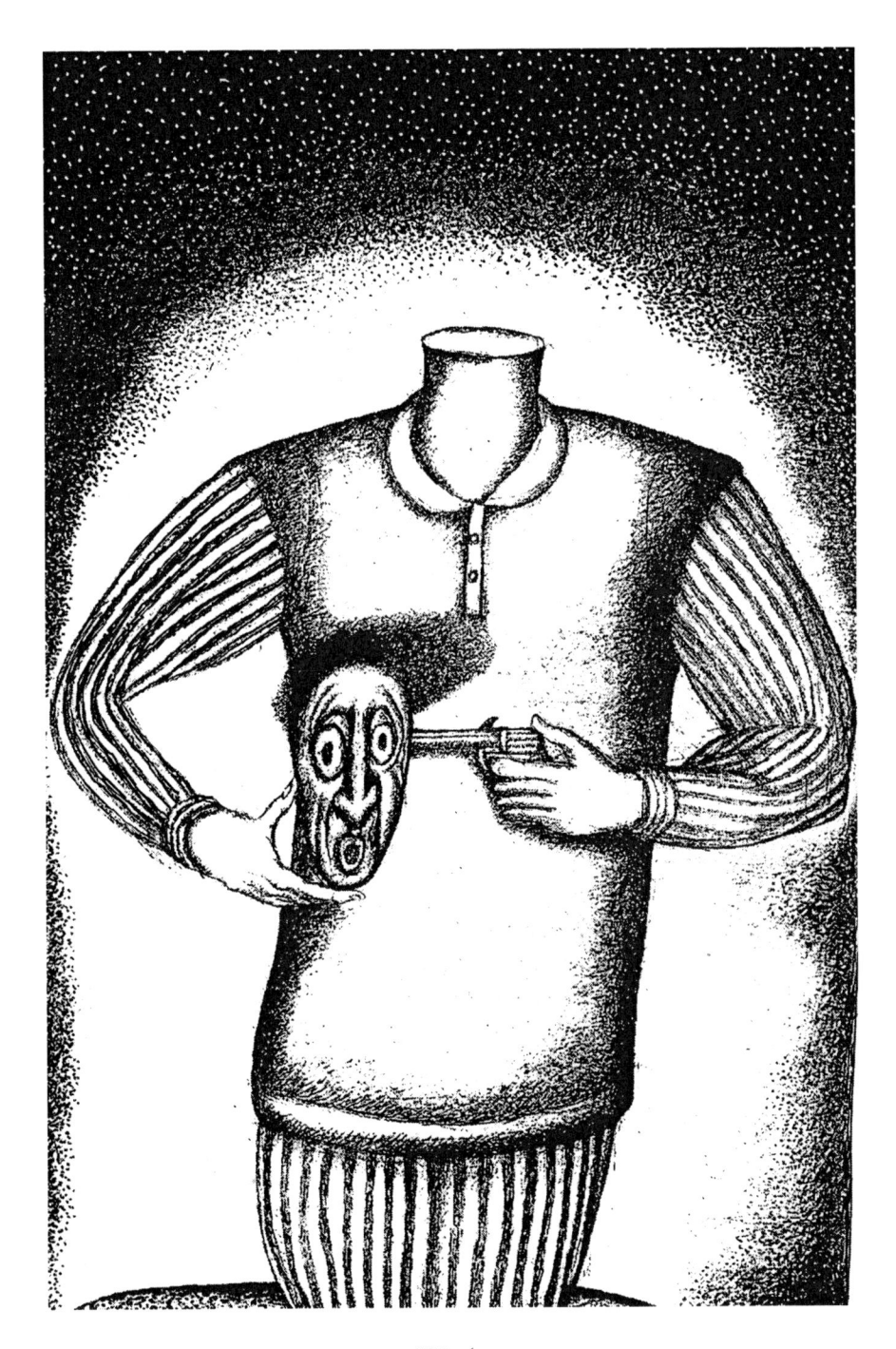

Hijacker

patterns of disease, pain and dissociation. The person who experiences fogginess, confusion and collapse when fearful can change his pattern so that fear does not overwhelm him and his body returns to a state of resilient strength in which he no longer collapses. Incrementally, he can develop patterns of wellbeing, as nature intended, involving vitality and clarity to take action and defend himself when threatened.

Observing the body as waves of emotions rise, peak and fall away is the most direct and effective way of gaining mastery over our feelings. This means becoming able observers and honing our skills so that each time we can sit a little longer in the 'fire' of our emotions. In this way, we allow our bodies to release the bound energy holding our patterns in place and shift towards their blueprints for health. Through repeating this process many times it is possible to completely change our emotional experience and to experience fear, anger, sadness, disgust, surprise, happiness, love and joy—the whole spectrum of emotions—in new ways, and to master them.

We have developed our emotional body patterns according to our life experiences. The good thing is that these patterns are subject to change. Because the body-mind wants to return to wholeness, emotions that need to be resolved will arise more often. Re-enactment and emotional outbursts are the body's way of trying to return to health. By viewing emotional discord as an attempt to move towards homeostasis with wellbeing, we can support each other in our return to wholeness. But we need to start with ourselves.

In the African bushveld, when lions go on the hunt they often work collectively. The eldest and weakest of the lions lays in ambush while the young hunters chase the prey towards him. At the last minute the old male jumps up and lets loose a mighty, terrifying roar. In fright, the prey does a one hundred and eighty degree turn and runs straight into the strong virile young hunters. If the prey could somehow realize what is in store, it would keep going straight towards the old lion and probably survive. Our emotions are often like the big roar of the old lion. They terrify us. But to live in wellbeing we cannot turn around and avoid them. We must move towards them—by going into the body.

The following chapters explore ways of using the Three Steps to go into the body and work with various emotions and states of being, including fear, anger, sadness, shame, love, joy and gratitude.

CHAPTER FOURTEEN

WORKING WITH FEAR

Escaping from danger is what all animals, including humans, must do at times in order to survive. When there is a sudden threat to our survival we need to act fast. Protection against danger is a hardwired instinct that cuts across all species. Even the tiny amoeba, when poked or threatened, constricts to protect itself from the invasion.

Because fear is a natural emotion that arises when we are threatened, feeling fear is part of being alive. It does not matter whether the threat is real or perceived. For example, a person walks along a path at night and sees a snake. He feels afraid. He backs off, shines a torch at the snake and sees that it is actually a length of rope. Whether it is rope or a snake, his fear response is initially the same.

We often feel embarrassed or ashamed when we are afraid because we have been conditioned to consider fear a sign of weakness. Absurdly, we have learned to 'fear fear'. When we deny fear, though, we cannot master it. As the meditation master Chögyam Trungpa advises us, 'in order to experience fearlessness, it is necessary to experience fear. The essence of cowardice is not acknowledging the reality of fear.'[31]

The journey to wholeness and mastery requires an intimate understanding and knowing of fear. To know fear is to transcend it.

Thwarted flight responses

We lose our capacity to move away from danger when our natural flight response has been thwarted or overwhelmed by past experience.

Take the example from Chapter Eight of Deborah, who is afraid of dogs. As a young child she was attacked and bitten by a dog. Nobody was around to assist her and she felt helpless and, of course, fearful. This triggered her body's fight-flight responses, with certain hormones being released into her bloodstream. Her autonomic nervous system's accelerator increased her body's energy, her heart and respiratory rates increased, and blood rushed from the organs and skin into the skeletal muscles in her arms, back, neck and legs. But she was too small to fight off the dog and too slow to escape. Her defences were thwarted and her body went into a state of freeze. It went still. This one experience erased her fight and flight responses from her strategies for survival and instilled the freeze response as her first and only line of defence.

In many modern day cultures, to run away instead of stand your ground is considered weak and cowardly. However, everyone would agree that if an elephant is charging at you it would be a good idea to get out of the way; to stand and fight would be foolhardy. But when our natural flight response has been thwarted or overwhelmed by past experience we may have lost our capacity to move away from danger—even in the face of a charging elephant! A thwarted flight response can manifest in subtle ways. For instance, a person walks into an office that has just been fumigated and reeks of poison, but he remains in the room. So he breathes the poison, develops a headache and becomes even less sensitive to his bodies' natural fear responses. Most people are unaware of the hundreds of ways a thwarted flight response can result, through everyday activities, in undesirable outcomes.

People who cannot defend themselves by exercising their 'fight' or 'flight' responses are generally more anxious and more likely to have an all-consuming fear of the future. Once they restore these natural responses, they feel more confident about being able to cope with threat and their anxiety and fear of the future diminishes. Their lives change radically as they think, speak and act in new empowering ways.

Befriending fear

It is necessary to explore fear and the body's relationship to it. It takes courage to stay present in the 'heat' of fear—in its groundlessness, its shakiness—and watch this intense wave weave its way through the body.

Fear can drive you into action or freeze you into immobility. When fear arises we may freak out, suppress it or dissociate. Usual responses to fear are to avoid it, deny it, or do whatever it takes to make it go away, including smoking a cigarette, popping a pill or trying to talk one's way out of it—for example, by repeating affirmations. We each have our habitual and deeply ingrained responses to fear, and these can occur in a split-second without us being aware of them.

The way of Alchemy is precisely the opposite. When fear arises, I invite you to move closer to it. Become familiar with it and remain with it as it courses through your body and shakes your very being. Become aware of your particular fear pattern. Do you dissociate? Do you distract yourself? As you sit in the heat of fear, what does your body do? Does it tighten? What happens to your breath and heartbeat? What happens in your head, both to your thoughts and to your physical feelings? Do your eyes blur? Does your head get heavy or light? Do your legs go weak or feel strong? Is there a knot in your belly?

Tracing the sequence of bodily events evoked by fear is a crucial part of befriending fear. As you stay with the body you notice that fear comes and goes in a cycle. Everything changes, nothing is permanent—and you see this at the level of the body. As you develop a capacity to stay with fear, you gain greater tolerance to its sensations and you no longer need to run away or distract yourself. It becomes easier to be present with these sensations and, at a deep experiential level, you learn to be with what is, accepting all that life brings. The more you can remain alert, with equanimity, even while fearful, the more you are in the now, the more you are present with life.

How to work with fear

By now you are familiar with the Three Steps, namely:

1. Become aware of your state of being at the level of bodily sensations.
2. Look for how the body is regulating.
3. Watch how the body changes for the better.

Now experiment with applying the Three Steps to the emotion of fear. I suggest three different ways to apply the Three Steps.

The first way is to think of something that scares you and evokes symptoms of fear. For example, think about sitting for an exam, or approaching a person of the opposite sex whom you desire. As fear arises, simply direct your awareness towards your body and feel how it organizes around the fear.

Apply the Three Steps. By doing so, you will start to master your fear. You will become aware of fear at a bodily level and develop the skill and capacity to watch it rise, peak and fall away.

The second way is to actually approach what you are afraid of. For example, pick up the phone to make a call you have been avoiding. As fear arises, stop and follow the Three Steps. Once the fear has settled go ahead and make the call. See what happens. If fear arises again, follow the protocol again. Perhaps the intensity of the fear will lessen to the extent that you find you can make the call. Afterwards, sit for a few minutes, feeling how it is to have made the call. Perhaps elation or excitement arises. Feel this and apply the Three Steps to this new feeling.

It is not possible to quash all fear in one go. Perhaps the first time you applied the Three Steps you were not able to make the call. Or maybe you did, but find that the next day you are not able to make a similar call because fear arises again. Our body-minds do not function in a linear fashion. Work done in awareness is never wasted. Persist slowly. Sooner or later you will find that you are regularly making these types of calls, or engaging in other behaviour and activities that formerly made you freeze in fear.

The third way is to catch yourself experiencing fear in the midst of life. Simply stop and apply the Three Steps.

When working with fear, it is often beneficial to help the body complete its flight response. Fear and anxiety usually provoke a physical urge to escape, but as noted earlier, the flight response may have been thwarted. By running slowly on the spot or even just make running movements while seated, we allow the body to follow through with this natural instinct. A great alternative is to walk around slowly. As you perform any of these movements—for anywhere between thirty seconds to a few minutes—be mindful of your body, particularly your legs. When you feel you have moved enough, sit down and allow the body to down-regulate by following the Three Steps. Remember: if you begin to shake or tremble, allow it to occur; these are healing sensations.

As you continue to practice the Three Steps, the flight response will gradually restore itself and you will no longer need to help the body complete it through movement. Now you can just watch and observe the wave of fear rise, peak and fall away. Fear will still be a frequent visitor yet will not overwhelm you, and the more you watch the passing waves the easier it will become to be with them. Soon, the waves will come fewer and further between. You will be surprised that you no longer experience the debilitating effects of fear, and you will catch yourself doing many things that you would never have dreamed of doing. A whole new life unfolds as your body reorganizes and composes a new life melody.

Note: If you go into freeze when fear is triggered, please refer to Chapter Sixteen.

Examples of working with fear

I would like to share my personal story of working with fear.

I had dissociated from the sensations of fear to the extent that, in the beginning, I couldn't identify the actual sensory experience of the emotion of fear, just many of the associated bodily reactions. My fear of fear was so great that I had saved myself from sensing it by dissociating from it. Like many people who say 'I feel no fear', I was correct. Yet it was still directing my life from behind the scenes.

As I began to observe my signature pattern of fear, it was difficult to be patient enough to sit with fear because part and parcel of that emotion is to prepare the body for activity. There was a surge of energy in my body ready for fight and flight, which was triggering my various strategies of action. Sitting still and watching my bodily sensations meant going against my lifelong behavioural patterns of movement.

When I would sense the urgency and restlessness of fear, I would run slowly on the spot for a short time as a way of completing the flight response and helping my body to begin discharging. Then, I would sit and monitor my body. Sometimes there was so much energy and restlessness that I needed to rotate my wrists and open and close my fingers slowly. Then I could sit and watch the discharge.

My mind was often racing, so focusing on bodily sensations helped to quieten it; otherwise, anxious thoughts would have kept triggering the stress response and I would have been stuck in a state of high activation for longer periods.

I found that all sorts of difficult sensations—horrible, yucky, buzzy, electric, hot and tight—were driving my anxiety. I found that I had a pattern of fear that included my throat becoming constricted to the point that it felt like it was being squashed. This alone was scary enough to drive me to act in all kinds of ways so that I could 'free myself' and breathe easily. All I wanted to do was get away from these horrible sensations, to rid them from my body. But I persisted and continued to observe this high activation, and then the discharge—particularly in my arms and legs.

Watching the discharge sensations did three things for me. Firstly, focusing on my arms, hands, legs and feet reduced the intensity of the horrible sensations I was experiencing in the rest of my body. It was like resting at an oasis in the middle of a hot, dry desert. Secondly, by broadening my awareness to the rest of my body I was not stuck in the hell of arousal and constriction in my throat, chest and belly. Feeling a pounding heart, quickened breath, tightened chest and throat, along with surges of heat and buzzy sensations, can be overwhelming. Broadening my awareness helped me to survive these sensations, and they became more manageable. Thirdly, I was able to now see how my body was discharging and righting itself through the tingling and warmth in my hands and my feet.

Sometimes I would tremble. At times the trembling was light and barely discernible; other times it was strong and visible. The first few times I trembled, it was scary. Moreover, noticing that I was trembling increased my fear and I interrupted the trembling by clenching my muscles in my arms and legs and also by distracting myself. I had to remind myself that trembling was my body's way of releasing a high charge, and that it was good and I should let it happen. This took practice, patience and perseverance.

Often, I wished that I would never tremble again. I thought that by allowing trembling to happen a few times, my body would change dramatically and move into a magical realm of non-trembling. To this day, trembling still occurs from time to time. Trembling is part of the body's amazing repertoire for releasing a huge charge within us. It is completely natural, and the more I witnessed it, the greater my tolerance grew for being with and accepting the trembling.

This was also the case for most of my other discharge sensations. The more I witnessed them, the more I became accustomed to and tolerant of them. In the beginning, however, it was difficult to keep my attention on my discharge sensations. Even the tingling in my feet and ankles was horrible and would propel me away from my body and into my thoughts. But I became accustomed to the practice of gently returning—after noticing that I was thinking—my awareness to my bodily sensations.

Step 3—to watch how my body had changed for the better—was often difficult to remember to do. Sometimes, after observing discharge, I would feel a bit better and rush on with my life. Other times, I knew I was feeling better but found it difficult to pinpoint the actual bodily changes that were making me feel better. It was quite some time before I was able to discern the positive changes. I began to notice that my breathing was easier, my heart was no longer pounding, my belly was more at ease and my mouth and throat were moist and not nearly as constricted as before. My muscles were more relaxed and the buzzy electric feelings were gone. I also noticed that my eyesight was clearer, and I developed the habit of looking around and witnessing my surroundings from this sense of calm. My unique signature pattern of fear was changing for the better.

I was under the belief that by practicing the Three Steps ten or fifteen times I would master fear—my life would be transformed and that would be it. I have since practiced the Three Steps many hundreds of times. My life is transformed and I have a greater mastery of my emotions. Fear still arises at times, and when it does I continue to watch and be with it. I have found that I am more present and focused, and that I don't get pulled into unnecessary thoughts about the future. I also find I am less drawn into dwelling on the past. When I do, I use it as a valuable opportunity to process by pausing and becoming aware of my body.

My body's regulation is now much stronger, I am less restless, and I have a greater capacity to sit and watch the bodily sensations of fear and other emotions from a still space. In the beginning, I needed to use movement—like running on the spot or rotating my hands or feet—in order to encourage my body to discharge. As my capacity to sense, tolerate and regulate increased, the less I needed to do to help my body regulate. Now, I just watch and go deeper.

Immediately after my divorce, I often felt loneliness. Strong fear would arise and I would catch myself having an urge to rush out to my favourite coffee shop. Time and again, I stopped and watched the wave. Sometimes, I did not stop myself, but once I got to the coffee shop, I would regulate while waiting for my coffee.

I also noticed that I often felt the need to speak to a friend when I was feeling afraid and lonely. So, just as I was reaching for the phone, I would stop and monitor my state of being and allow regulation to happen. Again, this didn't always happen. Sometimes I needed to connect with a friend, and then I would monitor my state of being after the call and apply the Three Steps. I realized that life would keep bringing me—and all of us—opportunities to experience and befriend fear and other emotions. The challenge is, when strong emotions arise, to stop and go inside. The more we do this, the greater we increase our tolerance and shift patterns for the better. This is the way of the body, the way to master our emotions.

Throughout this process, it has been helpful for me to remember that actions taken in times of stress are often motivated by fear; therefore, they may well be less than ideal courses of action. When I was able to move through anxiety before making decisions my whole life started to change. The impulsiveness which had been a hallmark of my life began to shift. Less and less do I think back with regret to what I have just said or done.

Let us now return to Deborah, who was bitten by a dog as a child. As the dog attacked her, she went into a state of freeze and experienced weakness in her joints, particularly her knees, pelvic area, shoulders and elbows. As the dog bit her thigh, she felt excruciating pain.

Twenty years after the dog-bite, Deborah was still fearful of dogs. Most phobias result from having undergone an overwhelming emotional experience. In Section Two we saw how mental models and classical conditioning and operant conditioning form patterns that shape our present experiences and our anticipation of the future. Remember Hebb's Axiom: As neurons fire together they wire together. With Deborah, neurons representing fear fired (A), and so did the neurons associated with the weakness in the joints and muscles of her arms and legs—we can call these neurons of helplessness (B). At the same time, neurons representing the phenomenon of freeze fired (C), as did those of confusion (D) and those connected with the pain in her thigh from the bite (E). A+B+C+D+E fired together, wired together and became her constellation of fear. Subsequently, every time Deborah felt fear—even when the fear was unrelated to dogs—her signature pattern of fear, or her fear constellation, fired again, conjuring up the same physiological patterns.

Deborah was not conscious of how or why her body responded to fear in that particular way. All she knew was that she went 'weak' when fearful, and so she avoided situations that triggered her fear. She did not possess appropriate strategies to defend herself when she felt threatened, so she began to feel that the world is a dangerous place, and meekness became one of her predominant character traits. (Remember: Deborah's signature pattern of fear is just one example. Each of us develops unique signature patterns and, consequently, individual strategies in order to ensure our survival and feel safe. These strategies are informed by our individual experiences.)

Through repeated practice of the Three Steps, Deborah became mindful of her signature pattern of fear. By faithfully following the steps, she was increasingly able to witness the wave of fear as it rose and peaked. She worked at completing her fight and flight responses. She supported the discharge sensations and was patient while watching her body return to balance as the wave would recede. Her body received the needed support and time to transform and return to health.

Over time, Deborah found that she no longer became weak in the joints and experienced 'freeze'. Having use of her arms and legs in confrontational events created new possibilities and strategies for her. She could stand up for herself when appropriate, or choose to simply remove herself from the situation. Having a greater repertoire of strategies transformed her life. Every interaction became an opportunity to reprogram her mental models. Deborah became more confident, her self-esteem grew and, overall, she felt safer and more at home in the world. Today, Deborah is an empowered woman living a new life.

I worked with a businessman who had regular panic attacks. It became apparent that he had a history of near-drowning because his pattern of fear included bodily memories of being drowned. Although the triggers for his fear were related to business or relationships, he would bodily relive this distressing experience. His implicit memories of drowning had fired together, wired together and now—although he had long forgotten his near drowning experience—all fear led to sensations of drowning. The event was instrumental in the formation of his signature pattern of fear. His throat would constrict, his breath would stop, his chest would burn and the same frantic sensations of suffocation would well up inside of him.

After a few sessions, he shared with me that he had nearly drowned when he was a teenager. Through our work together, he was able to shift his pattern of fear. He no longer experienced the same overwhelming sensations of drowning when fear arose. His throat no longer clenched shut, he could breathe, his chest did not burn and he no longer felt frantic sensations. Even in fear he had the capacity to take action to right difficult situations. He had more choices and could experience fear in a new way without being so overwhelmed. His journey to master fear continues.

Another illustration of how timely help and the right kind of support works wonders involves a forty year-old woman named June.

June suffered from anxiousness for as long as she could remember. Her hands would shake uncontrollably, which caused her such great embarrassment that she would avoid socializing. She would walk around with tight fists in order to stop this shaking from occurring. She had no answer for the horrible sensations of anxiety riddling her body. In vain, she had seen many doctors and tried many modalities of therapy in her quest to rid herself of this debilitating 'dis-ease', which infiltrated every aspect of her life. She believed she was a weak person and that there was no hope for her condition.

It took a single one-hour session to educate June about how the body regulates fear and to guide her through the Three Steps. When trembling arose I reassured her that it was simply a way for her body to discharge energy. I taught her how the body releases the energy of fear through sensations like warmth, tingling and trembling. After a short time, trembling stopped and she reported feeling calmer and more together. I guided her to witness how her body had returned to a calm state. As we progressed through the same one-hour session, fear arose once more, so again I supported her through the Three Steps. June ended the session in a calmer and more confident state.

After educating June about the body's innate healing capacity and its natural self-regulatory mechanisms, and showing her how to work with the

Three Steps, she was in a position to support herself whenever her pattern of anxiety arose. Each time she cycled through anxiety to a calmer and more secure state, she felt more confident that she could handle anxiety. She strengthened her capacity to feel the uncomfortable sensations associated with anxiety and also strengthened her resilience, which meant returning to a calm state more quickly. She no longer felt stuck and anxious, about anxiety, which led her to feel progressively less anxious.

June had the courage to open herself up to this powerful method. She now feels much more confident and goes out more often. She is empowered through having the skills to move through her anxiety whenever, however and from wherever it arises. She sleeps better and does not get headaches as often. Colleagues and friends tell her she is a new person since she interacts fully and is not so defensive. She is more assertive at work, is able to assume more responsibility and has been promoted.

How did June come to be a new person leading a new life? Her body and brain were stuck in a pattern of fear and anxiety, over which she had no control. Once her body was supported in cycling through the arousal and allowing it to regulate and relax into a calmer state, a new pattern was forged in her brain and nervous system. The more June supported this new pattern the stronger her self-regulation became and she was no longer stuck in debilitating cycles of fear.

Starting on the small waves

Panic, anxiety, worry and concern all exist along a continuum of fear. We have hundreds of opportunities throughout our lives to practice and watch waves of fear, rise, peak and fall away. But first we need to be aware that fear is a normal phenomenon and part of being alive. Then we need to practice the Three Steps when our fear is relatively mild so that we can manage the sensations and build confidence. Imagine surfing for the first time. Do you surf the largest waves or start on the small ones?

Start on the small waves of fear and build your balance and skill before taking on the larger ones. Sometimes it may be helpful to find a Three Steps practitioner or a Somatic Experiencing therapist who can help you to gain some capacity so that you can then manage on your own.

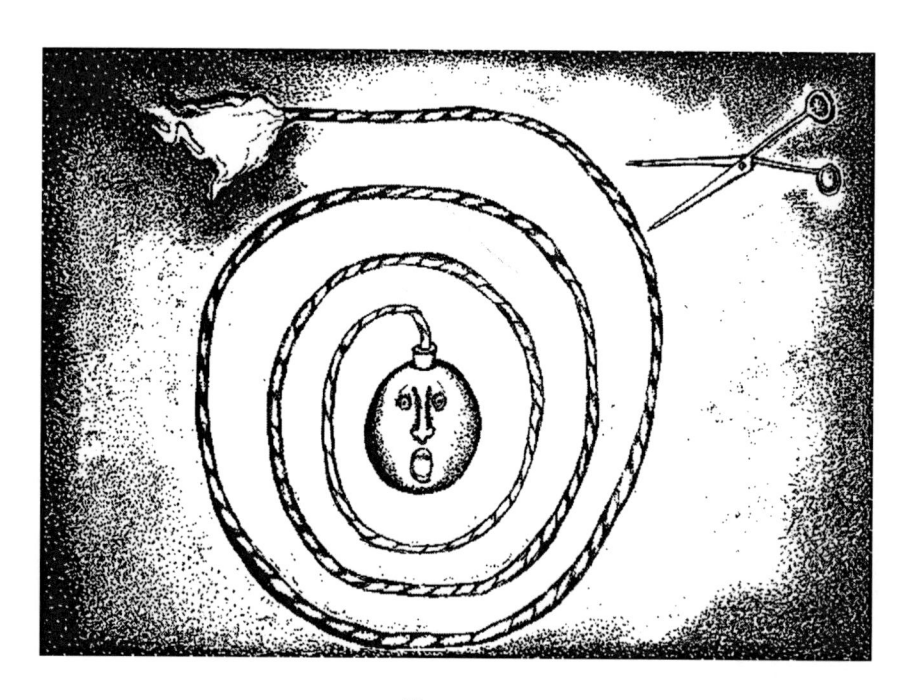

Vortex

CHAPTER FIFTEEN

WORKING WITH ANGER

Like fear, anger is about protecting and preserving our lives. Appropriate expressions of anger are beautiful energetic manifestations. Inappropriate acting out, such as physical violence and verbal and emotional abuse, is disastrous to our overall wellbeing. We get stuck in patterns of angry behaviour that play out daily, affecting our health and destroying our relationships. Conversely, when anger has been thwarted and a person is meek, mild and timid, this also negatively impacts his health and overall wellbeing. And when anger is sidetracked or repressed it can smoulder and build, like a volcano waiting to erupt at any time.

Anger is a manifestation of the 'fight' side of our fight-flight response. The emotion or feeling of anger is a manifestation of the cocktail of hormones and peptides released into the bloodstream, body and brain as the autonomic nervous system accelerates our body-mind to prepare us to fight, attack or even kill—just as a lion needs to kill its next prey in order to survive. When healthy, this aggressive energy is a natural part of our makeup and is required for us to be assertive and bold. It is what motivates us to pursue our ambitions and to create.

When the fight response becomes overwhelmed it may become dysfunctional, resulting in pathological conditions associated with hostility, rage and violence. On the one hand, we may act out aggressively; on the other, we may become passive-aggressive. We may compulsively judge and blame others, or even blame the economy or the state of the country for our problems.

The importance of feeling empowered

When we do not feel empowered we either act out in order to prove that we are powerful, or shrink back to avoid confrontation. In such instances, when we are acting aggressively, we may not subjectively feel that we are strong. The key point is that whether our strategy is to fight or to shrink, we are not able to access or experience our power. We do not have an internal awareness of our power, and you could say that we are dissociated from it. We become caught in a loop of acting out aggressively and feeling victimized.

Fortunately, the world is filled with opportunities that challenge us so that we can experience our lack of power, find resolution and return to a whole state in which we can subjectively experience ourselves as empowered individuals. Once we have a sense of our inner strength, we no longer feel a need to fight. Naturally, our outer experiences reflect our inner worlds, so we find we become challenged less and less in ways that lead us to resort to violence. We feel threatened less often or find creative, assertive ways to resolve threats when they do appear.

Empowerment exercises

As a teenager I practiced a martial art called wing chun. I loved the form, which involves a lot of handwork, and one of its exercises was 'pushing hands'. Here I introduce you to a version of pushing hands I have integrated into the Three Steps.

The first pushing hands exercise allows us to get a sense of our strength, our power. I regularly come across many physically strong people who have no sense of their own power. I have worked with incredibly strong bodybuilders and sportspeople who do not feel strong inside. They compensate for this lack of felt power through excess weight training, trying to build up their bodies until they feel strong. The perception of strength, however, must originate from within.

This exercise requires two people; one pushes and the other provides resistance. The pushing is done in a gentle and respectful way.

- Stand comfortably, with your feet placed firmly on the ground, shoulder width apart. One foot is forward, similar to a boxer's stance.
- Place one of your palms against your partner's opposing palm. Take turns pushing and providing resistance.
- When you are pushing, your partner slowly applies pressure, mirroring the pressure of your palm against his or hers—no more and no less. As the pusher, experiment a little with the force you are exerting

against your partner. Try and get a sense of the power within. Feeling your power is more important than pushing your partner over.
- The slower you practice the exercise, the greater will be your awareness and possibility of sensing your power.

Practice this pushing hands exercise for one minute and then sit down and apply the Three Steps.

A few pointers for practicing the exercise:

- Some eye contact is beneficial, but too much can be overwhelming. If you feel the eye contact is too much, use this discomfort for processing. Stop and sit down. You may close your eyes or keep them open, whichever is more comfortable for you. Process using the Three Steps.
- Maintain balance while pushing. If you lose balance, right yourself, stop and process, using the Three Steps. Losing balance may cause high activation and processing at this stage will be beneficial.
- Play around with pushing a little further until you fall off balance. Then stop, right yourself and follow the Three Steps.
- When you are pushing, allow yourself to stop and process at any point. Perhaps when you are feeling your power it is good to stop and sense it fully by following the Three Steps.
- Occasionally, the one providing resistance can also play around by letting go of the resistance and seeing if your partner keeps his or her balance.
- If you suddenly feel very aggressive, stop, feel and process the aggression, using the Three Steps. Likewise, if you feel weak or that it's too much, stop and process.
- In one hour you and your partner can perform up to four rounds of the exercise, two for you and two for your partner.
- Perform this exercise several times over the course of a few months. Playfully explore and monitor your progress.

Becoming aware of anger

Often we are not aware of what triggers our anger. Many things may trigger our anger, including the way somebody walks towards us, or the way another driver overtakes us. We may often trigger our own anger, for example by doing something silly or stupid, or by forgetting something. Relationships, especially intimate ones, are great playgrounds for anger to arise.

Sometimes, we may find ourselves becoming angry while replaying an event in our minds—perhaps a situation, such as an argument, in which we did not cope with a threat successfully; or while thinking ahead to the future, maybe about confronting someone with an unresolved issue. As we replay these past or future events, anger may increase and we may start to call our 'adversary' harsh names or even fantasize about physically harming him or her. This can all take place in the theatre of our minds.

A patient friend who understands the Three Steps can be of great assistance in helping us to become aware of and process anger. Processing with a friend can be a particularly powerful way to heal. Often when we are talking with friends our emotions come to the fore more easily. If the friend also has the ability to process then the two of you can stop talking and follow the Three Steps. It just takes one of you to say, 'I need a few minutes to process'.

Whether with a friend or by ourselves, when we interrupt ourselves replaying anger-inducing events and direct our awareness towards the body we notice many physiological indicators of the urge to fight, to defend or to attack. Our hands may be in a defensive, blocking-type gesture, or clenched into fists, ready to punch out, or tense as if they are ready to slap someone. To prepare our fight-flight responses, our bodies pump more blood into skeletal muscles, such as in the arms, legs, hands and feet. The muscles become tenser as they prepare for action. The legs may feel more energetic as they gear up to support us and provide a strong, grounded stance, or even to kick out. The jaw may also be tense, either clenched or in some other way readied to either argue or shout, or even bite or gnash. The tongue may also be extra-energized, and so may the rest of the muscles in the face, as they organize themselves into a ferocious expression designed to warn off any threat. The eyes may tense up and glare (whenever I used to glare at my step-father when I was angry he would tell me that I had 'the devil in my eyes'). In addition, our overall posture will indicate aggression and a willingness to fight. Our orientation will be directed towards the threat. If the scenario is taking place only in the mind, our thoughts may be caught in a loop, replaying the situation over and over again.

In the midst of this replay, stop yourself! It is wonderful to experience the readiness to defend or attack, to feel the power of a geared-up body, the heart pumping furiously away, the short, quick, shallow breath high up in the chest. With all the adrenaline circulating in the bloodstream, the body may have a charged, even a hot and highly electric quality. There will be tension patterns, such as a tight stomach, neck, back and shoulders. You may even be shaking with rage. Sensing all these indicators may feel almost intolerable, like you are Mount Etna ready to erupt at any second.

It is this very sense of intolerability—especially when it occurs unconsciously—that leads us to lash out, or to shut down and dissociate in a freeze type of response, because the energy in the body is too much to handle. When a freeze response occurs we may feel helpless, so learning to successfully navigate such a response is a crucial step towards mastering anger. We will explore this in the next chapter on the freeze response.

Restoring Fight Responses

A wave of anger tends to rush in quickly, and often, by the time we are aware of it, it has already engulfed us. To begin working with anger, therefore, it is best to catch ourselves in mild outbursts. Spend a few moments noticing how your body feels in anger. Do you feel like hitting out or biting? Perhaps you'd like to slap or backhand someone? Or snarl? Or spit? Once you identify your preferred response, do it, but in slow motion. Allow your body to hit out, to spit, or to gnash your teeth. Really slow the movement down. You might be tempted to go all out and thrash around. This is not advisable, as it will likely only increase your activation and possible dissociation. Catharsis may feel good, but it is usually not as effective in mastering anger as working slowly and in awareness.

Perhaps, as you feel anger building, you sense preparedness in the arms and legs. Try putting your hands up as if you are going to push someone away. Then, with awareness, slowly push out. Explore this a few times: push out, let go, push out again. Repeat these motions until you feel satisfied. To accompany your movements, you may want to say something out loud, like: 'No!' or 'Stop that!' or 'I don't want you to do this anymore!' or 'Go away!' Another possibility is to grunt, growl or make guttural sounds.

It is important, as you do these exercises, to experience how you feel. As you act out these movements, perhaps you feel empowered. How it is to feel empowered? Savour this feeling. Enjoy it for a while.

Now continue with Step 2 of the Three Steps, looking for discharge sensations. If need be, refer to the directions for Step 2 in Chapter Eleven. Take as much time as you need to allow the anger to dissipate. It is important to remember that the body needs time to down-regulate, and that 'slowing down is speeding up'. By taking your time you are doing yourself the greatest favour possible. Notice in Step Three how you are feeling better.

You may have to repeat these exercises many times before you notice that you no longer need to push or hit out, and that you can now watch anger arise and perceive, through your body, its wave rising, peaking and falling away.

As anger arises you can watch the micro-movements of the charge circulating throughout your body and preparing your muscles to act, all the way from your shoulders, down your upper arms, into your elbows, your forearms, your wrists and hands; and likewise in your legs and your facial muscles. These involuntary movements may be perceptible to you, but hardly noticeable to an outside observer.

Just continue to watch. This is where tolerance and patience is needed: to observe the body without moving it voluntarily, and allowing it to shift naturally and complete its own involuntary movement. Once the body starts to discharge with the felt sensations of tingling, trembling, warmth or vibrations, it becomes more comfortable and resumes a baseline state of ease and alertness.

As you become more comfortable with sensations of anger, you will be able to process increasingly intense situations. Following a conflict, there are various emotions and states of being we can process. In fact, it may be these very 'aftermath sensations' that are keeping our patterns of anger in place. For example, if guilt always follows your angry tirades, you will likely not be able to let go of your anger patterns until you resolve your patterns of guilt. Once you have done this, you may make great strides in resolving your anger patterns. So whatever you feel after experiencing anger—be it guilt, shame, indignation or any number of other emotions—take the time to process by using the Three Steps.

Working with the Three Steps after a conflict also helps you to become more resilient, to bounce back faster. You will be able to find resolution more quickly, and over the long run, the pattern of replaying events over and over in your mind will reduce dramatically. Often, after a conflict situation, I would take some time by myself to go through the Three Steps. Each time I did this I strengthened my nervous system and resolved something. After the event, it would often play itself out repeatedly in my mind, so each time I would stop and go through a cycle of the Three Steps. If, after the cycle, my mind again returned to the event, triggering another bout of emotion, I would stop and process that as well.

Restoring fight responses and working with anger is long, hard and perilous work. It requires courage, determination and perseverance. Many times I would think 'Yes, I've got it! I just aced that conflict'—only to become overwhelmed by the next one. I sometimes wanted to give up, but somehow I kept going. It has been worth it, and I am a much nicer person to be with.

Whereas my fuse used to be very short, destroying many opportunities to collaborate, I am now able to patiently work with others. Before, my anger would hijack my attempts to share my skills; now my patience, compassion and tolerance are far greater and support my relating, teaching and learning. My relationships are richer and I find that my former aggression now manifests itself as creative energy. Projects I could only have dreamed of pursuing are, at present, pleasantly unfolding.

My personal journey with anger

Anger and I have gone on quite a journey together. Anger has frequently hijacked my relationships, leading me to act inappropriately and become distanced from the ones I love. Even mere discussions have often led to aggressive tactics on my part. Other times I have felt weak and helpless, unable to protect myself. I have cycled between being aggressive and being timid—there is no rule to say that a person is only aggressive or only timid, although some people may tend more towards one particular side of the spectrum.

Remember: anger is about protection. Anger long protected me from feelings of fear, shame, hurt, powerlessness and inadequacy—and their horrible, intolerable associated sensations. It felt far easier to seethe with anger than to experience these sensations. As soon as my 'radar' detected any slight to my integrity, anger flared up in my defence. In this way, anger was driven by my weakness. Moreover, I felt guilty for having become angry, and wrong for verbally or physically hitting out. As mentioned earlier, to master anger we also need to work with other emotions, such as guilt, shame and fear; and we also need to heal the pain and the hurt of the heart. The puzzle of anger is not complete until all the missing pieces have been put together.

I tried many methods of working with anger. They were not helpful, and I would still act out angrily, practically on a daily basis. This greatly distressed me, especially because it was damaging my relationships with those I loved. I felt helpless, having meditated for years and having tried all sorts of therapies, including many that advocated catharsis, such as pillow-hitting. I hit pillows every day for eight months! Even after working with some of the world's leading transpersonal psychologists and other therapists, someone would push my buttons and Boom!

Something was wrong and I did not know how to fix it, despite the different trainings and hundreds of workshops and meditation retreats, and thousands of hours of individual therapy sessions using various modalities. I had an abundance of training and knowledge, and was on a spiritual path of self-realization. But here I was, feeling helpless in the face of my 'hijacker emotions', particularly anger. The very emotion that was designed to empower and protect me had become my enemy, my downfall. Only after I started to work at a deeper level involving bodily sensations did I finally manage to initiate my healing process.

My turning point with anger occurred on an occasion when I travelled to an ashram outside of Delhi. My wife was scheduled to perform there and, consistent with Indian planning methods, nobody had begun assembling the stage and there were numerous other outstanding logistical and preproduction issues. I introduced myself to the gentleman in charge of the event, and immediately sensed that something was amiss. As we began to discuss the various matters at hand, his attitude became one of: 'Well, if that's the way you feel, then don't perform.'

I was in a fix. It was my wife's event; I was just hoping to smooth the way for her by taking care of some preproduction issues. I would have been quite happy to tell this annoying man to get stuffed, but that would only have made matters worse. Pressure began to build up inside me, especially in my chest, which felt like it would explode. Aha, I thought, what a fantastic opportunity to work! I excused myself and suggested that when Zia arrives, he discuss the way forward with her.

The situation, the context, the right person to provide resistance had all been perfect to evoke this volcano in my chest. As I walked into the ashram's garden, the volcano was still bubbling and waiting to explode. What to do with it? Act out? Suppress it? No, I chose to feel it fully by following the Three Steps. This helped my body to contain, resolve and shift my pattern of anger. It was tough to be with such overwhelming sensations, but it was of enormous value. From that day on, I have never experienced the immense pressure in my chest, which previously had been such a common phenomenon, even when I'd been confronted in small ways. It is now much easier for me to handle confrontation. I do not become nearly as beset, which allows me to employ more creative strategies for dealing with the situation.

In Peter Levine's Somatic Experiencing work, he advocates the completion of the fight, flight and freeze responses. In exploring my fight responses, I recalled having been at the receiving end of physical abuse. One instance was a fight I lost when a few boys ganged up on me to save their friend, the school bully, who was not faring well in his fight with me. As a means of completing the fight response, I re-enacted the fight with some friends to whom I had taught the Three Steps. We slowly acted out what had occurred all those years before. Whenever the activation inside of me would escalate, I would stop and process. Recreating the event was an effective way to evoke the body-mind patterns that needed resolution. I could then process and heal them. If you want to work through some of your past highly emotional events in this manner, I would recommend that you find a competent Somatic Experiencing therapist to assist you.

I used the Three Steps to process in various situations where I caught myself in anger. Over the next few years I changed, and as my body patterns shifted, my anger became more appropriate to the trigger. A small event started to trigger an appropriately small reaction. Please keep in mind that in no way do I advocate quelling or muzzling anger. When we cannot feel our power and have suppressed or become dissociated from our anger, it will take its revenge—usually in ways that are nasty enough to attract our attention until we welcome it back as a friend.

Working with anger: a recap

Supporting yourself through discharge and regulation back to balance is of indispensable assistance in the journey towards mastering anger. The key—as with any other emotion—is to reach a stage at which we can ride waves of anger without judgment, tolerating all that is happening and allowing the wave to peak and then fade away. To get to this stage we may have to go through a period of restoring our fight responses. Due to societal conditioning and past debilitating experiences, our fight responses may no longer be at our ready disposal. Or the opposite: we may constantly be triggered into outbursts of rage and acting out.

As with other emotions, begin by working with anger of relatively small intensity in order to get into the habit of stopping and using the Three Steps to work through the wave. Often, you will not be able to. So, after you have vented your anger in whatever way, try to sit and apply the Three Steps to work through the aftermath.

There is no need to act out these aggressive urges in the sphere of our interpersonal relationships. Not acting out or suppressing the powerful urges associated with anger and just letting them play out in the theatre of the body is the greatest gift we can give our children and spouses, our friends and colleagues.

CHAPTER SIXTEEN

WORKING WITH STATES OF FREEZE AND DISSOCIATION

The immobility or 'freeze' response is the body's third way of defending itself, in addition to fight and flight. In our culture of being 'tough like a soldier', the freeze state is not understood and highly condemned. This is unfortunate because freezing is a natural process and mechanism, over which we have no actual control. When we cannot fight or flee from a threat, the body-mind sends us into a state of immobility, one in which we cannot move. You have heard people say 'I was scared stiff'. Well, this literally happens.

In Chapter One I mentioned how I froze as I confronted my fear of heights on a high diving board. As a warm up, I had jumped from the lowest diving board. Then I jumped from the three-metre board; then the six-metre board. Each jump was exhilarating. There was fear each time, but it was manageable. Then I made my way up the ladder to the highest diving board of twelve metres.

I walked along the board, and two metres away from the edge fear pulsed through my body. My legs froze. I couldn't move them. In retrospect, my thinking brain still wanted to jump, but my second and third brains—the ones in charge of survival—deemed otherwise. So there I waited in the middle of the high diving board. What else to do? I was literally stuck.

The amazing thing about the freeze response is that it is a time-limited phenomenon. After some moments my legs began to ease up and my body filled with nervous energy. I took a few steps back, sat down and rested. After around ten minutes, which seemed an eternity, I got up to try again. As I neared the edge of the board—I think I managed to get a little closer to the edge—my legs froze a second time. Again, the freeze response thawed, my legs eased up and, with a pounding heart and my entire body vibrating furiously with huge energy and agitation, I walked to the edge and took that dreaded step....

Needless to say, I survived. I was elated. I went straight back up to jump again because the first jump had been too fast for me to savour the experience.

Freeze, as happened with me on the diving board, occurs automatically when excitation or activation reaches a certain physiological threshold. In Chapter Three the freeze response is likened to a circuit breaker, one that shuts down an overloaded physiology. It is a profound physiological state that contains a tremendous amount of activated energy. For all of us, there is a great likelihood of freezing when confronted with a highly-charged event. If, in the past, you have frozen in the face of a threat, freeze may be your preferred strategy and your fight and flight responses may not be available.

What does freeze feel like?

Many of us, when we experience the freeze response, do not know what it is, so we judge ourselves as being weak. Perhaps you have frozen when trying to speak in a meeting or after standing up in a conference to pose a question to the speaker. Or maybe the freeze response has manifested itself by becoming 'tongue-tied' during an argument, to the point that you can no longer express yourself.

The body actually has the capacity to freeze certain regions of the body while others continue to function normally. Another example is, when faced with a threat, a person's neck stiffens and he cannot turn his head towards—or perhaps away from—the threat, but he can move his arms and legs.

We may experience the freeze response as stiffness or heaviness, with the 'heavy' region perhaps feeling cold. Certain body parts, such as the arms and legs, may feel clamped or wooden, practically stuck. When we notice this freeze state it is helpful to observe it, using the Three Steps. Make sure you scan the body to notice what is happening in other regions. Return your attention again and again to the frozen area or areas to see what is happening there and to notice any changes. Oscillating attention from the frozen area to other areas allows us to observe how 'freeze' is time limited and how the constriction or stuckness thaws and transforms when given time.

When a frozen state begins to thaw, the body usually experiences heightened arousal. You may start to feel a strong emotion, have an urge to hit out or run away, or any number of other possible fight and flight responses. This is normal. Begin a new cycle of the Three Steps and process the responses.

You may also experience discharge sensations, such as trembling and shaking. In this case, start the Three Steps with Step 2—observing discharge sensations. Remember: this is alchemy in action, the body's way of changing deeply entrenched patterns.

Brace, collapse, rebound

Many people become stuck in a subconscious dynamic of bracing against collapse. This can happen when, for example, as anger arises, the high activation triggers the freeze response. When we freeze we may become weak and collapsed, but since we do not like to experience sensations of collapse, we brace ourselves as a way of propping ourselves up.

We spend such a large amount of energy bracing against collapse. To mimic how the body braces against collapse, try the following exercise.

- Hold your palms against each other, as if in prayer.
- Push your hands together as hard as you can. Keep pushing a little longer. Do you notice how much energy is being used? You may be getting tired, although an outside observer may not perceive any signs of effort. You, however, can feel how exhausting this is.
- Release the pressure and notice how you are feeling in your body. Notice how tired you feel.

Dealing with collapse and bracing

When, in everyday life, you find yourself bracing, try to feel the conflict in the musculature; your muscles feel weak and want to collapse and you brace against this almost like you are propping yourself up from the inside. The key is to notice how you are bracing.

Try to let go just enough to sense collapse. Even allow yourself into the collapse, sensing its helplessness. Perhaps there is a weak feeling in your shoulder joints. Now scan your body and observe how the rest of your body feels in this collapsed state. Notice your breathing, the sense of gravity acting against you. Allow yourself to rest in collapse. Become friends with it. Remember: collapse is time-limited. With patience and tolerance, you will come out on the other side.

Coming out of collapse, the body expands and restores its natural muscle tone. The posture shifts and naturally becomes more upright. The body feels more alive. To navigate a collapse, brace, rebound cycle requires time. In our daily lives we often do not have two minutes, let alone twenty! This is why our health and stress levels are deteriorating worldwide. We do not take the time to support ourselves in a way that is conducive to healing and resolution. The body demands resolution and will become symptomatic in order to catch our attention. There is no escape; sooner or later you have to turn inwards.

By accepting collapse—through the above exercise and in our day-to-day lives—we find that we do not need to expend so much energy bracing against it. After many times of witnessing, in awareness, your body collapsing and then reorganizing itself into an expansive, vital state, collapse will not occur as often. There will be greater mobility and ease in your body, because the energy formerly used for bracing is now freed up for creative pursuits. You will gain a deep level of trust in your body. This trust—that your body will find its natural homeostasis with wellbeing—is the ultimate resource in life.

Working with dissociation

Dissociative symptoms often defy rational medical examination
- Robert C. Scaer, MD

Remember the myth described in Chapter Three of how Isis 're-membered' Osiris's scattered body parts, it being an analogy for the work we must do to re-member our own body parts 'lost' through dissociation. These body parts become lost when, during and following states of freeze, we are unable to release horribly uncomfortable trapped energy sensations, so the areas in which they are trapped become walled off from our awareness.

'What a lot of hogwash,' I thought upon first hearing that I may not be able to feel certain parts of my body. It turned out that I was very much dissociated from large parts of my body. Intellectually, I knew I had two legs, a neck and a head. I could identify them and tell you: Here are my two arms, my two hands, my two legs and my two feet. But I was not really in touch with all these body parts, and only as I have re-membered them have I been able to recognize that they were actually lost to me. If we think of each body part as a member of our collective body-mind nexus, the terms 'dis-member' and 're-member' become strikingly apt.

When dissociation occurs, there is a corresponding disruption of conscious awareness, one in which we experience a distortion of memory, affect, perception, behaviour and physical sensations. Certain elements of a person's experience 'split' from others. Dissociation often causes a loss of sense of self, and this sense of unreality may be experienced as a 'fog-like' perception clouding one's consciousness. A lifting of this fog indicates improved cognition.

Dissociation may also present itself as an attention deficit disorder, whereby there is difficulty processing new information: heard, seen or read. It may be hard to make plans, take decisions or formulate lists of things to do. The fundamental ability to solve problems is hindered. Common sense, logic and judgment may be impaired. Forgetfulness, absent-mindedness and even a distorted sense of time may all occur.

Dissociative states can be triggered in split-seconds; for example, whenever a particular mental model is recalled, such as public-speaking, or perhaps whenever the body-mind experiences high arousal. The origin of the arousal—be it fear, panic, excitement, sexual arousal or any other stimulus—does not matter.

Dissociation diminishes our capacity to participate in life, and in a bid not to be exposed to more stimulation than we can tolerate, we may avoid much of what the world has to offer. At the extreme end of the dissociative continuum, people completely avoid socializing and withdraw into total isolation, becoming social recluses or hermits. Conversely, others may be drawn like moths to a flame to the stimulation of risk taking, extreme sports, and even intense socializing to get their 'fix' of endorphins associated with dissociation. In extreme sports athletes have to endure high levels of pain that may lead to dissociation and endorphin reward. Their behaviour may also be motivated by a need to feel empowered. This combination of endorphin reward and the need for empowerment can be very addictive.

Dissociation may dull moods and emotions—or heighten them. For example, the sense of fear may be muted, and a person may cycle from dullness to rage. Likewise, he may not be able to experience joy, love and pleasure, and may cycle from depression to panic. Intense emotion-related flashback memories also represent dissociation. Flashbacks are linked with high arousal states, confusion and, frequently, panic. Flashbacks may last from minutes to hours or even days.

I experienced some of the symptoms of dissociation in childhood and, as I grew up, they intensified dramatically. On a daily basis, by three in the afternoon my head would be overwhelmingly foggy and heavy. I couldn't think straight and would put off the simplest of decisions. I couldn't register anything I read and felt completely fatigued, barely being able to keep my eyes open. Between the ages of thirty-four and forty, these symptoms were at their worst. And they would have worsened still had I not intervened with the Three Steps.

One day as I worked on my computer the heaviness and fog in my head became too overwhelming. I lay down on the couch and explored the mist in my head with a sense of curiosity. I had done this many times before, but this time there was a greater capacity to stay in the mist for a longer period of time without falling asleep. As I witnessed, I seemed to go into an altered state of consciousness in which I was still aware of my body's sensations. I went deeper and deeper, losing all awareness of the outer, and from head to toe, my body became a cascading waterfall of tingling. It was a most wonderful feeling, like fairy dust being thrown all over me, as happens in cartoons.

For ages, it seemed, I witnessed this blissful state. Suddenly, it was time to come back and, quite quickly, I opened my eyes. The tingling was still happening, albeit more mildly, and was mostly in my arms and legs. I remained lying down and, as I returned to a state of wakefulness, looked around and oriented myself to the now. My head was clear. For many years I had suffered from a foggy, groggy, heavy head, which had made my life pure hell. Understandably, although I was excited about my head being clear, I was also cautious. This could be just a temporary state. One week later, however, there was still no fog. Wow!

When the fog lifted and the body-mind-numbing state first cleared, I found that I had become more reactive, experiencing greater arousal and activation. It was a difficult period. I was supposed to be getting better, but now I was more anxious and trigger-happy, and became angry more easily. What was happening was that the dissociative state that had previously numbed the 'new' sensations I was now experiencing was no longer being triggered. So I had to learn to tolerate these new sensations and, with the help of the Three Steps, resolve the high charge in my nervous system—instead of shutting them out again through states of dissociation.

Thankfully, as I experienced this onslaught of previously numbed sensations, I had the right tools to upgrade my system's 'electrical wiring' and handle a higher charge. However, certain activities or situations still evoked a familiar, but not as intense, dissociative state. So I kept applying the Three Steps in these various situations. Remember: each time we work with the Three Steps it is like doing nervous-system aerobics, and we strengthen the nervous system's resilience and, through equanimity and awareness, reprogram our mental models.

A highly charged nervous system is the root cause of many symptoms that lead us to seek medical help. Unfortunately, mainstream doctors do not possess the knowledge or expertise to resolve these symptoms. They may prescribe medication, diet and exercise to help manage the symptoms, but once you are on high blood pressure medication, it is for the long term. In the vast majority of cases, diabetes is managed but not cured, and the same goes for asthma, irritable bowel syndrome, chronic fatigue syndrome, migraines and insomnia. These are all symptoms of the autonomic nervous system trying to manage and resolve the excess high charge stuck within it.

Exercise is definitely useful, but it does not usually resolve the problem because certain conditions have to be met for the body to release the high charge it contains. In this way exercise can become another way of managing symptoms so that they do not worsen—but this is still 'managing', not healing. The Three Steps support our body-minds to heal the symptoms so that we no longer need to manage them. Once this happens, we can exercise purely for fun and enjoyment.

My journey to health has been a long one. I am fortunate to have had the wisdom not to drug myself into deadness, and to work with the alternative methods that led me to formulate the Three Steps. I am happy that I had the courage to persevere at times when nothing seemed to be working and everything seemed to be telling me to 'just get on with life'. Sometimes the appearance of imminent defeat is merely a veil for a big breakthrough. In this work, there is a pattern of breakthroughs, 'wows' and, often, setbacks. The process is like a spiral, or like the ebb and flow of water coming ashore at high tide; wave after wave reaches its limit on the beach and then retreats into the vast ocean.

In the Three Steps process we meet ourselves wherever we are. This may be a horrible place, or it may be a joyful one. By using the Three Steps you will develop a capacity to tolerate life's extremes and to be with love, joy, gratitude, anger, hurt and sadness equally, without dissociating at the drop of the hat.

I am happy to say that my fog-like perception has lifted and that I have gradually regained my life, and with much reward. My sense of perception is far greater than ever before. My sensitivity and capacity of awareness have improved a hundred fold. I am a lucky man to have lived in hell for a long time and to have found the road to redemption. Through the healing process I have gained great insights and capacities that were not part of my experience before the sickness, or prior to the appearance of my symptoms. In this manner sickness, symptoms, dis-ease—although they can put us through hell—can be seen as a path to liberation, and therefore a blessing in disguise.

Our dis-membered parts are like the missing pieces from the body's jigsaw puzzle. They are the holes in our bodily container, from which energy leaks. Once the holes are patched or otherwise fixed, we can contain energy without leakage. As we re-member our lost body parts we have greater containers to tolerate life's extremes. And as we become more whole we have greater substance with which to encounter and experience the world around us.

CHAPTER SEVENTEEN

WORKING WITH GUILT, SHAME AND SADNESS

Meeting a beautiful woman triggers my guilt, memories of my wife and how I fought with her through shaming and aggression. The familiar, insidious 'guilt sensations' spread throughout my body. I catch myself in thoughts of 'I was wrong' and turn my attention towards my body and how it is being taken over by this wave of guilt and shame.

Because of my regular practice, I don't become as physiologically shut down as before, but I do feel the shame as my spine shudders with an insidiously gnawing constriction, and I feel how my heart clamps down a bit, my tongue is swollen, metallic and buzzing, and my mouth tight. My entire body has tightened. I know that these sensations too shall pass. The wave has peaked, my body is discharging and I already feel my musculature loosening as the pendulum of self-regulation moves towards equilibrium.

'I am sorry. Please forgive me.' This is what I've learned to say once the wave has passed. It is a request to myself: please forgive me for the wrong I have done. It is an important step towards loving myself. If I cannot forgive myself, how can I forgive others? Like many of us, I am my own harshest critic.

After saying sorry and asking for forgiveness, I again turn my awareness inwards and watch what is happening in the body with this new state of being, this new wave.

Working with guilt is tough work. We need to slow down and surf each wave. Each cycle we are able to be with guilt is a step towards freeing ourselves of the debilitating effects it has on our body-minds. The key is to more often catch ourselves in guilty states of being and to process them.

By and by the waves rise, peak and fall away much more quickly. What may have been a fifteen-minute 'guilt cycle' now completes itself in two minutes, or even faster. Eventually, there will be no need to actually stop and process because awareness has increased to such an extent that we are able to maintain awareness of the wave while in action.

Shame

Shame has been used to discipline us, and we will do just about anything to hide those parts of ourselves that our family, peers and society at large deem repulsive or just plain wrong. In trying to avoid shame, embarrassment and humiliation, we devote huge vital energy towards protecting ourselves against these feelings. However, true to the Law of Attraction, what exists inside of us is what we attract into our lives, granting us plenty of opportunities to explore shameful feelings and turn them from base metal into gold. Befriending shame frees up an enormous wealth of energy which allows us to enjoy life in more creative ways.

The basic strategy for befriending shame is the same as that for guilt and other emotions. Simply use the Three Steps to be with them more often, becoming aware of these emotions' body-mind patterns and riding their waves.

Sensations of shame and guilt are horrible, so venture into them slowly. Even if the waves seem to move at a snail's pace, they will, in fact, pass. As bodily patterns of shame and guilt shift, the waves become less overwhelming.

When we can be with guilt and shame we have less need to shirk responsibility and place blame outside of ourselves. We find that we argue less, and many of our defence strategies that guard against our feeling guilty fall away. We are able to say, 'Yes, I did that!' We do not feel as threatened and, as a consequence, we are less protective and our hearts feel safer to open.

Working with sadness

The secret source of humor is not joy but sorrow; there is no humor in Heaven.
- Mark Twain

There is no way to deal with sadness other than to feel it, be with it and let it open our hearts. We only have two choices: close our hearts with our learned strategies and avoid feeling sad. Or feel as much as possible and befriend sadness, pain and hurt. Over time, as sadness becomes more manageable, we find that—lo and behold!—love and joy follow.

Sadness often stems from a sense of loss. A significant loss like divorce, death or the moving away of a friend can be a most difficult situation to come to terms with. Everyone emits certain frequencies, and our bodies resonate with the electromagnetic waves of a constant companion. When our friend is no longer with us, we naturally undergo a period of craving the friend and his or her frequencies. This period of craving is often accompanied by excruciatingly uncomfortable sensations; but it is also a blessing in disguise. It is life's way of bringing us the greatest opportunity to open our hearts and transform our lives at all levels. It is our choice what we do with the opportunity.

The journey through sadness seems hazardous, but the rewards are well worth the effort. We may feel that we will die if we stay present amid sadness's horrible sensations, which involve the whole body, particularly the throat, gut, lungs, eyes and heart. There is often a sense of wanting to cry and sluggishness—physical, mental and emotional. In sadness, the heart can feel so heavy that we might fear it will stop working; and if the heart—being 'the sun' of our body—stops, we die. These kinds of fears may lead us back to our protective habits, so we need to be patient with ourselves.

Protective habit patterns help us avoid feeling vulnerable, hurt and sad. This leads to hard, tight or numb feelings in the chest area as our musculature compensates for the pain we are avoiding. In fact, the entire body reorganizes itself to relieve the heart of the burden and protect it from pain. This is a dissociative mechanism in action. We may even have no awareness of our chest region.

When we allow ourselves to feel grief, it is only natural that we don't feel much energy or enthusiasm. It is normal to feel dull and find it difficult to make decisions or take as much action as we normally would. The body needs to rest and recover.

When we are overtired, we become more vulnerable to succumbing to negative thinking and sinking deeper into the abyss of depression. Tiredness reduces our capacity to be with difficult feelings like sadness. If you have the luxury of taking time off from work this is a great gift to give yourself. If not, it is also okay; just try to take it a little easier. Pace yourself, and take some time throughout the day to nurture your heart and process your feelings and sensations with the Three Steps.

Whatever comes up, observe yourself. Have the patience and courage to accept that this is the way it is. This attitude pays huge dividends, and you will dramatically speed up your recovery. But don't be in a hurry. With significant loss, it takes many months, even a few years, to mourn. Some days might be relatively easy and you may think: Oh, great, it's over! And the next day, when you wake up, sadness has returned. Befriend the sadness once again. Remember that you are not impeding your heart from opening.

I remember the beautiful feelings of gratitude, love and joy I experienced as my heart opened when I worked with my own sadness following the separation from my wife. This made the period of being with the pain of sadness well worthwhile.

Before my heart opened, when I was still in the throes of grief and sadness, I started to wonder whether my approach—using the Three Steps—was the right one. How could I still be grieving after a year? My heart hurt, I missed my wife and I was sad that my daughter was not living with me. My friends also fuelled my doubts by admonishing me: Don't wallow, get on with your life.

One of the reasons friends and family are not supportive of people in sadness is that they have suppressed their own sadness. When they come in contact with a person who is grieving, the grief triggers their repressed sadness, which they cannot tolerate. Rather than begin to feel their own sadness they say: Be strong. Get on with life. Don't dwell in sadness.

I have often worked with clients who have lost their spouses. An Indian lady in her sixties who lost her husband after forty years of marriage told me that her friends warned her that if she continued to cry when they visited her, they would stop coming. So she had to put on a brave face when her guests visited.

Suppressing sorrowful feelings and not supporting the body to return to a balanced state is bound to lead to long-term suffering. Because sadness is such a powerful emotion we require multiple strategies to consistently avoid its sensations. A primary strategy—and one that is most rewarded in our current era—is to busy ourselves with work. The results are long-term protection of the heart, with unconscious sadness and sorrow remaining for a lifetime at the core of our behaviour and decisions, and maybe even heart disease.

During my grieving process, I had a strong sense that I was not escaping or 'wallowing' in sadness, due to the quality of awareness that I brought to it. Awareness changes everything, and it made my sadness a way of clearing and evolving, of opening my heart. So I persevered.

I took some time off to be in Goa. I love the beach and the ocean and find them to be a great resource. Often, when I was feeling despair, I would walk on the beach and not enjoy my surroundings at all. I couldn't experience the beauty around me, only my pain. I felt doomed. Thankfully, I had cultivated a capacity to witness my body and be with painful sensations. It was excruciating, but I supported my body as much as possible with the Three Steps.

One day, as I was walking along the beach in the late afternoon, I began to feel, to my utter amazement, such immense gratitude. It came upon me so suddenly and powerfully that it was overwhelming. I thought: Wait, I'm in the midst of despair. None of my circumstances had changed; yet here I was, feeling grateful. Wow! Then I knew: it's not about what happens outside of us, but rather inside. I had heard this adage a thousand times, but it hadn't yet been my experience. It was a defining moment for me, the knowing that it's not the outer things that make us happy and grateful. Joyfulness, love and gratitude are all states of being that emanate from the heart. They are physical visceral experiences and they are all qualities we can experience even when the outer world is not going the way we like.

Over the next few months, I cycled through deep sadness and feelings of joy, love and gratitude, then back to sadness. I have to tell you that I still harboured a wish that sadness would go away for good, and that I would only experience joy, love and gratitude. There are always plenty of triggers to evoke sadness: a song, a memory, a smell, a friend, a place. So many triggers, so many opportunities. I found that the morning, as I was dressing, was a particularly vulnerable time for me. Again and again, I would stop in the midst of putting on my clothes and stand or sit with sadness for a few minutes, just experiencing it and watching my habit pattern of feeling disappointed that sadness had showed up again. Remembering to stop and be with painful sensations requires strength and courage.

Although I believed that I was through with sadness because I had processed it, I hadn't really befriended it. Imagine having a friend who comes to visit and you invite her into your house with the intention of never seeing her again! You are being crafty, not a friend. The atmosphere of her visit becomes charged with your underlying intention and your friend will feel, if only at a subconscious level, your resistance and stress. This resistance is likewise a habit pattern to be watched and befriended. Sadness, like any true friend, is always welcome to show up any time.

Our bodies usually have patterns of discomfort that manifest when sadness arrives. We can shift these patterns so that sadness feels much more comfortable in our bodies. For example, when I felt sad I would experience—amongst other things—intense pain in my throat, my face would hurt and so would my eyes. As I stayed with the discomfort and followed the Three Steps, my body was able to shift and release these difficulties a bit at a time. My body reorganized itself, and now when sadness arrives my throat is no longer overwhelmed, and my eyes and face do not hurt nearly as much. I've supported my body to employ its innate wisdom and craft a new pattern for sadness.

The only constant in life is change. To remember this in difficult times is priceless. Always remember, even in your deepest and darkest moments, that this too shall pass. In times of hopelessness and despair you will not be able to imagine the joy that will come. But it will come. Having navigated my worst nightmare I now feel like a new person. I am more open and loving, softer yet stronger, and definitely more resilient.

One of life's paradoxes is that by being with sadness, joy follows. Conversely, resist sadness and it will persist. As Osho tells us:

"Life consists of sadness too. And sadness is also beautiful; it has its own depth, its own delicacy, its own deliciousness, its own taste. A man is poorer if he has not known sadness; he is impoverished, very much impoverished. His laughter will be shallow, his laughter will not have depth, because depth comes only through sadness. A man who knows sadness, if he laughs, his laughter will have depth. His laughter will have something of his sadness too, his laughter will be more colourful".[32]

Some tips for working with sadness

- Place one hand over your heart, firmly and at the same time gently supporting. As I worked with sadness, when I was lying down I would place a pillow under the elbow of the hand supporting my heart. I would rest the other arm alongside my body, making sure this other hand was not closed so that my body could use it as a channel for discharging. I would alternate lying flat on my back with lying in a foetal position, supporting my heart with the hand that was higher up. Sometimes I lay on my belly, with one hand on my heart.

- If your eyes or throat hurt, likewise use touch for support. Sense these areas of difficulty, but also broaden your awareness to include the rest of your body.
- Many times you will not want to be present. You will just want 'time out'. This is a good time to resource yourself by choosing external resources to help you through. Perhaps invite a friend or two whom you find supportive. Take a walk, a hot bath, a cold shower, eat food you enjoy, watch a comedy—whatever helps you.
- When crying comes, this is good, especially for those who have not cried in a long time or rarely cry. Just cry and cry. Be conscious of crying so that you do not dissociate. As you cry, maintain awareness of the body. Allow yourself to feel the pain in the heart and the rest of the body so that crying does not become just another mechanism to avoid pain.
- It is sometimes fine to just feel the sadness in the body and the simultaneous urge to cry. In awareness, the right decision—whether to cry or not—will unfold. Let the waves come and watch them rise, peak and fall away. After many times of watching crying you may sometimes not cry.
- If you never cry, when the impulse comes, watch what you do to thwart it. Watch how you do something in your throat to swallow back the tears, or whatever your habit pattern is. Stay with the impulse longer without thwarting it. If you start to cry—even one tear—watch this and let it happen. Feel the moist, ticklish feeling of the single tear rolling down your cheek.

CHAPTER EIGHTEEN

WORKING WITH HABIT PATTERNS

Our habit patterns compel us to act in certain ways and to re-enact various events and situations, as described in Chapter Five.

In working with habit patterns it is helpful to begin with small habits. Take a daily routine like brushing your teeth. When brushing your teeth, stop and go inside. Say, for example, you notice a low level of anxiety. This anxiety is likely triggering anxious thoughts, such as about a forthcoming high-pressure meeting or the state of your finances. By solving the underlying anxiety that occurs when brushing your teeth, you create more calm in your life. Imagine that you are able to resolve the anxiety that drives ten of your daily habits. This creates an altogether different life experience, one that is much more calm, present and focused.

Other examples of everyday patterns to work with include: waking up, urinating, passing bowels, bathing, dressing, drinking, eating, searching for lost keys and other items, bending down to pick up something, opening and closing doors, driving, cooking, cleaning, and napping in the afternoon. We can expand our exploration to include any habit, from the ways we interact with people to how we relate to money to how we respond to a beggar in the street.

When working with any habit, it is helpful to keep in mind:

- The various stages before, during and after any particular event. As described in Chapter Seven, we can divide these stages into: a time leading up to the event, the event itself, and the time after the event. During each of these stages, our states of being shift and morph into each other in a seamless manner. Just as we can pause a movie and freeze one of its frames, we have the option of pausing and exploring a particular state of being, in all its detail at any stage. It is helpful to explore all these different stages.
- For example, as you put toothpaste on the toothbrush (before the event of brushing), pause and take time to become aware of what is

happening within. Follow the Three Steps. Then continue to brush your teeth. Halfway through brushing (the event itself), pause and run through another cycle of the Three Steps. After brushing (time after the event), sit down and follow the Three Steps once again. You can explore all the stages in one session or you can explore the various stages on different days. The order is not important; practice and awareness is.

- Watching the wave. The waves of our states of being—be they big or small—come and go just like waves in the ocean. They arise out of the ocean, swell and peak. After they 'break' at the peak, their water spills forth onto the beach, then peacefully recedes back into the ocean. The Three Steps supports the natural process of emotional waves to unfold. Sometimes these waves take just a few moments to unfold, as with minor irritability. Other times they may take a few days or more, as with intense bouts of anger or sadness.

Working with habit patterns of illness

Any illness is a golden opportunity to increase our capacity to watch the body and to shift behavioural patterns. This has been my experience.

I was lucky that, as a young boy, my grandmother was opposed to taking any medication. She believed that God would heal all. True to her word, when it came time for her to die, she refused medical intervention and passed on happily. I admired and was influenced by her strong faith and conviction.

However, I took medication during my teenage years, at times when I was afflicted with intense migraines. I continued to take medication until my late twenties, for headaches, flu and so on. Then I went on holiday with a good friend, Gary. He fell ill with a heavy dose of flu, and I saw how, by just resting and taking liquids, he recovered and was up and about within a few days. Gary believed our bodies have the wisdom and innate healing capacity to take care of themselves, as long as we support this process through rest.

Gary's example was inspiring, and I followed it the next time I had the flu. Boy! Was it terrible to suffer the symptoms of a stuffy, running nose, heat from the fever, and an aching body and head! My joints were in such pain that I thought I would die. Luckily, sleep came easily, so I slept as much as possible. I almost resorted to medication, but I'm glad that I stuck it out. It took a few days for the symptoms to clear and for me to regain my strength. I had successfully navigated flu without medication and realized what amazing bodies we have. They have their own internal pharmacies which, given the chance, heal more powerfully than any external intervention. After that experience, the more I navigated the tides of flu and fever the less sick I became and the stronger my immunity grew.

The Three Steps, combined with an understanding of the body's mechanisms of regulation, greatly supports us in navigating recovery from illness and in shifting difficult lifelong patterns in the process. Often, our physical symptoms, regardless of the particular ailment, are similar, and these are our bodies' ways of responding to the stresses of being ill.[33] As our personal collection of symptoms appear, the body becomes more sensitive, its energy wanes and we naturally want to rest. This creates the ideal circumstances to support our body-minds by taking a break from our busy lives and processing via the Three Steps.

During the time that I was recovering from the difficult separation from my wife and daughter, I came down with fever. My eyes were painful and burning; in fact, I was so hot all over that I felt like I was burning in hell. It felt like the darkest night of my soul. Thank God the fever only lasted one night. Amazingly, the next morning I had a new pair of eyes. I had given my body the time and support it needed to release the pressure and pain stored in my eyes.

The only reason that I was able to endure such a hellish night was the tolerance and resilience I had garnered. I had the skill to suffer consciously. I was able to practice what I preach. As I repeatedly cycled through thoughts of vengeance, I watched how painful this was for my body. After I processed one set of thoughts, other angry thoughts would arise, so I would go through another cycle. Not only did I gain a new pair of eyes, but I am also grateful that the feelings of vengeance and anger I was experiencing reduced considerably—if I had to put a number on it, I would say that they reduced by eighty percent. Many times, during illness, I have experienced 'new' sensations, as previously unavailable parts of my body suddenly come 'online'. I am constantly impressed at how well the Three Steps work.

Taking time out to process during illness may shift symptoms and bodily states that could otherwise take a lifetime to change. When you have a fever, it is important to rest a lot and drink plenty of water and other liquids, such as soup and ginger, lemon and honey water, and to eat fruit. Don't watch television, watch your body. Try to shift awareness back and forth between areas in your body that feel horrible and those that feel a little more comfortable. Try not to become stuck solely in the pain and constriction. The goal is to endure illness in a way that is as supportive as possible in helping the body to release and recover.

When processing, keep oscillating your awareness between the painful areas and the more comfortable ones. Spend a few moments exploring the discomfort and feeling its various nuances and then moving to an area of comfort. Or just follow the protocol of Step Two by exploring discharge sensations in the extremities. It is a skill to be able to keep your attention on the body and to move your awareness to a place of relative comfort. The brain is naturally drawn to areas of discomfort, which then catapult your mind away from the body and towards thoughts. Your job is to bring your attention back to the body and focus it on areas of relative comfort. Step Two focuses our attention on the arms, legs, hands and feet, and these are usually areas of relative comfort.

Working with our social engagement system

Social interactions are fantastic opportunities to grow and know ourselves. Interacting with one person may trigger sensations of inferiority; another person may evoke sensations of sexual attraction; another, a feeling of embarrassment; another, inadequacy; another, inspiration or joy. Just meeting someone may even catapult us into a highly activated and dissociated state. An invaluable way to grow is to pause and process our interactions as often as possible.

The head contains much of the apparatus we use to engage with others. We use the mouth and tongue for speaking, and our state of being expresses itself not only through words, but also through tonality. We use the eyes to see and connect with people; the eyes alone can convey all kinds of expression, from mild surprise to interest to attraction to anger. The face has forty-four muscles, which are hardwired with certain patterns that express our emotions. The neck orients itself towards those with whom we wish to connect, or towards a threat we are confronting.

However, through our conditioning we have learned to mask the natural expression of our true feelings—to the extent that we may have become dissociated from our original facial expressions. (High-impact accidents, physical abuse and dental work can all cause somatic dissociation of the face.) Dissociative patterns can lead to facial constriction or flaccidity, contributing to signs of an aging face; contrarily, by 're-membering' our faces we can slow down the aging process and even make rejuvenation possible.

We modulate our voices and put on false smiles, but try as we might we cannot completely hide our emotions; anyone with a keen eye or ear can recognize them. Charles Darwin was convinced that facial expressions do not vary from culture to culture, and Paul Ekman, an emeritus professor of psychology at the University of California at San Francisco and a world authority on facial expressions, agrees. Ekman spent forty years studying thousands of people's facial expressions, and in 1967 he travelled to study the Fore people in the highlands of Papua New Guinea. The Fore had never been exposed to movies, television, magazines, and had met few outsiders. When Ekman showed them photographs of faces with various expressions, they interpreted them exactly as Westerners would have.

Using his expertise, Ekman teaches law enforcement officers how to analyze expressions and interpret voices and gestures so that they can detect lying. Ekman has observed that when people try to hide their emotions, their true expressions may flash for one-fifteenth to one-twentieth of a second—just long enough for others to see them. After that, they can successfully 'wipe away' their expressions.[34]

When dissociation happens in the face we cannot feel the emotional expressions we are making. For example, a person's face contorts into an awful expression of disgust, but when someone else asks whether he is feeling disgusted he indignantly pronounces 'No, I'm not!' Dissociation from our face and its expressions also reduces our capacity to read the social signs expressed by others. This makes sense; how can we know others if we do not even know ourselves?

In the past, there was lots of activation in my mouth, accompanied by the most intolerable sensations of pain in my teeth and jaw. This pain occurred whenever my body-mind became charged, but due to the phenomenon of dissociation I was not aware of it. As I regained awareness of these areas, I became acutely aware of the pain and other terrible sensations in my mouth area. My tolerance and skill in working with the Three Steps helped to move me through this stage of the healing process to a place where a large percentage of these sensations dissipated. I now have greater comfort and ease in my mouth and jaw.

Dissociation allows us to carry on with our daily lives, and at the same time appear 'normal'. Remember, however, the sensations that are masked from our awareness are directing our behaviour from behind the scenes and are secretly contributing in composing our life melodies. To return to wholeness we need to regain our bodies and allow them to move naturally in and out of expression.

Try these methods of working with your social engagement apparatus:

- Move your face about. Smile. Frown. Growl. Scrunch up your eyes. Move your mouth from side to side, backwards and forwards, open and close it. Move your head around slowly and look around the room. Do this for about one minute. Then follow the Three Steps.
- Explore one expression at a time. For example, smile a few times, then follow the Three Steps.

Sometimes the slight playfulness involved in these exercises can activate us and, in a matter of seconds, propel us into dissociation. It may take a few minutes to begin sensing the body. In the meantime you may think, 'Oh, nothing is happening. I feel great!' Have patience and explore this feeling. After a few minutes, as regulation occurs and dissociation lifts, you may start to feel uncomfortable. As you become aware of the discomfort that sent you into dissociation, apply the Three Steps, allowing time for the body to renegotiate this activation. In Step One remember to explore what is happening in your entire body, not just your face.

There are hundreds of opportunities to explore our activation and facial expressions in social settings. As you greet someone in the street and move on, pause and become aware of your facial expression. Don't change it; allow it to remain. It will leave on its own and in its own time. After smiling, we often stop smiling abruptly. Try letting the smile linger, feeling how it is to smile. Then broaden your awareness to include the rest of the body, letting your smile just be. And follow the Three Steps.

As you develop tolerance and sensitivity, waves tend to pass more quickly and only a few minutes will be needed to regulate after each interaction. As your capacity increases, even while interacting you will be aware of your gestures, movements and bodily sensations as you allow them to flow and morph. As life happens you will constantly watch, always maintaining some perception of your body and its inner sea of sensations.

Love and compassion are necessities, not luxuries.
Without them, humanity cannot survive.

- Dalai Lama

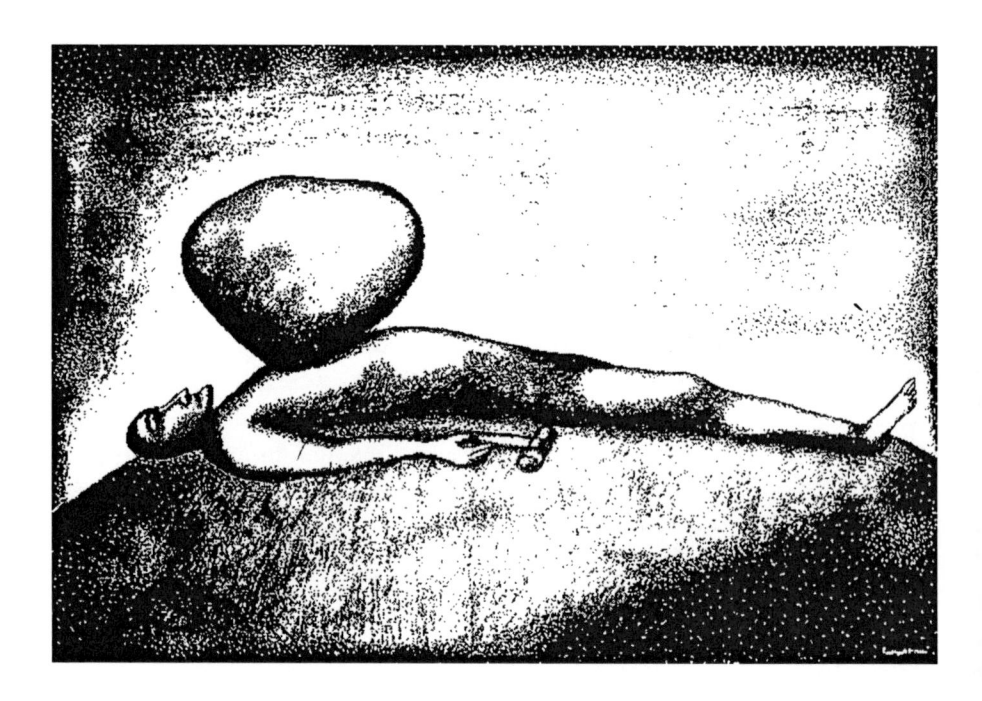

In life devote yourself to joy and love.
Behold the beauty of the peaceful dove.
Those who live, in the end must all perish.
Live as if you are already in heavens above.

- Khayyam

CHAPTER NINETEEN

OPENING TO THE HEART

Opening to the heart—cultivating the capacity to feel compassion, love, joy, and gratitude—involves the work described in the previous chapters. This journey also involves negotiating physiological patterns of states of being like longing, grief, the hurt of disappointment, the pain of betrayal, loss of trust, and sadness. In these states the heart may really feel 'broken', on the edge of collapsing. Your whole chest may feel clamped shut, as if a ton of bricks is pressing down on it, making it difficult to draw a breath. In such a state fear will surely arise. If you have not been working and preparing yourself by knowing your fear and beginning to shift your patterns of freeze and dissociation, you will automatically shut down. This is your body implementing its number one priority: survival.

In panic, you may believe that you are having a heart attack and admit yourself to hospital. I have negotiated this 'heart attack' state of being on numerous occasions. The first time was the scariest. I really thought I was going to die, and I surrendered with the attitude: what must happen must happen. These 'heart attacks' occurred repeatedly over a half-year period. Again and again I had the opportunity to be fully conscious and watch my body react; how my other organs, particularly my stomach, assisted by relieving some of the pressure from my heart. To witness the body in action as it protects the heart—to allow it, without interference, to complete deep levels of waves that we usually impede—is awe-inspiring.

To safely manage such extreme experiences you need to be well versed in the Three Steps and to have cultivated great tolerance, trust in your body, and strong self-regulation. It takes much preparation and should not be undertaken lightly. You may want to acquaint yourself with this type of work through individual sessions with qualified somatic practitioners, by attending Vipassana meditation retreats, and by participating in Three Steps workshops.

Making space for love

Uncomfortable sensations not only arise with strong emotions like anger, sadness and hurt, but they can also manifest with feelings of love and gratitude. If there are bodily patterns of discomfort, tension, constriction and pain when love is evoked then we will likely cycle out of the state quite quickly.

When love and gratitude come we also need to sit with them and let them be, just as we would when we work with any other emotion. Maintain an awareness of the sensory experience of love and gratitude while following the Three Steps. By broadening our awareness to include the whole body, we make space for the heart to open and emanate love and gratitude. As the heart opens we have a greater connection to all that is and we become established in experiencing the beyond, where words do not suffice....

Love often seems to be an elusive quality. Many of us have been betrayed and hurt, and have lost our loved ones. Due to past experience, love and pain may have become linked, so whenever we feel love, memories of betrayal, pain and loss are evoked. How can we make love our underlying experience so that it becomes the filter through which we perceive life?

Fortunately, as my heart was opening I found it easier to explore love. I found it beneficial to say the words 'I love you' and then watch what was happening in the theatre of my body. As I started to feel love, my chest area would expand. Continuing to watch patiently, I then noticed some discomfort arising, accompanied by thoughts about past betrayal, hurt and loss. Again, I would direct my awareness to the theatre of my body and, using the Three Steps, watch this new story play out. As I settled and returned to an easier state, I would repeat the words 'I love you' and watch.

In the beginning, I said 'I love you' not directed towards myself or anyone else—just the words. At other times I would also catch myself spontaneously feeling love. I made these sensations more conscious by taking time out to sit with them, thereby supporting my body as it re-organized itself to be able to contain these sensations of love.

Try it. Whenever you have a few moments, quietly say 'I love you'. Then watch and be with whatever comes up. In the morning before jumping out of bed, say 'I love you' and watch. At night before sleeping, say 'I love you' and watch. At various points throughout the day you may find yourself happily remembering your daughter or son, or another loved one. Stop and take a moment to experience this love. Sit for a few minutes and apply the Three Steps. Maintain the sensations of love in your awareness. As you keep one 'eye' on the love creating, say, an expansive feeling in the chest, with the other 'eye' broaden your awareness to include the rest of your body.

When the heart is in love this frequency of electromagnetic waves affects the entire body, leading to considerable change in the structures of the organs, tissues and muscles. By slowing down to observe and allowing the body to reorganize itself with the help of the Three Steps, we are speeding up our transformation and increasing our tolerance to this new state of being so that it becomes a trait. As our hearts open, a whole new life of love, joy and gratitude follows. Our decisions and strategies are no longer geared towards protecting the heart.

As love grows stronger and we can tolerate love, there is no need to try and evoke this quality. It just comes by itself. We do not need other people to be a certain way or things to happen according to a certain plan in order to experience love.

Love is a visceral physical experience we can feel and know and radiate to those around us. Imagine the type of world we will live in once we all take the time to build the foundations of love and joy. All we do in life—all our thoughts, words and actions—will arise from this space of love. Challenges will still come our way; the difference will be the way we respond—from love.

Making space for gratitude

Can you be thankful for all life has to offer you—bar none?

Can you feel grateful to existence for everything that comes your way, both 'good' and 'bad'?

Can you feel gratitude towards the messenger of bad news?

Can you feel gratitude towards the thief who has stolen your car?

Can you feel gratitude towards your cheating spouse?

You have probably heard that, according to the Law of Attraction, an attitude of gratitude brings forth more to be grateful for. Why then does such a simple thing to do pose such great difficulty? Why do we demonstrate an inkling of gratitude for a short time and then bounce back to our normal ways? Are we just paying lip service when we say thanks? Are we trying to manipulate the universe into giving us more? Or do we really feel thankful?

Try as we might, there is no fooling the universe. We can say a prayer of thanks before a meal, and one afterwards as well, but these prayers are useless if they do not generate a sense of gratitude. They are just parroting without meaning. It is habitual behaviour we learned growing up, having been taught that all good religious 'believers' must pray and be thankful. So, to be a good Christian or Muslim we utter a few words out of obligation. But how effective are these words if they are devoid of feeling? How helpful are they if the underlying motive behind the prayer is manipulation or fear that if we fail to pray we will be doomed?

At the same time that they were teaching us that we must pray, our parents and teachers may have employed coercion and punishment in order to elicit our 'thank yous'. 'Don't you say thank you?' they may have scolded us, causing us shame and embarrassment—uncomfortable feelings that became linked to gratitude. Or they may even have hit us for not saying thank you, so that fear, hurt and anger became linked to gratitude. Or maybe they were manipulative and abusive, admonishing us for not being grateful 'after all we have done for you'. Such experiences may have discoloured our experience of gratitude to the point that we have great difficulty in feeling grateful.

There have been many periods in my life during which I could not feel grateful. I could only experience a few short seconds of gratitude here and there. If someone had asked me 'Are you grateful?' I would surely have answered: 'Yes, of course!' Mentally, I was grateful that I had received some help or money or insight. But this was an attitude of the head, not the heart. My head knew that it is right to be thankful, but my heart was not responding in kind. Like love and all other emotions, gratitude is also a visceral physical experience.

Some say 'fake it till you make it'. This advice is not necessarily helpful when it comes to gratitude. We may be merely cultivating a habit of faking feeling grateful. Many times in my life I have undertaken this effort of cultivating an attitude of gratitude. I zealously made lists of all I was grateful for: money, my car, my work, my friends, my health, my family, the lists were endless. The more I was grateful for, I thought, and the more I mouthed it, the better. Daily, I took the time to remember these things and mouth them out. I would keep up this routine for a few months before dropping it like a hot potato—it was too stressful!

My exploration with the Three Steps has revealed new insights to me, one of which is that gratitude is a heart quality. If the heart is full of sorrow, hurt and despair, evoking gratitude will then trigger this sorrow, hurt and despair. I gradually understood how, as a means of avoiding having these feelings triggered, my body-mind had long helped me to not feel gratitude.

Increasingly, as I was able to be with sorrow and hurt, my heart started to breathe again and I was also able to feel gratitude. But it took time to develop capacity to tolerate sensations of gratitude, for the body to hold gratitude and allow it to come more often.

As with the previous 'I love you' exercise, try saying 'thank you'. Watch the body, allowing whatever takes place. Also, catch yourself saying 'thank you' in your day-to-day life. Try stopping and staying with the feelings that follow. You may find difficult sensations arising. Also, catch yourself while spontaneously saying 'thank you' to someone. Stop and process.

For me, sensations of gratitude were uncomfortable in the beginning and it wasn't easy to stay with them for long. The mind kept reverting to some old story, and the body would follow. As I applied the Three Steps I slowly developed capacity for these sensations and was consistently able to stay with them longer, allowing them to come more fully and intensely.

Generate thankfulness as often as you like, but always try to remember to watch the body. This is the key to alchemy. This is the secret. Eventually, there will be an underlying feeling of gratitude at the core of your experience of life from moment to moment.

CHAPTER TWENTY

CATCHING THE MOMENT

True happiness comes from mindfulness
- Thich Nhat Hanh

In the beginning we may need external stimuli like music to help us dance and celebrate in order to evoke a sense of joy, love and gratitude. As we continue to explore our inner world, the time comes when bliss, joy and love emanate from within, and no stimulus is needed. Then we can really share it with others. In the meantime we must use external stimuli wisely: to cultivate joy and love.

By catching ourselves in the joy of living, and by using the Three Steps to pause and watch the marvellous waves inside our bodies rise, peak and fall away, we prepare ourselves to contain these wonderful states of being. To be conscious while fully alive requires cultivating the body as a container for these experiences.

When we are having fun we may be active and do not bother to take the time to pause and feel the beauty of, say, the sun shining on our skin or the soft, warm seawater as we swim in the gentle waves, or the sensations of playfulness, joy and gratitude.

Catch yourself in the midst of feeling good and having fun. If you have just completed a task and feel good about it, stop and sense how this moment feels. Watch the wave. Sometimes apply the Three Steps, and sometimes, just for a moment or two, feel the sensations and then continue.

When dancing sense how it feels to dance, becoming aware of your bodily sensations. You might want to stop and stand still, being with these lovely feelings for a few minutes, applying the Three Steps. You might even want to walk a little distance from the music and the rest of the stimulation if it helps you to sit and go inwards.

As you walk down the street, you might be attracted to someone. Catch yourself. As you continue walking, focus on your bodily sensations. Or find a place to sit down and watch the body. Or just stand where you are and go inside.

Catch yourself when someone says something nice to you, or when you give yourself a compliment. Sit with your feelings, sensing the smile and glowing feeling welling up. Sometimes this feeling will morph into a state that is not so nice, so then apply the Three Steps.

We may actually be unable to tolerate many of the states of being we consider 'positive'. When they arrive we might experience high arousal, a state of excitement with sensations similar to those of fear. Sensations of love may lead to tension, constriction and stuckness in certain parts of the body. We may experience symptoms, such as a headache.

We may be conditioned to not feel 'good' feelings, such as pride in our accomplishments, or joy from having done something well. When joy and pride arise, we may immediately suppress these feelings. So now our work is to catch ourselves in these joyful and loving moments. This may take time and lots of patience. When pleasant emotions are followed by difficult ones, apply the Three Steps. Next time a pleasant emotion arises, perhaps you will be able to be with it a little longer.

When we learn anything new, we need to devote much effort and attention towards this new activity. After some time it becomes a habit, almost second nature. This process also applies to mindfulness. In the beginning, mindfulness requires lots of energy, and after we practice for some time—maybe six months, maybe a year, maybe more—it will happen naturally.

It is possible to consciously 'reprogram' ourselves so that mindfulness permeates everything we do. Each of the Three Steps has one common denominator: mindfulness. As we cultivate awareness of the body, mindfulness becomes rooted in our bodies and, without effort, continues from moment to moment. With mindfulness, keep catching yourself in your various shades and states of being. As you do so, you open yourself to a world of possibilities.

The more we pay attention to the 'good' in our lives—through the repeated practice of mindfulness—the more we cultivate habits of enjoyment and happiness. In this way we become aware of the different ways in which we enjoy life, and these become our frames of reference for living.

EPILOGUE

THE SINGING BOWL

With every moment we produce karma, the universal principle of cause and effect, action and reaction, that governs all life expressed via thought, speech and bodily actions. Our thoughts, speech and behaviour create a chain reaction in the world. We continually produce ourselves and our worlds. If you want to perceive your future, just become aware of your thoughts, speech and actions in the present.

'In every moment you are producing yourself,' Thich Nhat Hanh writes. 'You are producing the continuation of yourself. Every thought, every speech, every act bears your signature—you can't escape.'[35]

Your thoughts are motivated by your emotions. To change the type of thoughts you have you need to change the quality and frequency of your emotions. To do this, you have to explore, be with and re-tune your body at the level of sensations. Because these sensations are the glue that keeps your emotions, thoughts and actions in place, anything less will not be effective.

Paradoxically, when we invite so-called negative emotions in and develop a tolerance for them they have less effect on us; they don't hijack us anymore. And when we cultivate sensitivity and tolerance towards states of being like compassion, gratitude, joy, and love they have an increasingly greater influence on our lives.

The singing bowl is a wonderful metaphor for karma. I was introduced to it while attending a meditation retreat in Japan with a wonderful master, Kohrogi San. Singing bowls are a type of standing bell that sit with the bottom surface resting. Using a wooden mallet to strike the bowl, the sides and rim of singing bowls vibrate to produce sound. Singing bowls are widely used in spiritual traditions such as Buddhism and Hinduism for meditation, personal wellbeing and religious practice.

THE SINGING BOWL

Karma

When the mallet meets the singing bowl a warm sound reverberates into the environment. Imagine that you—that is, your body-mind, or biological musical instrument—are the mallet, and that the bowl is the present moment. The mallet swinging towards the bowl is you coming from your past, and as your biological musical instrument meets the present moment—the bowl—you create a sound that reverberates into the future. This sound attracts your life circumstances. It is your pied piper, playing the tunes that attract your life experience to you, and it is happening continuously.

Only the present moment is available to us, so what we do in this moment has far-reaching consequences for what we experience in the future. Only in the present moment can we bring awareness to our states of being and support our body-minds to shift patterns and create new life melodies. In this way we can weed out the thoughts, speech and actions that no longer serve us and we can cultivate happiness, love and joy.

The writing of the Three Steps

My having written this book is a testament to the efficacy of the Three Steps. As a teenage boy I was unable to write and share my thoughts with any clarity. Since the age of fifteen I have found ways of avoiding writing English essays, history projects and other papers. I even learned a generic essay by rote and wrote it out in my final exams. Even in my adult life, I seldom wrote emails and sending sms's also presented difficulties.

When I first wanted to write this book, I could not find any help. The thought of writing it, even with help, totally perplexed me. I would go blank, feel irritated and experience all kinds of excruciatingly painful and horrible sensations. No wonder I avoided writing. Then I applied the Three Steps to the issue of writing. This book is the result.

If I can write a book you can do anything you want. A friend joked about me becoming a rock star and my reply was that if I can write a book then becoming a rock star would be easy. The icing on the cake of this project was that, while writing it and my creative juices were flowing, I penned a children's book and had it illustrated at the same time. The children's book was inspired by my beloved seven year-old daughter, who requested that I write a book for her too.

The Three Steps helped me to avail of my creativity. This book, the children's book and much more is in the pipeline. The Three Steps has helped me to explore the emotions that were hijacking my life, such as constant anxiety, regular rage attacks and a huge fear of abandonment. I also had an intolerable fear of what the future held, depression and a sense of despair. The Three Steps has released me from the clutches of chronic fatigue syndrome, multiple chemical sensitivities, food intolerances, and has helped me to manage major neck pain, and chronic back pain.

Along the way I discovered that when the heart is threatened we resort to our fight-flight strategies, and that to go to the next level of healing we have to be with the sorrow, the hurt and pain of the heart in a new way that supports the healing and transformation of lifetimes of conditioning.

Just working with fear and anger is not enough. This can take us to a certain level, but to go deeper, to transcend fear and anger, we have to endure the pain of the heart. To abide in love, joy and gratitude, which are all higher heart states, we have to brave the murky waters of hatred, vengeance, grief, sorrow, anger and fear.

The next time you experience difficulty, thank life for bringing this amazing opportunity to master yourself. Thank the entire universe for conspiring to bring you the right people and the right context for you to experience what you are now experiencing. This may be difficult. In the heat of the moment, you may feel terrible. You may be trembling with fear, or frozen in humiliation, or feeling helpless or hot with rage, or sad and hurt. Most often, there will be horrible sensations you cannot bear. These sensations are at the core of your actions. These sensations drive your compulsions, your addictions, your behaviour, the way you protect and shield yourself, the way you delude yourself, and the way you manipulate situations.

Part of the spiritual journey is to be with what is, whatever that may be, and to stay alert and present. However, being alert can be rather hot at times. 'Sitting in the fire' can feel like being fried or boiled alive. It is wise to have tools to help you stay present and manage the high activation. The Three Steps will help you cook, but not burn to a cinder. This technique will help you build your container one brick at a time and regain your body awareness one part at a time.

The inner revolution

There have been many revolutions in our history. There was the Russian revolution, the German revolution and the French revolution. There are currently uprisings in places like Tunisia, Egypt, Libya, Yemen, Bahrain and Syria. But what use are these revolutions if the hearts of the people leading them are hurt and closed. Then we get just another Stalin, Hitler or Mugabe. There is no fundamental change, just a few new faces imposing their particular system of domination and control, which is still based in fear and survival.

The revolution has to be an inner revolution, an opening of the heart. It is time for each of us to make this leap.

For a new consciousness to emerge we need to master our survival responses and our emotions. To evolve we need to move from a survival-based society to a heart-based one. As our hearts open, our way of thinking and acting will automatically shift. The more of us who open our hearts, the easier it will be for a new world to transpire. Nothing else is required; just a lot of people opening their hearts. The mystery of life will take care of everything else.

We are living in exciting times. Humankind is on the brink of a quantum leap. What this entails we are not sure, but it is a time of transition, a time for a new society not through revolution but through transmutation, through alchemy of the heart. The background of love can then become the springboard for all our thoughts and actions. This love is not just a concept or an esoteric belief. Love is a visceral, physical experience, and can become the lens through which we view the world.

The coming years are bringing unprecedented change our way. We are reaching a crucial time in human history. A tipping point is approaching. It seems like there is a race to see which alternative will occur: ultimate destruction or a new way. Which will it be?

We are destroying the planet. Like a cancer we keep multiplying and spreading, destroying vegetation and habitation. Hundreds of species of animals are on the verge of extinction. Our water supply is deteriorating. Our food supply is becoming unhealthy. We are obsessed with consumerism, money and stock markets. We are afraid, angry and hungry. Hunger drives our consumer behaviours, our need for accumulating more and more. But we will never be satisfied.

The patterns of hunger, fear, and greed need to be shifted from the core at the level of sensations. Until this happens, billions of dollars in the bank will not bring you a sense of safety, love and joy. These have to be gained from within. When you have them, then you can enjoy the billions in the bank too.

Using the Three Steps

There are many ways of using the Three Steps. Personally, I have processed for thousands of hours, and I continue to grow in awareness, love and wisdom. Some of you may follow me with the intense desire for transformation of the heart and utilize the wisdom in this book to effect profound and sometimes rapid transformation. Others may use the Three Steps to change a particular longstanding habit pattern and then relegate the technique to the back burner. Still others may read this book, find it enlightening yet not apply the Three Steps to their lives in any way. This too is okay. You have read, and just by reading knowledge is gained. This may open the way for an inner journey when the time is right for you.

My wish is that these powerful insights into the body-mind become common knowledge, like old wives' tales every family knows, so that whoever wants to effect change can do so—simply by applying the Three Steps.

As we work with the Three Steps, our bodies become organs of perception which perceive the mysteries of the silence and stillness beyond the mind. As we do this inner work and abide in love, joy and gratitude, and as our compassion for ourselves and others grow, we contribute to the awakening of the collective consciousness. This will herald a new way of life, one filled with love, gratitude and joy.

What a gift to give to our children.

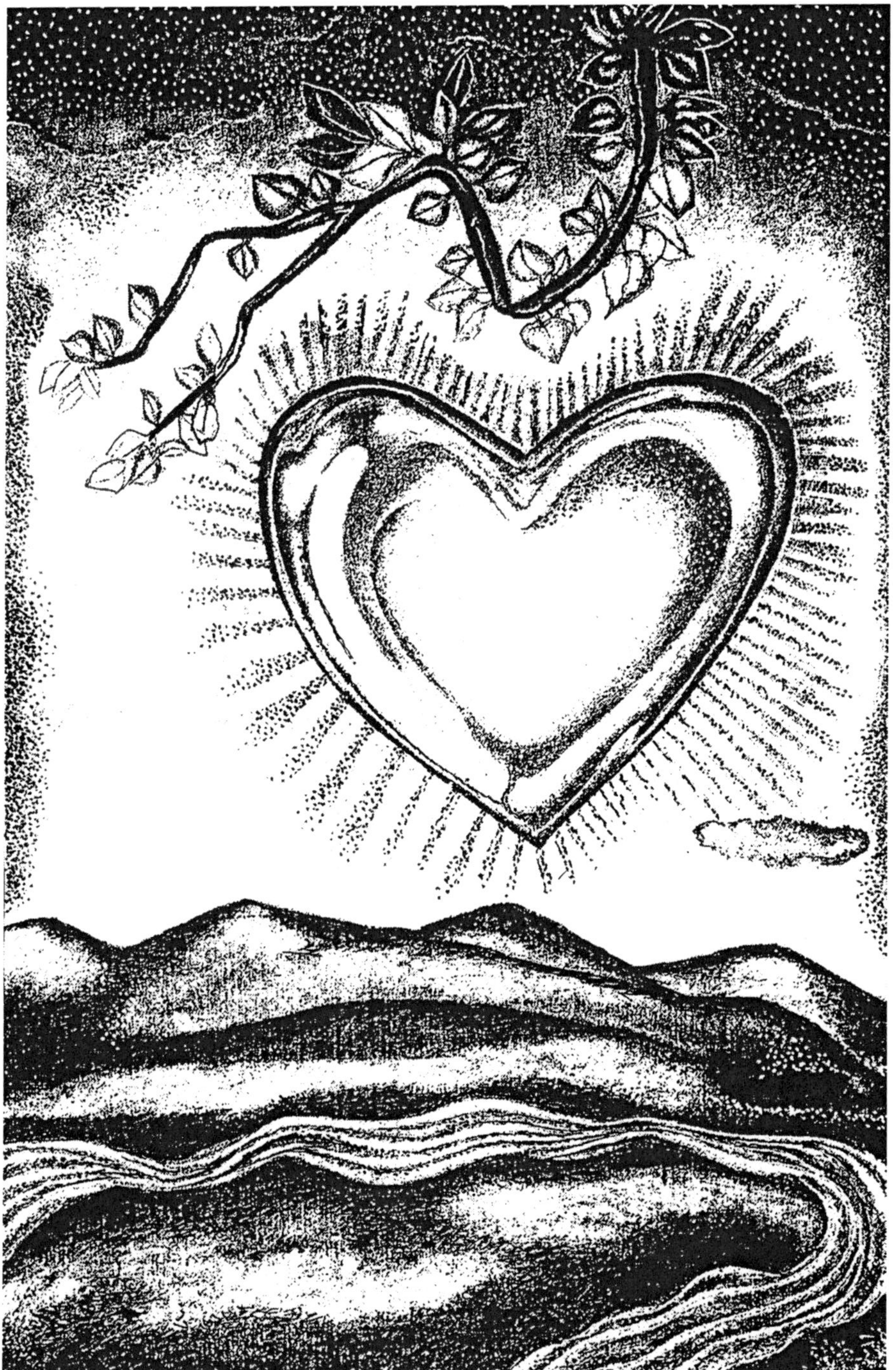

END NOTES

1. Damasio, Antonio (2003). Looking for Spinoza: Joy, Sorrow, and the Feeling Brain. Orlando: Harcourt, Inc., p.30.

2. Freedman, Joshua (2007). The physics of Emotion: Candice Pert on Feeling Good. http://www.6seconds.org/blog/2007/01/the-physics-of-emotion-candace-pert-on-feeling-good/

3. Dana Tomasino, Heartmath Research Center. New Technology Provides Scientific Evidence of Water's Capacity to Store and Amplify Weak Electromagnetic and Subtle Energy Fields.

4. Ridley, Charles (2006). Stillness: Biodynamic Cranial Practice and the Evolution of Consciousness.

5. Mccraty, Rollin, Raymond Trevor Bradley and Dana Tomasino (December 2004-February 2005). The Resonant Heart. Heart Fields.

6. Gershon, Michael (1999). The Second Brain: A Groundbreaking New Understanding of Nervous Disorders of the Stomach and Intestine.

7. Cited in Heller, Diane Poole Somatic Experiencing Participants' Manual. Milan.

8. Siegel, Daniel (2001). The Developing Mind: How Relationships and the Brain Interact to Shape Who We Are. New York: The Guilford Press.

9. Schacter, D.L. and Buckner, R.L. (1998) Priming and the Brain. Neuron. 20, pp. 185-195

10. Jacoby, L.L. (1983). Perceptual Enhancement: Persistent Effects of an Experience. Journal of Experimental Psychology: Learning, Memory, and Cognition. 9 (1), pp. 21-38

11. Gladwell, Malcolm Blink (2007). The Power of Thinking Without Thinking. Back Bay Books, p. 53

12. Risen, Clay. The Lady Macbeth Effect. http://www.nytimes.

com/2006/12/10/magazine/10Section2a.t-9.html

13. Skinner, B.F. http://en.wikipedia.org/wiki/B._F._Skinner

14. Scaer, Robert C., MD (2001). The Body Bears the Burden. New York: The Haworth Medical Press, p. 86.

15. Van Der Kolk, Bessel (1989). The Compulsion to Repeat Trauma: Re-enactment, Re-victimization, and Masochism. Psychiatric Clinics of North America, Vol. 12, No. 2, pp 389-410.

16. Fox, H. E., Steinbrecher, M., Pessel, D., Inglis, J., and Angel, E. (1978). Maternal Ethanol Ingestion and the Occurrence of Human Fetal Breathing Movements. American J. of Obstetrics/Gynecology, Vol. 132, pp 354-358.

17. Chamberlain, David, Ph.D. (1997). The Fetal Senses: A Classical View. http://www.birthpsychology.com/lifebefore/fetalsense.html

18. Dowling, A .L .S., Martz, G. U., Leonard, J. L., & Zoeller, R.T. (2000). Acute changes in maternal thyroid hormone induce rapid and transient changes in gene expression in fetal rat brain. Journal of Neuroscience, Vol. 20, pp. 2255-2265.

19. Verny, Thomas (2002). Tomorrow's Baby: The Art and Science of Parenting from Conception through Infancy, New York: Simon & Schuster.

20. Damasio, Antonio (2003). Looking for Spinoza: Joy, Sorrow, and the Feeling Brain. Orlando: Harcourt, Inc., p.37.

21. Damasio, Antonio (2003). Looking for Spinoza: Joy, Sorrow, and the Feeling Brain. Orlando: Harcourt, Inc., p.37

22. Damasio, Antonio (2003). Looking for Spinoza: Joy, Sorrow, and the Feeling Brain. Orlando: Harcourt, Inc., p. 200.

23. Einstein, Albert, cited in J. Hadamard (1945). The Psychology of Invention in the Mathematical Field. Princeton, NJ: Princeton University Press, p.142.

24. Benson, Herbert Timeless Healing (1996) http://www.mbmi.org/basics/

whatis_rresponse_TRR.asp

25. http://www.lessons4living.com/relaxation_response.htm

26. Sarno, John (1991) Healing Back Pain: The Mind-Body Connection. New York: Warner Books.

27. Stress, definition of stress, stressor, what is stress? Eustress? http://www.stress.org/topic-definition-stress.htm

28. Siegel, Daniel (2001). The Developing Mind: How Relationships and the Brain Interact to Shape Who We Are. New York: The Guilford Press, p. 132.

29. Ledoux, Joseph (1998) The Emotional Brain: The Mysterious Underpinnings of Emotional Life. Simon & Schuster, p. 303

30. Siegel, Daniel (2001). The Developing Mind: How Relationships and the Brain Interact to Shape Who We Are. New York: The Guilford Press, p. 123.

31. Trungpa, Chogyam (2004) The Collected Works of Chogyam Trungpa, Volume Eight. Shambhala Publications, p.35.

32. Osho (2009). The Book Of Wisdom.

33. Seyle, Hans (1956). The Stress of Life. New York: Mcgraw-Hill.

34. Duenwald, Mary (2005). The physiology of facial expressions. A self-conscious look of fear, anger, or happiness can reveal more than a lie detector. www.discovermagazine.com.

35. Thich Nhat Hanh, Buddha Mind, Buddha Body: Walking to Enlightenment, Mumbai, Jaico Publishing House p. 69.